D0960239

A FOREST OF TIME
American Indian Ways of History

A Forest of Time introduces undergraduate and graduate students, Western and Indian history scholars and buffs, and general readers to the notion that American Indian societies transmitted and interpreted their own histories in their own ways for their own reasons. Through discussions of legends and oral histories, creation stories and folktales, it illustrates how various Indian peoples related and commented on their changing times. Drawing on his own research as well as recent scholarship from ethnohistory, anthropology, folklore, and Indian studies, Dr. Nabokov offers dramatic examples of how the American Indian historical imagination has put rituals and material culture, landscape, prophecies, and the English language to the urgent service of keeping the past alive and relevant. This book also supplies useful references as it demands that we engage with alternative chronicles of America's multicultural past.

Peter Nabokov is Professor of American Indian Studies and World Arts and Cultures at the University of California, Los Angeles. He has lived and worked among the Navajo, Lakota, Crow, Penobscot, and Alabama–Coushatta Indian nations. His previous books include *Two Leggings: The Making of a Crow Warrior* (1967), *Indian Running* (1981), the prize-winning *Native American Architecture* (1989), which he coauthored with Robert Easton, and *Native American Testimony: From Prophecy to Present, 1492–2000* (2000).

"Among those who study Native American culture, Peter Nabokov is one of the most engaging and important writers. Everyone interested in the philosophy of history and how Native Americans have understood their own histories should savor this fresh and valuable book."
– Gary Nash, *University of California, Los Angeles, and Director, National Center for History in Schools*

For Ray Fogelson

A Forest of Time

American Indian Ways of History

PETER NABOKOV

University of California, Los Angeles

CAMBRIDGE
UNIVERSITY PRESS

PUBLISHED BY THE PRESS SYNDICATE OF THE UNIVERSITY OF CAMBRIDGE
The Pitt Building, Trumpington Street, Cambridge, United Kingdom

CAMBRIDGE UNIVERSITY PRESS
The Edinburgh Building, Cambridge CB2 2RU, UK
40 West 20th Street, New York, NY 10011-4211, USA
477 Williams town Road, Port Melbourne, VIC 3207, Australia
Ruiz de Alarcón 13, 28014 Madrid, Spain
Dock House, The Waterfront, Cape Town 8001, South Africa

http://www.cambridge.org

First published 2002
Reprinted with corrections 2002

Printed in the United States of America

Typeface Sabon 10/13.5 pt.   *System* LATEX 2$_\varepsilon$ [TB]

A catalog record for this book is available from the British Library.

Library of Congress Cataloging in Publication Data
Nabokov, Peter.
A forest of time : American Indian ways of history / Peter Nabokov.
p.   cm.
Includes bibliographical references and index.
ISBN 0-521-56024-1
1. Indians of North America – Folklore.   2. Indians of North America –
Historiography.   3. Tales – North America.   4. Oral tradition – North America.
I. Title.
E98.F6 N33   2001
973′.0497 – dc21   2001025955

ISBN 0 521 56024 1 hardback
ISBN 0 521 56874 9 paperback

Contents

Preface   *page* vi

INTRODUCTION: Short History of American Indian
  Historicity   1

ONE: Some Dynamics of American Indian Historicity   29

TWO: Within Reach of Memory: Oral Traditions, Legends,
  and History   58

THREE: Almost Timeless Truths: Myth and History   85

FOUR: Commentaries and Subversions: *Memorates,* Jokes,
  Tales, and History   105

FIVE: Anchoring the Past in Place: Geography and History   126

SIX: Memories in Things: Material Culture and Indian
  Histories   150

SEVEN: Renewing, Remembering, and Resisting: Rituals and
  History   172

EIGHT: Old Stories, New Ways: Writing, Power, and Indian
  Histories   192

NINE: Futures of Indian Pasts: Prophecy and History   218

Index   241

Preface

It is the generative premise of this book that different cultures relate and use their pasts in different ways and sometimes for different reasons. There is nothing original about the idea. Over the past quarter century, scholars from a number of disciplines have been learning many new things about the relationships between indigenous peoples in Africa, South America, and the South Pacific and their notions of history. In North America, however, which once reflected ethnohistory's cutting edge, the study and appreciation of American Indian views of history have lagged behind.

This book refocuses attention on motivations and practices through which American Indians have remembered their diverse pasts. It corrals the often scattered state of scholarship and writing, by non-Indians and Indians alike, on this subject. Rather than an update of writings about historical events from the non-Indian, academic perspective, the book is a preliminary inquiry into what has variously been called the "folk history," "historical consciousness," "Native historiography," or "historicity" of Native societies of North America. It is also an inventory of approaches and a guide to sources for others to carry these explorations further.

Thinking about history, especially about the historical discourses of non-Western societies, is too important to be left to historians alone. This overview draws freely upon the work of Native writers and scholars, folklorists, anthropologists, linguists, historians of religion, and generations of American Indian oral historians. Some may dismiss my efforts as

little more than a glorified literature review. They may complain that I fail
to interpaginate Indian cases with themes of concern to contemporary
historians – issues of human agency, alternatives to Master Narratives,
experiments with multivocality and narrativity, and older debates over
Great Men storylines and how best to periodize the past. That's their
job, but this tool kit may help. The ideas I have cribbed and cobbled
together from more informed researchers, Native peoples, and scholars are topically arranged and footnoted to produce an introductory
handbook for any students or ordinary readers who have wondered
why and how Indians transmitted and made sense of their range of
histories.

This is emphatically not a case for a unified Native American historical philosophy. Years ago, the Tewa Indian scholar Alfonso Ortiz stated,
"There is simply no *the* Indian viewpoint in the writing of history."[1]
But broadly similar strategies, generally common genres, and recurrent
vested interests for recalling the past, which are shared by many tribal
traditions, do organize my chapters. Inevitably, a survey like this walks
the tightrope between provisional generalization and provocative exception. I am always on the lookout for commonalities in historical
thought among cultural traditions, yet I also want to leave the diversity
of still unplumbed Native historical concepts and practices as open as
possible.

Hence the title of this book, adapted from Chippewa historian David
Beaulieu's issue with the European model of history, which he analogized
as "a [Euro-American] tree with many different branches, the idea of
variations on a common theme." In its place, Beaulieu proposed a more
egalitarian alternative that he, in turn, attributed to Navajo historian
Ruth Roessel, "a forest of many different and varied trees," with its
stand of independent tribal approaches to recollecting and using the
past including a Euro-American trunk and branches as only one among
many.[2] But this arboreal symbol for American Indian cultural diversity

---

[1] Quoted in "Commentary," in *Breaking Barriers: Perspectives on the Writing of Indian
History*, edited by D. L. Beaulieu (Chicago: The Newberry Library, 1978), p. 33.

[2] "Papers on Indian Historiography," *Meeting Ground: Center for the History of the
American Indian*, 2(1) (Chicago: The Newberry Library, 1975), p. 17. This sentiment is
echoed in contemplations that novelist Thomas Berger creates for his protagonist, the
Cheyenne adoptee Jack Crabb, in *The Return of Little Big Man*: "I came up with the

may have a wider root system, serving in one instance to make a point about epistemological diversity or in another to supply a mnemonic metaphor for tracing the evolution of a given tribe's accounts about itself.[3]

In July 1844 an Ojibwa orator told a Jesuit, "My brother, you have come to teach us there is only one way, for all people, to know the Great Spirit.... My brother, there are many species of trees, and each tree has leaves that are not alike...."[4] The Hidatsa of North Dakota's Middle Missouri River likened their tribe's corpus of origin stories to "the branches of a tree" so that, explained the narrator Bears Arm to folklorist Martha Warren Beckwith, "if we related a branch, [we] can tell where it belongs in the tree and what comes before and after."[5] The Blackfeet of northern Montana told Clark Wissler that "The parts of this weed all branch from the stem.... So it is with the versions of a myth."[6] And Alanson Skinner heard from the Menomini of Wisconsin that "One ritual is an arm or branch of the lodge, and the myth accounting for its origin forks off from the main branch."[7] Even the Lakota author Luther Standing Bear, renowned for his two autobiographies, maintained in

---

idea that time belongs to everybody and everything and nothing can lay claim to any part of it exclusively, so if you talk about the past as though there was just one version of it that everybody agrees on, you might be seen as stealing the spirit of others, something which the Cheyenne always had a taboo against" (Boston: Little, Brown & Company, 1999), p. 75.

[3] Using trees and forests as mnemonic analogies for intellectual or cultural development, and for schematizing the hierarchical placement of cosmological domains or social or moral relationships, is a practice not limited to Native America; it is described for sixteenth-century France by Frances Yates in *The Art of Memory* (Chicago: University of Chicago Press, 1966), pp. 186–187.

[4] Denys Delage and Helen Hornbeck Tanner, "The Ojibwa–Jesuit Debate at Walpole Island, 1844," *Ethnohistory* 41(2) (Spring 1994), p. 319.

[5] Martha Warren Beckwith, collector, *Mandan–Hidatsa Myths and Ceremonies*, Memoirs of the American Folk-Lore Society XXXII (New York: The American Folklore Society, G. E. Stecherd & Co., 1938), p. 268.

[6] Clark Wissler and D. Duval, *Mythology of the Blackfoot Indians*, American Museum of Natural History, Anthropological Papers, V. 2 (New York: The Trustees, 1908), p. 5.

[7] Alanson Skinner, *Medicine Ceremony of the Menomini, Iowa, and Wakpeton Dakota, with Notes on the Ceremony Among the Ponca, Bungi, and Potawatomi*. Museum of the American Indian Notes and Monographs, V. 1 (New York: Museum of the American Indian, Heye Foundation, 1928), p. 102.

1933 that written history was second best to oral tradition because "a people enrich their minds who keep their history on the leaves [is this his double entendre?] of memory."[8]

As for the "Ways" of my subtitle, I am evoking the nonjudgmental tack that Indians often take when commenting upon the inclinations of other peoples. Once I asked a Crow Indian friend why a Shoshone Sun Dance I had recently witnessed differed in certain respects from the Crow version. "Oh," was all he would speculate, "I guess that must be their way." I also welcome the hint of the Navajo suffix (-ji, commonly translated as "-Way") that connotes a ceremonial activity, a shading that suggests that for many Indian peoples their sense of history and its conduct are not just secular or abstract pursuits. For them, no less than for any modern or New historian, the "doing of history" can become a pathway to rediscoveries of identity, home, and inner purpose.

I must not be coy about this book's origins. Editor Frank Smith guided me through an essay I wrote for Cambridge's *History of the Native Peoples of the Americas – North America*, entitled "Native Views of History," and then encouraged me to expand it. While Frank stressed that this should be a short book, I added instances from my own experience when probing Indian ways of history was the only way I could make sense of things – the "stories about stories" about history that bring it all home.[9]

After Frank Smith, the Cambridge *History* editors Bruce Trigger and the late Wilcomb Washburn also stood behind my original essay and encouraged this expansion. Raymond D. Fogelson and William S. Simmons have been faithful mentors and contributors behind this book. To Frederick Hoxie I am thankful for collegiality during my predoctoral fellowship in 1981 at the D'Arcy McNickle Center for Indian History at Chicago's Newberry Library, for many discussions about Crow Indian culture history, and for hosting my documentary workshop on material

---

[8] Luther Standing Bear, *Land of the Spotted Eagle* (New York: Houghton Mifflin Company, 1933), p. 27.
[9] I lift this phrase from William Cronon, who urges environmental historians to write "stories about stories about nature" because "narratives remain our chief moral compass in the world" ("A Place for Stories: Nature, History, and Narrative," *Journal of American History* 178, n. 4 [March 1992]), p. 1375.

culture and history on August 21–24, 1991, at the Newberry Library, on which Chapter 6 is based. The late Alfonso Ortiz was always a generous listener and friend, as well as a crusader for Native interpretations of Indian–white relations. Wendy Rose graciously gave me a copy of her typescript, "Native North American Types of Non-Oral Literature." Well before Vine Deloria Jr., wrote the preface for my anthology on Indian–white relations, his writings and correspondence were exemplars for doing the right thing. When Marilyn Kriney of Thomas Y. Crowell, Michael Millman of Viking-Penguin, and my agent Susan Bergholz helped to make that anthology a reality, they also laid a foundation for this deeper investigation. Sophisticated fieldwork and elegant writing by Frank Salomon on Native South American historicities have inspired me. Other social scientists who kindly commented on my essay or whose works spurred me include Ramond J. DeMallie, Jay Miller, Douglas R. Parks, Alan Roberts, Matthew Snipp, and Peter Whiteley. Historians who graciously provided reactions were Carter Blue Clark, William Cronon, Philip Deloria, Jan Vansina, and Richard White. From folklore and literature I am thankful for suggestions from Ken Lincoln, Daniel F. Littlefield, Jr., Jarold Ramsey, Barre Toelken, Gerald Vizenor, and Andrew Wiget, and, as always, for the training and enthusiasm of Alan Dundes. Other friends who made contributions include Grant Bulltail, Kirsten Erickson, Bruce Feld, Bill Firman, Gary H. Gossen, Valerie Kack-Brice, Tim McCleary, and Wayne Olts. To Laurie Miller of *The Fine Line*, Cody, Wyoming, and Ken Wade, librarian at UCLA's American Indian Studies Program, I am especially grateful.

———◦———

Short History of American Indian Historicity

Many of us who have received formal training in how to follow the often
subtle rules for determining what sort of evidence may be deemed reliable,
and thus admissible, in this alien, European art form called history have
come to love it as a discipline. We have also learned to distrust it.... A
people's stories about themselves, their world, and their past may leave
many things unsaid, but on the whole, the things that do get said, and the
way they are said, give a clearer picture of that people than any work of
history can give.[1]

D. L. Birchfield, Choctaw

Visiting the back country where a lot of American Indian history took
place and still unfolds can yield more than touches of local color. You enter the past in three dimensions, seasonal climate, and diurnal time. You
recognize the topographical appeal of bygone settlement sites, the food-
procuring or home-protecting attractions of creek side, estuary, floodplain or forest fringe, and the practicality of high grounds for surveillance
or defensible draws in a skirmish. You are even tempted to deduce former
aesthetic sensibilities. Then the places themselves talk back.

Longtime residents pull out old family photos and walk you to where
their relatives lived and are buried. Tribal librarians escort you around
former agency grounds. An elder personalizes with flair and irony the
underside of events you thought you had down pat. Some physical reality

---

[1] D. L. Birchfield, "The Case Against History," in *The Oklahoma Basic Intelligence Test*
(Greenfield Center, N.Y.: Greenfield Review Press, 1998), p. 105.

touched by the personalities of your research falls into your hands. Once I kicked through a second-growth pasture where the nineteenth-century protagonist of my first book, a Crow Indian warrior, chose to be photographed opening his sacred medicine bundles beside the twisted trunk of his favorite cottonwood. My boot caught a sliver of that very tree – seventy years after the old man sang his vision songs on the spot. As I tilted its distinctive bowed shape out of the matted grass, I heard the old man's stepson suck in his breath behind me, and I laid it back.[2]

First lesson about Indian pasts – they're often personal and ever present.

This sort of immersion processes its data through your senses, whose observational and analytic skills you have been honing ever since you first played hide and seek. Even when the sites have become tract housing or freeway, today's encounters with such places become springboards for sharper questions about why things happened the way they did, frequently with salutary effects on the narratives you produce. And when you have the good luck to saturate yourself in the grit and spirit of historical sites, and then read a classic work by someone who only conjured them up in their head, the extra mile legitimizes your entry into the conversation.

That was my experience living in Puebla, Mexico, when I was fifteen and reading William Hickling Prescott's *Conquest of Mexico*. Every night my imagination was swept by swashbuckling Spaniards and their triumph over the Aztecs. Half-blind when he wrote *Conquest* in Boston between 1839 and 1843, Prescott could not walk the Mesoamerican landscape where Cortez's ruthless few brought down Montezuma's shaky coalition of subordinated Central Mexican tribes. But among the conscious choices he made in his Bedford Street library was to suppress the nativist side of the story.

Although for an hour each day Prescott suffered his daughter's reading to him from the conquest chronicle of Alva Ixtlilxochitl, descendant

---

[2] National Park historian John Hussey recognized this experiential power of place in 1958: "The person who walks on the very field where Cornwallis surrendered receives a vivid impression, a thrill of *kinship with the past*" ("The Role of History in the National Park System," "Mission 66" file, History branch files, NPS, Washington, D.C., 1958, emphasis mine).

of a native prince, he had little patience for such Aztec intellectuals, who, from the early colonial period on, preserved in illustrated books and other writings their people's myths, religious poems, migration narratives, and historical perspectives. Prescott's journal on writing his *Conquest* betrays little awareness of the native texts that were anthologized shortly after the conquest by Fray Bernardino de Sahagun.[3] At one point he even confesses, "I hope my readers will take more satisfaction than I do in the annals of barbarians,"[4] and he adds in another entry, "nor do I think they will bear expatiating on to any great length. But the overturning of their old empires by a handful of warriors is a brilliant subject, full of important results, and connected with our own history."[5]

If my nights raced with Prescott's Spaniards, my days found me pursuing village festivals such as La Conquista at Huehotzingo to the north, where plumed Indian dancers made more of the Aztecs' initial defiance against the Spaniards than of their own ultimate defeat on the battlefield, or Los Tastoanes in Jalisco, where masked dancers evoked both the martyrdom of Spain's patron saint, Santiago, *and* sacrifices to their old deity, Xipe-Toltec, so as to mediate between the imported and indigenous halves of the Mexican soul. Most weekends found me in Cholula, where local Indians led me through cornfields to caches of pre-Columbian pottery shards and terra cotta heads with the goggle eyes and prominent fangs of their old rain god Tlaloc – the same visage that glared from pots that I picked up in local Indian markets.

But nowhere did I see the lie put to Prescott's story of European triumph more persuasively, or the spirit of Mexican Indian survival

---

[3] Beyond the scope of this book are analyses of uniquely hybrid, indigenous historical genres produced in Mexico and South America, such as one finds in Elizabeth Hill Boone's "Migration Histories as Ritual Performance" in *Aztec Ceremonial Landscapes*, edited by David Carrasco (Niwot: University Press of Colorado, 1991), Frank Salomon's "Testimonies: The Making and Reading of Native South American Historical Sources," V. 3, Pt. 1, in *The Cambridge History of the Native Peoples of the Americas* (New York: Cambridge University Press, 2000), and *From Oral to Written Expression: Native Andean Chronicles of the Early Colonial Period*, edited by Rolena Adorno, Foreign and Comparative Studies/Latin American Series, N. 4 (Syracuse, N.Y.: Maxwell School of Citizenship and Public Affairs, Syracuse University, 1982).

[4] C. Harvey Gardiner, editor, *The Literary Memoranda of William Hickling Prescott*, V. 2 (Norman: University of Oklahoma Press, 1961), p. 17.

[5] C. Harvey Gardiner, editor, *The Literary Memoranda of William Hickling Prescott*, V. 1 (Norman: University of Oklahoma Press, 1961), p. 229.

exhibited with greater authority, than at the pre-Columbian pilgrimage center of Tepeyac. Located fourteen miles north of Mexico City, this sacred hill had witnessed human sacrifices to Tonantzin, a preeminent Aztec mother goddess associated with the moon and fertility. Only ten years after Cortez's victory, atop that promontory a brown-skinned Virgin of Guadalupe spoke in the Nahuatl tongue to an impoverished Indian convert we know as Juan Diego but who answered to "He Who Talks Like an Eagle" in his native tongue. She magically inscribed his *tilma*, a peasant cloak woven from maguey cactus fibers and tied at the neck, with her figure, floating above a crescent moon. Fusing Aztec and Catholic iconography, it remains the image of Tepeyac's brown virgin, not the lions of King Carlos V, that embodies the cultural legacy of the Hispanic Americas.[6]

More alert to the different agendas of white and Indian histories when I sought out the town of my birth near Lake Cayuga in the heart of upper New York State's Iroquois Indian territory decades later, I was leerier of Francis Parkman's master narratives that described the brutality and intellectual inferiority of local Indians. Despite ill health, Parkman had walked the grounds of his narratives and talked with Indians – Lakotas in the Black Hills, Penobscots in Maine, and Senecas in New York State. But his re-creations of their behavior still hewed to unflattering stereotypes of Indians drawn from Jesuit testimonies and popular literature. While scholars may credit Parkman's writings with a precocious display of "a sense of Native Americans as important historical agents," the man was even more explicit than Prescott about his disdain for Indian ways of history.[7] In 1861 Parkman wrote of Iroquois sources for their wars with the Erie Indians, "Indian traditions are very rarely of any value as

---

[6] See Stafford Poole, *Our Lady of Guadalupe: The Origin, and Sources of a Mexican Natural Symbol, 1531–1797* (Tucson: University of Arizona Press, 1995); Eric Wolf, "The Virgin of Guadalupe: A Mexican National Symbol," *Journal of American Folklore* LXXI (1958): 34–39, and Victor Turner and Edith L. B. Turner, "Mexican Pilgrimages: Myth and History," in their *Image and Pilgrimage in Christian Culture: Anthropological Perspectives* (New York: Columbia University Press, 1978), pp. 40–103.

[7] Melissa L. Meyer and Kerwin Lee Klein, "Native American Studies and the End of Ethnohistory," in *Studying Native America: Problems and Prospects*, edited by Russell Thornton (Madison: University of Wisconsin Press, 1998), p. 183.

historical evidence"[8]; in 1877 he railed again that "Indian traditions of historical events are usually almost worthless."[9]

Narratives that outsiders deem irrelevant to one historical discourse may remain of central significance in another. As I photographed old log cabins in the Indian hamlets that extend across northern New York State, I was aware that some front lawn figurines carved out of wood were not simply Indian equivalents of pink flamingoes. They displayed the matrilineal clan totems of resident families, an ancestry that derived from the first of three grand narratives that established the Iroquois sense of an intermingled heritage, identity, and destiny. When I drove down the old Iroquois Trail from Buffalo to Albany – today's Interstate 90 – I already knew how this route played its metaphoric part in their second epic story, the founding of the Iroquois League, in which their entire territory was analogized as a gigantic, protective, multi-tribal longhouse with this trail as its central corridor. Then a follower of the Longhouse Religion with whom I chatted on the banks of the Allegheny River Resevoir pointed to the old location of the Cornplanter Grant (now inundated by Kinzua Dam) where the prophet Handsome Lake underwent his vision in 1799. Handsome Lake's life and teachings produced their third guiding narrative, the "Good Word," which is still recited each year. Nor did this stacking of "main stem stories" prevent the Iroquois from maintaining other documentary memories of localized history of the type that Francis Parkman collected but then buried in small-print footnotes.

Over the years, such realizations persuaded me that any accounts of Indian–white relations deserved multiple representations. If we were to truly tell these stories "in the round," how could they not reflect contrasting or overlapping vested interests, differing modalities of accounting

---

[8] Francis Parkman, *The Jesuits in North America in the Seventeenth Century*, Part Second (Boston: Little, Brown and Company, 1930 [1867]), p. 545. As if unwittingly undercutting his adamancy, immediately after this comment Parkman cites an Iroquois account to authenticate their antipathy for their Algonquian foes, which "historical evidence" does substantiate.

[9] Francis Parkman, *Count Frontenac and New France Under Louis XIV*, V. 1 (Boston: Little, Brown and Company, 1897 [1877]), p. 164. What makes this attack on Indian credibility especially ironic is Parkman's own falsifications of data, exposed by Francis Jennings and others, which supported his positioning of Indians on the lower rungs of the evolutionary ladder (*The Ambiguous Iroquois Empire* [New York: W. W. Norton & Company, 1984], p. 19, fn. 24).

and interpreting, and culturally divergent senses of what it all meant? And while one was drawn to periods of cultural contact that highlighted those contrasts, I also asked, why should we not explore indigenous historical thoughts for their own sake, even as they might illuminate the years before any Euro-Americans were around? To approach these questions, a review of our belated interest in native attitudes about the past seems appropriate.[10]

The Prescott–Parkman "school of suspicion" regarding Indian historical traditions was nothing new. "What can a nation that has not letters tell us of its origins?" asked Dr. Samuel Johnson, "I have always difficulty to be patient when I hear authors gravely quoted as giving accounts of savage nations, which accounts they had from the savages themselves."[11] And speaking of origin narratives of the Creeks, Choctaws, and Algonquians, the nineteenth-century evolutionist Daniel G. Brinton complained that "Sifting them all, we shall find, in them, little to enlighten us as to the pre-historic chronology of the tribes, though they may furnish interesting vistas in comparative literature."[12]

But Brinton's tacked-on qualification reminds us that equally rooted in the American grain was a "school of empathy" toward Indian cultures, aesthetics, and oral traditions.[13] Among the few holdouts for an Indian ability to record history accurately was the late-eighteenth-century missionary John Heckwelder, who spent nearly forty years serving Christianized members of the Delaware Tribe and transcribed their accounts of white arrival and intertribal relations.[14] Another was the

---

[10] For an overview from a Native perspective, see Dean Morrison's "In Whose Hand Is the Telling of the Tale?" in *American Indian Studies: An Interdisciplinary Approach to Contemporary Issues*, edited by Dean Morrison (New York: Peter Lang, 1997), pp. 5–25.

[11] Quoted in Clement W. Meighan, "Ethnohistory and Rock Art," *Journal of New World Archaeology* 4(2), May 1981, p. 1.

[12] Daniel G. Brinton, *Essays of an Americanist* (Philadelphia: Porter & Coates, 1890), p. 24.

[13] I borrow this "suspicion–empathy" dichotomy from my colleague at the University of Wisconsin-Madison, Frank Salomon, who used it to characterize approaches in the anthropology of religion.

[14] John G. E. Heckwelder, *An Account of the History, Manners, and Customs of the Indian Nations*, Transactions of the Committee of History, Moral Science, and General Literature of the American Philosophical Society 1, Philadelphia, 1819, and "Indian Traditions of the First Arrival of the Dutch at Manhattan Island," *Collections of the*

INTRODUCTION

early-nineteenth-century anthologist James Jones, whose childhood exposure to the Gay Head Indian community on Martha's Vineyard "early led [me] to place a greater value upon the traditions of the Indians than has been attached to them by those who do not view them as a series of authentic annals. For myself, I hold them in the light of historical records, mixed up indeed with much that is fabulous, but not in greater degree than the early annals of other unenlightened nations, who could not perpetuate them by means of letters."[15] And the conversion experiences and cultural profiles by Chippewa Indian author-missionary George Copway also placed strong store on the reliability of old Indian oral histories.[16]

Positioned somewhere between the two camps regarding the viability of Indian historical narratives was the explorer-artist George Catlin. Although he, too, praised Indian traditions, he had in mind their artistry, not their empirical accuracy. Assuming his customary Indian-friendly tone, in 1832 Catlin reported that the Mandans of the Upper Missouri took "great pride in relating their traditions, with regard to their origin; contending that they were the first people created on earth." Yet his very next sentence undercut the Indian claim: "Their existence in these regions has not been from a very ancient period."[17]

Against what historian Francis Jennings has characterized as Parkman's "venomous type who did not hesitate to falsify his source materials to make them support his Social Darwinian preconceptions,"[18] one might position what Philip S. Mason praises as the "great understanding and sympathy for the Indian"[19] displayed by early Indian agent

New York Historical Society, 2nd Series, V. 1 (New York: Printed for the Society by H. Ludwig, 1841).

[15] James Athearn Jones, Traditions of the North American Indians, V. 1 (London: Henry Colburn and Richard Bentley, 1830), pp. xiv–xv.
[16] George Copway, Indian Life and Indian History, by an Indian Author: Embracing the Traditions of the North American Indians Regarding Themselves, Particularly of That Most Important of All the Tribes, the Ojibways (orig.: The Traditional History and Characteristic Sketches of the Ojibway Nation [1850]; reprint, New York: AMS, 1978), and Life, Letters & Speeches of George Copway, edited by A. LaVonne Brown Ruoff and Donald B. Smith (Lincoln: University of Nebraska Press, 1997), p. 7.
[17] George Catlin, Letters and Notes on the Manners, Customs, and Conditions of the North American Indians, V. 1, 3rd ed. (London: published for the author by Tilt and Bogue, 1842), p. 80.
[18] Jennings, The Ambiguous Iroquois Empire, p. 19.
[19] Philip P. Mason, "Introduction" to The Literary Voyager or Muzzeniegun by Henry Rowe Schoolcraft (East Lansing: Michigan State University Press, 1962), p. xx.

and folklore collector Henry Rowe Schoolcraft. If Parkman's Indians were brutish, menacing, and uncivilized, Schoolcraft's were amiable and colorful, and exhibited expressive talents.

Schoolcraft's voluminous compilations – what Mason considers "probably the first 'oral history' program in America"[20] – commenced in 1822 after Michigan Governor Lewis Cass mailed questionnaires to traders, military men, and Indian agents requesting information on "the earliest incident they recollect in their history" and their knowledge of migrations, memorable events, and tribal wars. With the Iroquois evidently in mind, Cass was especially curious about "what belts have they, by which these wars, or any other events in their history are commemorated."[21] After he married into an eminent mixed-blood Chippewa family, Schoolcraft provided data beyond Cass's wildest dreams.

Schoolcraft praised Great Lakes Indian speeches and stories for their poetic charm. But he, too, blew hot and cold as to whether they constituted reliable history. Even his Indian mother-in-law had her doubts. Whites probably possessed "the truth, because you had things past and present written down in books," she confided to Schoolcraft's wife, "[but] the stories I have heard related by old persons in my nation, cannot be so true, because they sometimes forget certain parts and then thinking themselves obliged to fill up the vacancy by . . . their fertile flights of imagination. . . ."[22]

And while Schoolcraft allowed that Indians were an "intellectual people," he was more responsive to the artistic "allegories" he discerned in their narratives. Some may have "concealed part of their historical traditions and beliefs," he wrote in 1845,[23] but a year later he sided with his mother-in-law: "a people who live without letters, must expect their history to perish with them. Tradition soon degenerates into fable, and fable has filled the oldest histories of the world with childish incongruities. . . . To restore their history from the rubbish of their traditions is a hopeless task." Yet in the same speech to the New York

---

[20] Mason, "Introduction," p. xvi.
[21] Excerpted in Henry Rowe Schoolcraft, *Schoolcraft's Indian Legends*, edited by Mentor L. Williams (East Lansing: Michigan State University Press, 1956), p. 289.
[22] Henry Rowe Schoolcraft, *The Literary Voyager or Muzzeniegun*, edited by Philip P. Mason (East Lansing: Michigan State University Press, 1962), p. 6.
[23] Schoolcraft, *Schoolcraft's Indian Legends*, p. 305.

Historical Society he held out hope. "Who shall touch the scattered bones of aboriginal history with the spear of truth, and cause the skeleton of their ancient history to arise and live? We may never see this; but we may hold out incentives to the future scholar to labor in this department."[24]

But the "suspicious" school would not accept fence straddling. Parkman blasted the Delaware Indian stories collected by missionary Heckwelder regarding their troubles with the Iroquois as "utterly unworthy of credit."[25] Prescott, likewise, judged Heckwelder "too obviously & intentionally an apologist for the Indians to merit implicit confidence."[26] As for Schoolcraft's anthologies, Parkman found them "stuffed with blunders and contradictions, giving evidence on every page of a striking unfitness either for historical or philosophical inquiry."[27] Of Copway's rendition of Ojibwa history and legends he had only scorn, dismissing the Indian author as "endowed with a discursive imagination and facts grow under his hands into a preposterous shape and dimensions." Within a few years, the third of the nineteenth-century's master narrators, Hubert Howe Bancroft, contributed his doubts about finding usable material among the "Wild Tribes by whom most of our territory was inhabited" (in contrast, Bancroft meant, to the "Civilized Nations" of Mesoamerica, whose chronicles he found "not altogether mythical"):

> These fables lack chronology, and have no definite historical signification which can be made available.... Myths are mingled in great abundance with historical traditions throughout the whole aboriginal

[24] Henry Rowe Schoolcraft, "Incentives to the Study of Ancient American History," *New York Historical Society Proceedings*, Appended Address (1846), reprinted in part in *Schoolcraft's Indian Legends*, p. 303. Schoolcraft's appreciation for the poetics of Indian oral tradition did not transfer to his tougher critiques of Indian writers who put those traditions in print; for instance, he felt that Tuscarora writer David Cusick's claim of thirteen sequential Iroquois leaders who presided at Onondaga in northern New York State was "a mere excursion of a North American Indian into the fields of imagination" (quoted in Scott Michaelsen's *The Limits of Multiculturalism: Interrogating the Origins of American Anthropology* [Minneapolis: University of Minnesota Press, 1999], p. 48).

[25] Francis Parkman, *The Conspiracy of Pontiac and the Indian War after the Conquest of Canada*, V. 1 (Boston: Little, Brown and Company, 1901; Preface to First Edition written August 1, 1851), p. 34.

[26] *The Literary Memoranda of William Hickling Prescott*, edited and with an Introduction by C. Harvey Gardiner (Norman: University of Oklahoma Press, 1961), V. 1, p. 230.

[27] Parkman, *Jesuits in North America*, p. 76.

period and it is often utterly impossible to distinguish between them, or to fix the boundary line beyond which the element of history is absolutely wanting. The primitive aboriginal life, not only in America but throughout the world, is wrapped in mystery.[28]

This polarization between the suspicion and empathy perspectives echoed Euro-America's ambivalent projections about Indians in general, which abides to the present day. Whether Indians are regarded as benighted savages or nature poets continues to say more about some binary opposition in our national psyche than about anything intrinsic to Indian culture or character, past or present. As rendered in the discourse over historical consciousness, however, no voice of the late nineteenth century asked whether the hidden motivations, rhetorical strategies, or nationalistic presuppositions that informed their own historical compositions, which Prescott confided to his journal and Parkman held even closer to his chest, might also underlie what they derided as the entertaining fabulations or illogical distortions of native narratives.[29]

A more grounded appreciation for Native historical consciousness soon percolated from the field studies of Frank Hamilton Cushing, James Mooney, Alice Fletcher, and Frances Densmore, among others. From the late nineteenth century on, as these ethnographers listened to living tribespeople, their notes touched upon Indian ideas about history without necessarily highlighting them as such. In northern Montana, where George Bird Grinnell tried to reconcile contradictory migration stories about Blackfoot origins, he translated their toponyms for historical clues and then supplemented his argument for northerly origins with supportive folklore from neighboring tribes.[30] The Omaha scholar Francis La Flesche maintained that among his eastern Plains brethren, "The burden of memorizing and transmitting with accuracy, from one generation to another," fell to specially designated individuals chosen from key social

[28] Hubert Howe Bancroft, *Primitive History*, Vol. V, *The Native Races of the Pacific States of North America* (New York: D. Appleton and Company, 1876), p. 135.
[29] Francis Jennings deconstructs these premises for Anglo-American historiography in his pithy essay "On the Undoing of History," Appendix C, pp. 398–406 of *The Ambiguous Iroquois Empire*.
[30] George Bird Grinnell, "Early Blackfoot History," *American Anthropologist* V (April 1892), pp. 153–164.

units.[31] Analyzing clan legends he collected among the Arizona Hopi, Cosmos Mindeleff realized that they described small agricultural clans first entering the Painted Desert one by one over some time, a piecemeal arrival that modern research has supported.[32] Also in the American Southwest, Adolf Bandelier discerned that in narratives concerning a hero named Montezuma, the Rio Grande Indians were preserving oral traditions revealing early commerce between Meso-American and North American native peoples.[33] Working closely with a Six Nations Indian leader, the Tuscarora scholar J. N. B. Hewitt painstakingly translated their founding of the Iroquois League narrative without any apology for its interweaving of supernatural, mythic, and historical elements.[34]

Geographical distance, plus the lag in intellectual agendas (and status) between isolated hands camped out in Indian country and their colleagues (and often supervisors and paymasters) in America's swiftly professionalizing museum and university establishments, inhibited moves toward synchronizing ground-up data with top-down theory. Nor were the times propitious for scholars staking out theoretical reputations to investigate Indian attitudes toward the past. From the mid-nineteenth century until the 1950s, whatever "history" meant to the governing anthropological paradigms allowed little room for cultural diversity.

To social theorists of the mid-nineteenth century, any discussion of "history" was co-opted by what would later be criticized as the "conjectural history" of evolutionists such as Edward Tylor, Herbert Spencer, and Lewis Henry Morgan. Their progressivist vision saw all human societies climbing the same evolutionary ladder toward civilization, with Indians pulling themselves up the lower rungs as they ascended out of savagery and through barbarism toward civilization. While this entitled them to membership in humankind's cultural-biological time,

[31] American Anthropological Society of Washington meetings, *American Anthropologist* 7 (1905), p. 368F.

[32] Cosmos Mindeleff, "Localization of Tusayan Clans," Appendix 1, in Victor Mindeleff, *A Study of Pueblo Architecture in Tusayan and Cibola*, 8th Annual Report, Bureau of American Ethnology, 1886–1887 (Reprint, with an Introduction by Peter Nabokov; Washington, D.C.: Smithsonian Institution Press, 1989 [1891]).

[33] Adolf F. Bandelier, "The 'Montezuma' of the Pueblo Indians," *American Anthropologist* V (October 1892), pp. 319–326.

[34] J. N. B. Hewitt, "Legend of the Founding of the Iroquois League," *American Anthropologist* V (April 1892), pp. 131–148.

it still minimized their creative or reflexive abilities in the production of human histories.

The ensuing reversal in anthropological theory did not grant Indians much more access to the sweep of their own events. Reacting against the armchair evolutionists and their overarching schema, the American school of "historical particularism" established by Franz Boas focused on collecting the bits and pieces of American Indian field data. It was not that history was anathema to Boas; "the study of the present surroundings [of a tribe]," he once wrote, "is insufficient [to explain its culture]: the history of the people, the influence of the regions through which it passed on its migrations, and the people with whom it came into contact, must be considered."[35] But only through controlled comparison of those field data, Boas argued, might one reconstruct those interchanges between neighboring tribes of concepts and skills that constituted any region's culture history. For Boas, therefore, history boiled down to diffusion. He may have introduced the plural into culture, as Rosemary Zumwalt puts it, but it would take another fifty years before anyone did the same for history.[36]

The Boasians' dependence upon reconstructing the "memory culture" of their tribal informants also led to the reification of slice-of-time cultural profiles in which, according to Raymond J. DeMallie, "the process of retrospective description falsely stabilizes an idealized, remembered culture as unchanging norm rather than as historical moment... [and yields] the lack of consideration of cultural plurality, of symbols of ethnicity, or of persistent identity systems...."[37] So focused were most Boasian analysts upon a narrow definition of usable historical data as defined by two or more proximal traits (whether obtained from living

---

[35] As quoted in Leslie A. White, *The Ethnography and Ethnology of Franz Boas* (Austin: University of Texas, Texas Memorial Museum, Bulletin 6, 1963), p. 44.

[36] Rosemary Levy Zumwalt, *American Folklore Scholarship: A Dialogue of Dissent* (Bloomington: Indiana University Press, 1988), p. xii. Up to this time, writes Marshall Sahlins, "Heroic history proceeds more like 'Fenimore Cooper Indians'– to use Elman Service's characterization: each man, as they walk single file along the trail, careful to step in the footprints of the one ahead, so as to leave the impression of One Giant Indian." Sahlins, *Islands of History* (Chicago: University of Chicago Press, 1985), pp. 36–37.

[37] Raymond J. DeMallie, "Preface" to *Indians of the Plains* by Robert H. Lowie (Lincoln: University of Nebraska Press, 1982), p. xii.

Indians or "historical researches") to be compared by trained outsiders that we hear few suggestions of any historical consciousness possessed by cultural insiders.[38]

Under anthropology's ensuing canon, British structural-functionalism, not even a diminished role for chronological reconstruction was encouraged. Here was an unapologetically "ahistorical" program that envisioned the small-scale, nonliterate, and preindustrial subject societies of European colonialism as fixated on the present and geared like pieces of clockwork toward achieving internal consistency and interinstitutional equilibrium. The fieldworker's job was to elucidate "the psychological reality of today," according to Bronislaw Malinowski, a prolific structural-functionalist, since "the 'past remembered' – that is, its vision in man's memory – need not, in fact cannot be reconstructed." As for any Native historical perspectives, they were nothing but a "mythological vision" in which "the past becomes in retrospect the Paradise lost forever.... To trust to the memories of old men or to current accounts of what used to be would, for purposes of reconstruction, be futile."[39]

This ahistorical bias turned positively antihistorical with the revival among scholars like the historian of religions Mircea Eliade and even the

---

[38] This anthropological silence on Native views of history is especially conspicuous in the historical speculations by Boas's West Coast counterpart, Alfred L. Kroeber, collected in *An Anthropologist Looks at History* (Berkeley: University of California Press, 1963), the same scholar who once remarked, "I have never heard from a Zuni the least reference to a historic event" ("Zuni Kin and Clan," *Anthropological Papers of the American Museum of Natural History* 18(2) [1917], p. 203), and who apparently turned a deaf ear when his Zuni informants shared "stories of the chimiky'ana'kowa, or 'The Beginning,' which are regarded as historical truth," or the other Zuni historical genres alluded to by Dennis Tedlock (*Finding the Center: Narrative Poetry of the Zuni Indians*, translated by Dennis Tedlock [Lincoln: University of Nebraska Press, 1972], p. xvi).

[39] Bronislaw Malinowski, *Dynamics of Social Change* (New Haven: Yale University Press, 1945), p. 29. Among folklorists one heard similar disputes over the historical value of classical sagas and epics. "How can the historicists winnow out fabulous monsters and dragons and call the residue fact?" is how folklore historian Richard M. Dorson interpreted the famous opposition of Lord Raglan (in *The Hero* [New York: New American Library, 1936], 1979) to claims that stories of Achilles, King Arthur, or Leif the Lucky contained trustworthy data. "If part of the narrative is fiction, why not the whole?" (in Dorson's helpful overview, "The Debate Over the Trustworthiness of Oral Traditional History," *Folklore: Selected Essays* [Bloomington: Indiana University Press, 1972], p. 200).

structural anthropologist Claude Levi-Strauss of a humanistic sentiment that viewed history itself as a toxin introduced by colonialism. Indian encounters with Europe wound up decimating Native life, destroying their natural environments, undermining Native confidence in their own cosmologies, and shattering their structures of thought. This was inevitable, according to Eliade, for "traditional" society adhered to "cyclical time, periodically regenerating itself," which stood in opposition to "the other modern [notion], that of finite time, a fragment."[40] To cyclical time Eliade attached moral superiority, as it was "sacred" and "exemplary," whereas finite time was profane and degenerate, with history itself practically tantamount to "suffering."[41] In anthropologist Claude Lévi-Strauss's more sophisticated rendering of this polarization between cosmology and history, his famous "cold" and "hot" societies, historical consciousness itself loomed as a defining factor:

> The "cold" societies which we call "primitive" are not that way at all, but they wish to be. They view themselves as primitive, for their ideal would be to remain in the state in which the gods or ancestors created them at the origin of time. Of course this is an illusion, and they no more escape history than other societies. But this history, which they mistrust and dislike, is something they undergo. The hot societies – such as our own – have a radically different attitude towards history. Not only do we recognize the existence of history, we make a cult of

[40] Mircea Eliade, "The Yearning for Paradise in Primitive Tradition," in *Myth and Mythmaking*, edited by H. A. Murray (New York: G. Braziller, 1960), p. 12.
[41] Mircea Eliade, *The Myth of Eternal Return, or Cosmos and History* (Princeton: Princeton University Press, 1954), fn. 97. Eliade's dichotomy is a prominent example of a persistent tendency to place what Jill Lepore calls a "great divide" between "primal" societies like those of the Indians and "Western" ones like that of Anglo-Americans. A popularizer of American Indian metaphysics, Jamake Highwater, reels out a string of such recurrent simplistic contrasts as he claims that Indians are to Euro-Americans as holistic:linear, static:dynamic, atemporal:temporal, communal:individualistic, experiential:"formal, emotional, or decorative," and, of course, "spiritual":profane (Jamake Highwater, *The Primal Mind: Vision and Reality in Indian America* (New York: Harper & Row, 1981). Would that human cultures could be so compartmentalized and compared so efficiently; more likely, such a spewing of binaries does disservice to both cultural oppositions. As for the motivation behind the creation of such ideal types, social critic Richard Rodriguez has observed that "[American] Indian memory has become the measure against which America gauges corrupting history when it suits us" ("Mixed Blood, Columbus' Legacy: A World Made *Mestizo*," *Harper's Magazine* 283, November 1991, p. 49).

it.... We internalize our history and make it an element of our moral conscience.[42]

One problem for both ahistorical and antihistorical positions was that around the world those field ethnographers kept bumping into all kinds of history – of the Boasian diffusionist stripe that their data enabled them to reconstruct, but also of indigenous sorts to which their informants proudly clung and were willing to share. Moderate structural-functionalists like the British E. E. Evans-Pritchard certainly found this to be the case for Africa. He pinpointed historical consciousness as a sufficiently critical sociological variable to ask where and when Africa's range of what he called "incapsulated" historical practices reflected differences in time-reckoning traditions, or customs related to inheritance, or social emphases on royal genealogy, age sets or royal successions, or even the impact of geography.[43] In America the anthropologist Fred Eggan explored similar questions in the Pueblo Southwest as he delved into the historical perspectives that were embedded in Hopi oral traditions. Soon it became Eggan's hope that "The future writers on Indian history will give us the other side of the coin emphasizing the Indian's view of his world."[44]

Some were already trying. The late 1930s witnessed the Roosevelt administration's Indian New Deal, which recruited anthropologists to apply their skills toward resurrecting Indian independence and pride in the political and cultural spheres. As for historians, however, up to this

---

[42] Claude Lévi-Strauss and Didier Eribon, *Conversations with Claude Lévi-Strauss*, translated by Paula Wissing (Chicago: University of Chicago Press, 1991), p. 125. An anthropological rejoinder to this famous Lévi-Strauss formulation is the rich collection *Rethinking History and Myth: Indigenous South American Perspectives on the Past*, edited by Jonathan D. Hill (Urbana: University of Illinois Press, 1988).

[43] E. E. Evans-Pritchard, "Anthropology and History," in *Social Anthropology and Other Essays* (New York: The Free Press, 1962), pp. 172–191. Actually, Evans-Pritchard borrowed the term "incapsulated" history from R. G. Collingwood's *An Autobiography* (Harmondsworth: Penguin Books, 1939) and meant by it the beliefs that contemporary people had about past events. Unlike Collingwood, however, who later pronounced that "The historicity of very primitive societies is not easily distinguishable from the merely instinctive life of societies in which rationality is at vanishing-point," Evans-Pritchard counted native peoples among those contemporaries (R. G. Collingwood, *The Idea of History*, 2nd ed. [Oxford: Oxford University Press, 1994], p. 227).

[44] Fred Eggan, "Anthropological Approaches to Ethnological Cultures," *Ethnohistory* 8(1) (1961), p. 8.

---

time their perspective had advanced little beyond the Prescott–Parkman model of writing about Indians. Still dominating their interpretations was Frederick Jackson Turner's influential 1893 thesis on "The Significance of the Frontier in American History." This essay extolled the aggressive ideology of an individualistic (Euro-American) spirit that had flowered on "free" (usually Indian) land. Turner's heirs only furthered their discipline's marginalization of the independent cultural histories of Indian peoples and their profoundly communal priorities.[45] In 1952 historian Bernard De Voto, certainly no advocate of Indian historicity, admitted that "American historians have made shockingly little effort to understand the life, the societies, the cultures, the thinking, and the feeling of the Indians."[46]

[45] For a Native historian's take on Turner's thesis see Donald L. Fixico, "Indian and White Interpretations of the Frontier Experience," in *Native Views of Indian–White Historical Relations* (Chicago: The Newberry Library, 1989), pp. 8–20. As Gray B. Nash elaborates on the absence of Indian history before and during the Turner-dominated years, "Within an interpretive framework that stressed the lack of class conflict or even deep social antagonisms and emphasized stability and continuity in American history it was hardly possible to focus on the experience of Indian people in North America. Indeed, within the schematization of the consensus school it was virtually obligatory to ignore Indian history over the last four centuries and to develop historical anmesia about their long history of relations with the European invaders, who colonized the continent in the early seventeenth century and interacted continuously and abrasively with them over the next three hundred years." "Whither Indian History," *Journal of Ethnic Studies* 4(2) (Fall 1976), p. 69.

[46] Out of one side of his mouth De Voto could say this, as quoted in J. K. Howard, *Strange Empire* (New York: W. Morrow & Company, 1952), p. 8, while out of the other side he would write to Garrett Mattingly in 1948 that "I don't trust an Indian tradition further than grandpa, if that far." *The Letters of Bernard De Voto*, edited by Wallace Stegner (Garden City, NY: Doubleday, 1975), p. 293. Thirty years later the situation was hardly improved, as Reginald Horsman wrote, "The most influential historical trends of the past ten years have largely bypassed Native American history. Only a minority of books have attempted to take Indian history out of its traditional framework by introducing new themes and approaches.... The new social history has helped transform writing on black history, but Native American history too often remains parochial.... Native American history needs jolting out of the well-worn ruts in which it often travels" (from "Well-Trodden Paths and Fresh Byways: Recent Writing on Native American History" in *Reviews in American History* [Baltimore: Johns Hopkins University Press, December, 1982], pp. 234, 242). Also see the review essay on the dearth of Indian representation in Western history overviews of the 1960s and 1970s by Wlliam G. Robbins, "The Conquest of the American West: History as Eulogy" (*The Indian Historian* 10(1) (Winter 1977), pp. 7–13). It would take until 1995 for one of Indian history's most eminent Native practitioners to go further, calling on his colleagues to "address those historical questions considered important by Indian communities [and also to] present

But a by-product of the Indian New Deal's crusade to redress the past was the Indian Claims Commission (ICC), which, from 1946 to 1978, addressed a stockpile of unresolved land disputes and festering Indian grievances.[47] Not many Indians were involved, unfortunately, since generally, writes anthropologist Nancy O. Lurie, "it was simpler and more persuasive to trot out white scholars with impressive credentials, degrees and publications, to speak about the evidence from the Indians."[48] But drafting briefs for these hearings did kickstart the careers of ethnohistorians who now returned to the archives on behalf of living Indians to piece together better pictures of aboriginal land use. In 1932 the University of Oklahoma Press also inaugurated its "Civilization of the American Indian" series (which numbered 235 volumes, and still counting, by the year 2000). Initially, Oklahoma published colonial period studies, but then began issuing its trademark profiles of specific tribes that carried obligatory opening chapters summarizing the cultural background before devoting their bulk to Indian–white relations (more recently, however, entire volumes have been allotted to past and present tribal personalities).

Critics would point out that the prime movers (and protagonists and intended readers) of this "tribal history" formula were basically non-Indians whose books caught fire only when they chronicled a given tribe's subjugation and the Euro-American military campaigns against its resistance, and that they drew almost exclusively on non-Indian sources and interpretations. But they were an improvement. And as the ICC cases of the 1950s and 1960s encouraged scholars to apply more sophisticated methods to reconstruct "contact history" and redraw Indian territories for which tribes may have not been properly compensated, their new Indian-centered summaries soon made those older storylines seem increasingly obsolete.[49]

a Native American perspective as worthy of incorporation into the tale" (R. David Edmunds, "Native Americans, New Voices: American Indian History, 1895–1995," *American Historical Review* 100 [3] [June 1995], p. 738).

47 *Irredeemable America: The Indians' Estate and Land Claims*, edited by Imre Sutton (Albuquerque: University of New Mexico Press, 1985).

48 "Epilogue," in *Irredeemable America*, p. 371.

49 According to James A. Clifton, the scholarly sins of early volumes in the Oklahoma series included unfamiliarity with Native languages, no acknowledgment of specific

Of course, this scholarly attention also reflected the intense popularity of Indians in the late 1960s, with political activism and cultural romanticism inspiring droves of readers to revisit Indian history and religious traditions. Some scholars saw ethnohistory as Indian studies' brand new day; to others it was old wine in new bottles. And when a foremost ethnohistorian, James Axtell, defined its parameters as "the use of historical and ethnological methods and materials to gain knowledge of the nature and causes of change in a culture defined by ethnological concepts and categories,"[50] it was clear that this return to primary sources, and the claims hearings that boosted ethnohistory's popularity, still had minimal interest in extracting Indian "historicity" from their researches. In Richard Dorson's words, the ICC scholars clearly fell back upon "The chronological and documentary method of convention of history."[51] When cases did reach court, the seal of expert witness was conferred, as Nancy Lurie observed, upon informed scholars rather than native historians. It would take almost a decade after the ICC heyday before the Zuni Tribe of New Mexico's three-case effort to reestablish tribal boundaries and protect sacred places made native oral testimonies the crux of an Indian case – and key to the Zunis' precedent-setting victory.[52]

Among the few disturbed by the neglect of "meanings" in this new ethnohistorical project was Calvin Martin. But his 1978 clarion call for an enlightened ethnohistory, which would merge cultural anthropology's

Indians as historical actors, perpetuating stereotypical terminology, recycling clichés, overreliance on dated secondary sources, and a failure to extract from primary documents "Native American views, tactics, sentiments, and strategies in dealing with Americans." "The Tribal History – An Obsolete Paradigm," *American Indian Culture and Research Journal* 3(4)(1979), p. 90. Clifton's critique was reiterated in Mildred Mott Wedel and Ramond J. DeMallie's objections to most Plains Indian histories, as exemplified by a 1975 purported ethnohistory of the Lower Brule Sioux, which confined anthropological discussion to its introduction, focused on a white-oriented history of the reservation, and ignored "any of the cultural dynamics that, from the Indian point of view, make up the real story of the reservation experience" ("The Ethnohistorical Approach in Plains Indian Studies," in *Anthropology on the Great Plains*, edited by W. Raymond Wood and Margot Liberty [Lincoln: University of Nebraska Press, 1980], p. 119).

50 James Axtell, *The European and the Indian: Essays in the Ethnohistory of Colonial North America* (New York: Oxford University Press, 1982), p. 5.

51 Richard M. Dorson, "Ethnohistory and Ethnic Folklore," *Ethnohistory* 8 (1961), p. 16.

52 See *Zuni and the Courts: A Struggle for Sovereign Land Rights*, edited by E. Richard Hart (Lawrence: University Press of Kansas, 1995).

stress on native cultural categories of thought with the new ethnohistorian's close-grained reconstruction of Indian histories, add a focus on culture contact and ecological and economic change, and explore insights from psychological anthropology, still placed the motivation for, management of, and interpretive structure for such investigations squarely in academic hands.[53] Not even the feisty "New Western Historians" who in the 1980s redirected ethnohistory's more sophisticated eye to a range of underrepresented themes such as women and mixed-bloods, and the impact of environment and economics, entertained the possibility that there might be alternative authorities, unsuspected genres, and internal consistencies within American Indian folk histories. Nearly forty years ago, Charles Hudson suggested that "the analysis of a society's folk history should proceed hand in hand with an analysis of that society's world-view or belief system."[54] More recently, commenting on Raymond J. Fogelson's analysis of a Cherokee legend concerning a precontact rebellion against a religious elite, Robert A. Brightman urged, "some of us should be writing or recording Indian historical consciousness of Indian religious history."[55] Insofar as academic history is concerned, this challenge remains largely unmet.

Less burdened than other humanistic disciplines by a system of professional advancement that prized theoretical innovation, some folklorists appeared a tad more at ease with other cultural views of what "'really happened' as judged by *their* sense of credibility and relevance," in the words of Charles Hudson.[56] In the same sense that the qualifier "folk" helped to ground other, often ignored cultural dimensions of vernacular practice, such as "folk religion" and "folk medicine," Hudson's term "folk history" nicely embraced native expressions of their timely experiences. Also, some field folklorists took seriously the root of "lore" (*laere*, meaning "wisdom") and credited their informants with undervalued bodies of often veiled knowledge.

---

[53] Calvin Martin, "Ethnohistory: A Better Way to Write Indian History," *The Western Historical Quarterly* 9(1) (January 1978), pp. 41–56.

[54] Charles Hudson, "Folk History and Ethnohistory," *Ethnohistory* 13 (1966), pp. 64–65.

[55] Robert A. Brightman, "Towards a History of Indian Religion: Religious Changes in Native Societies," in *New Directions in American Indian History*, edited by Colin G. Calloway (Norman: University of Oklahoma Press, 1988), p. 238.

[56] Hudson, "Folk History and Ethnohistory," p. 64.

But in and out of academia, the availability of such down-home data was more often discounted. The ethnohistorian James Axtell comforted his colleagues that they "need not feel unduly sensitive about their lack of personal research among contemporary tribal cultures" because few descendants of "their historical subjects" survived, and even if they turned up, they had probably "lost much of their historical cultural context."[57] Similarly, the folklorist Richard Dorson was assured by Anglo residents of Michigan's Upper Peninsula that he had come a half-century too late to learn anything from their Chippewa neighbors, whom they derided as mostly drunks and freeloaders anyway. But when Dorson made his respectful interest in their traditions known to these same Indians, they invited him over and regaled him night after night, filling his notebooks with reputable legends, unique versions of trickster tales, storytelling contests, their takes on local history, and even humorous responses to the prejudice that surrounded them.[58]

Second lesson about Indian history and historicity: take nobody's word for their non-existence, and take the time to find them for yourself.

As the notion that nonliterate societies possessed traditions for the selection and dissemination of historical material began to intrigue anthropologists, they wrestled over terminology. Some adopted "historical consciousness" for what Emiko Ohnuki-Tierney calls "the culturally patterned way or ways of experiencing and understanding... [and] constructing and representing history."[59] She herself preferred "historicity" so as "to avoid the inference that how people think of and experience history is always conscious."[60] Existing definitions seemed up for grabs: while Charles Hudson defined folk history in accord with

---

[57] James Axtell, *The European and the Indian: Essays in the Ethnohistory of Colonial America* (New York: Oxford University Press, 1981), p. 10.

[58] Richard M. Dorson, "Indians Stuffed and Live," in *Bloodstoppers & Bearwalkers: Folk Traditions of the Upper Peninsula* (Cambridge: Harvard University Press, 1952), p. 17.

[59] From Dr. Ohnuki-Tierney's useful introduction to her edited collection, *Cultures Through Time: Anthropological Approaches* (Stanford: Stanford University Press, 1990), p. 4.

[60] In his *Keeping Slug Woman Alive: A Holistic Approach to American Indian Texts* (Berkeley: University of California Press, 1993, p. 67n), Gregg Sarris concurs that "To what degree Pomo were conscious of the historical process and intentionality applied to a specific strategy of resistance – disguising the tactical, political nature of

Dr. Ohnuki-Tierney's emphasis on its determining patterns, to anthropologist Robert Carmack it was demoted to just another synonym for ethnohistory.[61] Concerned that ethnohistorians were still neglecting Indian interpretations of critical events and notable persons in the past, the anthropologist Raymond D. Fogelson half-humorously coined the neologism "ethno-ethnohistory" to indicate "a kind of anthropological ethnohistory in which a central role would be given to intensive fieldwork, control of the native language, use of a native time perspective, and work with native documents."[62] And to tongue-twist even further, Fogelson tripled the prefix in his "ethno-ethno-ethnohistory," by which he meant "native writing of native history from a native perspective," and which we might even ridiculously tweak further into "ethno-ethno-ethnohistorICITY" in order to emphasize the present essay's elusive quarry: the underlying whys and wherefores for all expressions of American Indian historical thought, whether of the spoken, written, crafted, or danced varieties.[63]

It was mostly outside of North America, unfortunately, that in the 1960s and 1970s what George Marcus and Michael Fischer have called the "historical consciousness of ethnographic subjects" became a hot

---

the 'blending' in a conspiratorial way – is unclear and perhaps not a relevant concern. The anthropologist Tim Buckley said to me, 'I think that such tactics and processes are very rarely so conscious or intentional or conspiratorial; I think something more intuitive, cultural (and therefore somehow even grander) goes on in these specific kinds of cases.' "

61 Robert M. Carmack, "Ethnohistory: A Review of Its Development, Definitions, Method, and Aims," *Annual Review of Anthropology*, V. 1, edited by Bernard J. Siegel, Alan B. Beals, and Stephen A. Tyler (Palo Alto, Calif.: Annual Reviews, Inc., 1972), p. 239.

62 Raymond D. Fogelson, "On the Varieties of Indian History: Sequoyah and Traveller Bird," *The Journal of Ethnic Studies* 2(1) (Spring 1974), pp. 106–107.

63 To quote from Bernard S. Cohn's crucial distinction between the separate tasks of historical and historicity research: "The first reaction of anthropologists to the fact that natives had other kinds of pasts than they did was to apply their own conception of 'real events' to statements that natives made about the past and to construct *for them* 'objective' histories about what 'really' happened. . . . [But now] [t]he texts and codified oral traditions are read not to establish chronologies nor to sift historical fact from mythical fancy, but to try to grasp the meanings of the forms and contents of these texts in their own cultural terms" ("Anthropology and History in the 1980s," in his *An Anthropologist Among the Historians and Other Essays* [New York: Oxford University Press, 1990], pp. 68–69, emphasis mine).

ethnographic frontier.[64] Reinvigorating the theoretical strain that sought emic categories of world view and symbolic thought in order to decipher the behaviors of other historical actors, the prospect of parallel and equitable cultural histories now attracted some of the discipline's strongest minds. As Marshall Sahlins announced in his rallying cry for this pluralization of history:

> The problem now is to explode the concept of history by the anthropological experience of culture. The heretofore obscure histories of remote islanders deserve a place alongside the self-contemplation of the European past – or the history of "civilizations" – for their own remarkable contributions to an historical understanding. We thus multiply our conceptions of history by the diversity of structure. Suddenly, there are all kinds of new things to consider.[65]

To cite only a few exemplary works from this generation: Sahlins and Robert Borofsky[66] delved into South Pacific islanders' interpretations of violent encounters that cast fresh light on their interpretations of historical events as repetitions of patterns "constituted by heroic events in the past"[67] and also on their behaviors as change agents. In Africa the pioneering if narrowly empiricist analyses of oral history by Jan Vansina[68] laid a foundation for the more nuanced attempts of John and Jean Comaroff to write a "'neomodern' historical anthropology" for South Africa's colonial period that uncovered forms of indigenous counterhistories that were frequently coupled with resistant symbolic practices.[69] From northern Luzon in the Philippines, Renato Rosaldo revealed how the Illongot people's conception of history's flow as a "path"

---

[64] In George E. Marcus and Michael M. J. Fischer's *Anthropology as Cultural Critique: An Experimental Moment in the Human Sciences* (Chicago: University of Chicago Press, 1986, p. 97), this historicizing turn is nicely summarized.

[65] Marshall Sahlins, *Islands of History* (Chicago: University of Chicago Press, 1985), p. 72.

[66] Robert Borofsky, *Making History: Pukapukan and Anthropological Constructions of Knowledge* (Cambridge: Cambridge University Press, 1987).

[67] James G. Carrier, "History and Self-Conception in Ponam Society," *Man* 22(1) (1978), p. 129.

[68] Jan Vansina, *Oral Tradition* (Chicago: Aldine Pub., 1961) and *Oral Tradition as History* (Madison: University of Wisconsin Press, 1985).

[69] John Comaroff and Jean Comaroff, *Ethnography and the Historical Imagination* (Boulder: Westview Press, 1992).

through a well-trodden landscape was periodized in tribal memory by encounters with outsiders, most notably distinguishing their experiences during an earlier *pistaime* (peacetime) from those following Japanese incursions in 1945 and the speeded-up turbulence thereafter.[70] For Latin America, Richard Price produced his stereoscopic ethnography of the Afro-American Saramaka, an escaped-slave community ensconced in Suriname. His book printed "insider" histories and "outsider" commentaries side by side to remind readers how dearly the Saramaka guarded, as a collective inheritance, their history-as-knowledge. But the political pertinence of their geographically detailed, always personalized *fesi-ten* (first-time) struggles for liberation were lodged less in straight narratives than in place names, clichés, proverbs, prayers, lists, and other almost liturgical genres, which ensured that they never forgot the price their forefathers paid for their freedom.[71]

Most of these culture-historical studies still stuck "to the beach," that is, to situating themselves in early episodes of cross-cultural encounters, first contacts or their fairly immediate aftermaths.[72] But deciphering the unfolding cultural logic of these high-tension periods, what Sahlins has called the "structure of the conjuncture," still left unplumbed any native expressions and applications of their own historical discourses when no Europeans were around. If any unfinished historical tasks remained on the horizon, they entailed imaginative ways to upstream – in the spirit of what African anthropologist Robin Horton once called a "thought experiment" – into those precontact mists when earlier tribal peoples summoned their interpretations of intentionality to make "useable" sense of historical experiences.

By and large, unfortunately, this historicist vanguard steered clear of the Native North American ethnographic fields so well tilled by

[70] Renato Rosaldo, *Ilongot Headhunting 1883–1974: A Study in Society and History* (Stanford: Stanford University Press, 1980).

[71] Richard Price, *The Historical Vision of an Afro-American People* (Baltimore: The Johns Hopkins University Press, 1983).

[72] Truth to tell, many of the new historical anthropologists still felt more comfortable with Western systems of chronological thought, as evidenced by the virtual exclusion of Native perspectives found in the collections *History and Tradition in Melanesian Anthropology*, edited by James G. Carrier (Berkeley: University of California Press, 1992) and *History, Power and Identity: Ethnogenesis in the Americas, 1492–1992*, edited by Jonathan D. Hill (Iowa City: University of Iowa Press, 1996).

earlier ethnographers. There were notable exceptions – Loretta Fowler's work among the Arapahoe,[73] Peter Whitely's among the Hopi,[74] William S. Simmons's coverage of New England native communities,[75] and a handful of others that will be cited in this volume. But whether for reasons of areal fashion (doctoral students at this time were often steered away from Native North America) or because social scholars, intimidated by Vine Deloria, Jr.'s barbs against their kind in his notorious *Custer Died for Your Sins: An Indian Manifesto* (1969), did not want their usually voiceless subjects banging on their front doors, anthropology's early love of Indians definitely waned during the 1970s and 1980s.

Nor was the budding crop of indigenous scholars encouraged to adopt much radical reflection on their own histories, either for resurrecting and reexploring their forefathers' intellectual traditions or for formulating their independent interpretations of Indian–white relations. Projects for collecting Indian oral traditions were largely administered by non-Indians. Local tribal histories of specific groups were rarely picked up by national publishers. The few think tanks that targeted fellowship programs for up-and-coming Indian scholars held politely progressive but essentially establishment expectations for their graduates. Rarely were their sharp young Fellows exposed to revolutionary political-economic critiques of the sort that energized the emigré Latin Americans, North Africans, and Southeast Asians who would become their countries' intellectuals and liberators. Except for a handful of politicized Indian academics such as Jack Forbes, Ward Churchill, and Roxanne Dunbar Ortiz, by the time most American Indian scholars encountered their Marx, Sartre, Fanon, Foucault, and Said at the close of the twentieth century, the hot allure of the thinking activist had been supplanted by the cooler stance of the postmodern ironist, the pragmatic posture of the legal advocate, or the personal advancement to be enjoyed as a tribal enterprise entrepreneur.

---

[73] Loretta Fowler, *Arapahoe Politics, 1851–1978: Symbols in Crises of Authority* (Lincoln: University of Nebraska Press, 1982).

[74] Peter M. Whiteley, *Deliberate Acts: Changing Hopi Culture through the Oraibi Split* (Tucson: University of Arizona Press, 1988).

[75] William S. Simmons, *Spirit of the New England Tribes: Indian History and Folklore, 1620–1984* (Hanover: University Press of New England, 1986).

In dispersed journal articles and the occasional anthology, however, in more recent years there has appeared an encouraging trickle of specific, often localized studies on American Indian historicity. And a new generation of Native historians such as Dane Morrison, Devon A. Mihesuah, and William Pencak has begun questioning the applicability of grand narratives, progressivist storylines, or the New Social History to the complexity of American Indian experiences.[76] I have tried to keep abreast of these resistant trends and to cite as many examples as I can in this volume – whose overall purpose is to encourage everyone to consider researching, engaging with, and enriching their own work through whatever they can learn about American Indian forms of historical consciousness. As James Clifford summarizes most of the earlier scholarship reviewed in this chapter, "Historical visions with deep sources in the Americas were inconceivable – recognized, if at all, only as legend or myth." In his view, however, today,

all this has changed. Indigenous stories of contact recenter familiar stories of discovery, conflict, acculturation, and resistance. The line between myth and history can no longer be drawn along a border between Western and non-Western epistemologies. And in the wake of growing arguments over the culture and political location of historical narratives, it becomes harder and harder to sustain a unified, inclusive historical consciousness capable of sorting and reconciling divergent experiences.[77]

[76] For examples, see Morrison's "'In Whose Hands Is the Telling of the Tale?'" in *American Indian Studies: An Interdisciplinary Approach to Contemporary Issues*, edited by Duane Morrison (New York: Peter Lang, 1997), Mihesuah's edited volume, *Natives and Academics: Researching and Writing about American Indians* (Lincoln: University of Nebraska Press, 1998), and Pencak's "Placing Native Americans at the Center: Indian Prophetic Revolts and Cultural Identity," in *Issues in Native American Cultural Identity*, edited by Michael K. Green (New York: Peter Lang, 1995). See also the critique by Maori scholar Linda Tuhiwai Smith, who condemns Western notions of history as overly totalizing and broad-scale, evolutionary-biased, human-glorifying, monovocal, morally insensitive, given to glib binary comparisons, and fundamentally patriarchal in "Imperialism, History, Writing and Theory," from her *Decolonizing Methodologies: Research and Indigenous Peoples* (New York: Zed Books, 1999).

[77] From James Clifford's "Fort Ross Meditation," an exceptional discussion of folk history, in *Routes: Travel and Translation in the Late Twentieth Century* (Cambridge: Harvard University Press, 1997), pp. 319–320.

Wishful thinking. Seriously weaving Indian ways of history into America's academic and publishing systems remains an uphill battle. For one thing, non-Indian scholars must accept the fact that in research enterprises involving Indian history, Native collaboration is mandatory and is usually predicated upon the ultimate benefits to the tribes. They must also appreciate that given their "presentist" mandate, most Indian historical forms are forever "under construction." What is deemed traditional, historical, or even sacred to one generation may subtly shift categories in the next, and Indians should not be penalized for keeping their histories pertinent. And scholars must also agree to walk the ground, talk with the people, and stick around long enough for the temporal sway of these separate Native worlds to penetrate their minds and hearts.

Another obstacle is the fact that Indians have a harder time than most minorities in breaking out of stereotypes that deny them the right or discount their ability to manage their futures creatively or to have their representations of their alternative chronicles of their many different pasts taken seriously. To appreciate what Indian "ways of history" remain up against, one need only hear a national TV commentator berate Indians for clinging to "remnants of their religion and superstitions that may have been useful to savages 500 years ago but which are meaningless in 1992,"[78] or read an op-ed piece in the country's leading newspaper alluding to their innate antipathy for change through the comment "We can no more stop history than the Indians could turn back the Mayflower,"[79] or peruse a similar knee-jerk prejudice in the closing pages of Francis Fukuyama's salute to the global triumph of liberal democracy, *The End of History and the Last Man*.

Searching for a summarizing analogy for the inevitable "homogenization of mankind" (which Fukuyama argued would result from the fusion of international institutions, transnational economic development, and the superiority of democracy over totalitarianism), he sought a counter-image to outmoded cultural relativism with its "thousand shoots

---

[78] CBS "60 Minutes" commentator Andy Rooney, as published in his March 10, 1992, nationally syndicated newspaper column.

[79] Gail Collins, "Where Were You in 1002?," *New York Times*, December 24, 1999, p. A23.

blossoming into as many different flowering plants." Instead of a future peppered with small, autonomous ethnic states, Fukuyama dredged up the progressivist analogy of human history as a "long wagon train strung out along a road."[80]

Like pioneering families pushing through uncharted territory, some societies "will be pulling into town sharply and crisply, while others will be bivouacked back in the desert, or else stuck in ruts in the final pass over the mountains." As the only threat to humanity's progressive movement, however, Fukuyama identifies some creatures who are still lurking beyond its fires. Helplessly in the grip of America's hoariest archetype, his next sentence goes, "Several wagons, attacked by Indians, will have been set aflame, and abandoned along the way."

A few pioneers become so disoriented by the firefight that they head in the wrong direction (here one recalls the seventeenth-century Indian captive escapees from New England puritanism, whom ethno-historian James Axtell describes assimilating, as if with some relief, into the heartholds of Catholic Canadian Indian society).[81] But the book closes with Fukuyama expressing confidence that enough wagons will finally pull into a safe and civilized municipality so that "any reasonable person looking at the situation would be forced to agree that there had been only one journey and one destination."

Fukuyama's return to the rusty theory of unilineal evolution has no room for those recalcitrant feathered few whom he portrays as so antag-onistic to liberal, rational democracy that he refuses even to include them among the other deluded holdouts for cultural relativism.[82] In all the world, this champion of the American way must single out the first

---

[80] Francis Fukuyama, *The End of History and the Last Man* (New York: Avon Books, 1993), p. 338.

[81] James Axtell, "The White Indians of Colonial America," *The William and Mary Quarterly*, 3rd. Series 32(1) (January 1975), pp. 55–88.

[82] This "disappearance" of Indians as evolving historical players and commentators echoes the omission of their historical consciousness in academic intellectual history. To note how irrelevant to American Indian concepts are trends that Bernard Bailyn has identified as driving contemporary historiography – "the fusion of latent and man-ifest events; the depiction of large-scale spheres and systems organized as peripheries and cores; and the description of internal states of mind and their relation to external circumstances and events" – is to appreciate why to date no American historian has attempted a book on Indian historicity ("The Challenge of Modern Historiography," *American Historical Review* 87(1) [February 1982], p. 22).

Americans as the sole human group not only to stand outside of history altogether, but to remain a peril to its very existence.[83]

One can only hope that this shameful but not unfamiliar exclusion has cleared the way for appreciating the alternative Native American modes for using and remembering the past that will be surveyed in the following chapters.

---

[83] While Fukuyama evokes the negative "bloodthirsty savage" stereotype to exempt Indians from historical processes, historian Richard White exposes how its symbiotically opposite, positive image, that of the "child of nature," is often employed to the same end: "in yet another version of the old western story of savagery – noble and ignoble – Native Americans merge with nature. They become 'primal peoples' at one with the world around them. Only whites and assorted other non-Indians are peoples of history: this is why our flattery of 'primal peoples' and their traditional knowledge – for we do intend to flatter – is an act of such immense condescension.... At best, Native Americans matter only as a litmus test to determine if our actions are good or bad. But, as they become one with nature, they also cease to matter as either historical or modern peoples. They stand outside history" ("Using the Past: History and Native American Studies," in *Studying Native America: Problems and Prospects*, edited by Russell Thornton (Madison: University of Wisconsin Press, 1998), p. 218.

ONE

————◀◦▶————

Some Dynamics of American
Indian Historicity

I am going to tell stories of the old days now. All of you lie down and
stretch out on your backs, otherwise you will be humpbacked, my father
used to say. Then he would tell us stories and teach us.[1]

Miwok

In the fall of 1975, I was rifling through the upright files of the Doris
Duke Oral History collections in the University of New Mexico library
when one transcript stopped me cold.[2] About six years earlier, a Duke
fieldworker had talked with an elderly Navajo in Tuba City, Arizona.
For openers, the visitor turned an archaeological textbook to a map of
North America with swooping arrows indicating the routes supposedly
trod by Paleo-Indian peoples after they crossed the Beringia Land Bridge
and migrated south to populate two continents.[3] Through an interpreter,
he asked what the old man thought of that scenario for Indian origins.[4]

[1] L. S. Freeland, *Language of the Sierra Miwok*, Indiana University Publications in
Anthropology and Linguistics, Memoir 6, *International Journal of American Linguistics* (Baltimore: Waverly Press, January 1951), p. 178.

[2] For background on this project see C. Gregory Crampton, "The Archives of the Duke
Projects in American Indian Oral History," in *Indian–White Relations: A Persistent
Paradox*, edited by Jane F. Smith and Robert M. Kvasnicka (Washington, D.C.: Howard
University Press, 1981), pp. 119–128.

[3] John McGregor, *Southwestern Archaeology* (New York: John Wiley & Sons, 1941),
p. 114.

[4] From transcript of Tape #761, pp. 1–10, interview conducted on January 2, 1971, for
the Doris Duke Oral History Project, Special Collections, University of New Mexico,
Albuquerque.

Not extracting a simple answer, his translator begged for patience – "he's telling it little by little" – but then he added, "it doesn't sound very little to me, though." The interpreter and informant put their heads together. "He said that he would like to tell you," the translator finally explained, "but...he will be punished for it...I mean the medicine, he can't tell how it works...he said that if he told all his secrets like that he would fall to pieces...."

As for pathways from Western Alaska south, "He said that, 'maybe some other guys came over like that, but us Navajos came a different way.'" At this, the old man launched into what sounded like contradictory origin stories. One was a fragmentary narrative in which cicada-like insects "won this world for us, won this land here, the reservation" after crawling up through the earth's underlayers. The second account had white corn kernels, "actually the mother of the Navajo tribe," and the sun, "the father," talking together, with Navajos born from the corn kernels' underarms. With that the old man clammed up.

Trying another tack, the interviewer asked a question about an illustration of a chronological sequence of arrowheads originating from Arizona's Desert Culture. Again the interpreter and elder went into their huddle; again the translator spoke, somewhat apologetically: "He says that...this isn't true. Whoever wrote it, just thinks about it, just thinks about it...and just makes up a theory about it...." As for who actually chipped those Folsom and Clovis arrowheads? "The horny toads carved it, he said that he has never seen them make it, but some of these old men that he is telling about, they have seen it...."

Finally, the translator explained the old man's reticence. "He says there are too many people that might know secrets like that, [that] is why the young generation, they are kind of breaking up the tradition, breaking up like that. By keeping the secret for such a long time, that now... the Navajo nation is the biggest nation in the world, well, not the world, but in the United States."

At the time, I was scouting material for an anthology of Indian–white relations as expressed through the experiences and words of Native peoples. Clearly, this candidate was a wash. Once I teased out its meanings, any adequate preface would be lengthier than the document, and even then my readers would be scratching their heads. It wasn't a story, it wasn't tagged to some notable event or personality, it wasn't explanatory of history in any recognizable way. It was a clumsy translation of a halting exchange containing fragmentary references to unfamiliar, nonhuman beings and alien conceptual categories about which the speaker felt nervous talking. But I couldn't put it down.

So much lay between the lines. The tensions between two value systems crackled off the page. The interaction was pregnant with contrasting assumptions and priorities regarding the past. What could be gleaned from this intriguing round over differing cultural attitudes toward history? Why did the vested interests that underwrite any culture's retrospective points-of-view seem like genres passing in the night?[5] Unpacking this Navajo anecdote and using Navajo notions of history as an object lesson, let me introduce some central dimensions and dynamics involved with American Indian ways of "doing" history.

Roles of the Indian Historian

If the old Navajo did not feel at liberty to divulge his people's private past, one might ask, who could?

In the case of the Navajos, designated ritual "singers" or "chanters" (*hataalii*) were expected to be familiar with sacred narratives, paying special attention to those portions invoked during ceremonies. But this did not prevent generations of other Navajo storytellers from offering clan migration accounts or historical recollections of more secular reservation times. "To Navajos," writes Navajo author Lucy Tapahonso, "a person's worth is determined by the stories and songs she or he knows, because it is by this knowledge that an individual is directly linked to the history of the entire group."[6]

---

5 For useful contrasts between Navajo and Anglo notions of history, and their ties to notions of identity, see James C. Faris, "Taking Navajo Truths Seriously: The Consequences of the Accretions of Disbelief," *Papers from the Third, Fourth, and Sixth Navajo Studies Conferences*, edited by June-el Piper (Window Rock, Ariz.: Navajo Nation Historic Preservation Department, October 1993), pp. 181–186, and Paul G. Zolbrod, *Dine Bahane: The Navajo Creation Story* (Albuquerque: University of New Mexico Press, 1984), Note 1, pp. 407–409.

6 Quoted in *Native Heritage: Personal Accounts by American Indians, 1790 to the Present*, edited by Arlene Hirschfelder (New York: Macmillan, 1995), p. 153.

Aspiring Navajo ritualists were trained in making prayer sticks, creating ground paintings, learning songs, prayers, and ritual formulae, and, for the class of master chanters, memorizing the lengthier narratives that scripted their curative rites.[7] The Navajo chanter Frank Mitchell, renowned for his mastery of the complex Blessingway ceremony, drew a comparison between his method for recalling this material and the practice of Anglo historians:

> Of course it is the story that tells us the order of the songs all straight, the story of how the songs began. That's why it is simple to remember all these songs. It is just like your history, your American history. You always remember who is the first president and the second president; who invented this and who invented that. Of course you have those facts in books; you do not memorize them, and you do not keep them in your mind. But with us we have all that memorized, you see, in the story.... The story is like a trail. You see, a trail runs in certain ways, and if you have gone that way more than once, you know every little thing that is on the trail.... And if you want to skip two or three songs, why you skip that much of the trail and continue from a point further on.[8]

The selection and training for the role of a traditional Indian historian varied by tribal region and time period. But in these small-scale societies, where everyone observed other people's offspring or their own age-mates at close range, one child's aptitude for remembering, recording, and narrating would probably be noticed and encouraged early on. Pima Indians stayed alert to youngsters who demonstrated an aptitude for recollecting traditions. When they matured into recognized historians eligible to engage in the male-only "smoke talk" of history-recounting, wrote Frank Russell, boys from upcoming generations were "regularly sent

---

[7] For the apprenticeships of Navajo specialists and their use of foundational chant myths, their shorter "lay" versions, and narrative elements that figure during rituals, see Franc J. Newcomb and Gladys A. Reichard, "Chant and Chanter," in *Sandpaintings of the Navajo Shooting Chant* (New York: Dover, Publications, 1975), p. 8, and Gladys A. Reichard, *Navaho Religion: A Study of Symbolism* (New York: Bollingen, 1963), pp. 276, 325.

[8] Frank Mitchell, *Navajo Blessingway Singer: The Autobiography of Frank Mitchell, 1881–1967*, edited by Charlotte J. Frisbie and David P. McAllester (Tucson: University of Arizona Press, 1980), p. 230.

[to them so] that they may listen for four nights to the narratives of how the world was made and peopled: whence the Pimas came and how they struggled with demons, monsters, and savage enemies."[9] Self-selection was also probable, as intellectually gifted or prophetically inclined individuals carved out historian roles for themselves, or fate offered the blind or crippled this productive outlet for their sedentary or otherwise marginalized condition.

In the more stratified world of pre-European southeastern chiefdoms and their successor tribes, like the Cherokee and Creek, one might expect to find more institutionalized roles and stricter regulations for tribal historians, as the French chronicler Antoine Du Pratz gathered from early-eighteenth-century Natchez of southern Louisiana: "I have been told that there were also graduates in the telling of myths. . . . These graduates, of whom there were several in each town, were evidently the repositories of learning, the keepers of the sacred myths, the historians, and the guardians of the supernatural mysteries."[10] It certainly helped when they were also animated performers, as Ella E. Clark, an English professor and anthologist of northern Plains and Plateau Indian narratives, learned at the feet of oral historians in the northern Rockies: "Their facial expressions, voices, and gestures almost told the tale without words as they entertained eager listeners with amusing stories, tales of adventure and war, horror stories, and myths and legends of the wondrous days of long ago. In fact, some stories were told graphically in the sign language."[11]

Among the Ojibwa (Anishinabe) Indians of the Great Lakes, the duties of ritual priest and historian – the *kanawencikewinini*, meaning "reserve man," the individual who "read" the mnemonics scratched into sacred birchbark scrolls – were collapsed into a single role.[12] In the highly

---

[9] Frank Russell, *The Pima Indians*, 26th Annual Report of the Bureau of American Ethnology, 1904–1905 (Washington, D.C.: U.S. Government Printing Office, 1908), p. 206.

[10] Quoted in John R. Swanton, *Social Organization and Social Usages of the Indians of the Creek Confederacy*, 42nd Annual Report of the Bureau of American Ethnology (Washington, D.C.: U.S. Government Printing Office, 1928), p. 367.

[11] Ella E. Clark, *Indian Legends from the Northern Rockies* (Norman: University of Oklahoma Press, 1966), p. 16.

[12] Thomas Vennum, Jr., "Ojibwa Origin-Migration Songs of the *Mitewiwin*," *Journal of American Folklore* 91 (1978), p. 753.

structured Iroquois Confederacy, a member of the Onondoga tribe was assigned the high-status role of "keeper of the wampum records" for the entire Confederacy. Customarily recruited from the Wolf Clan, his historical expertise also cast him as mediator whenever disputes arose during meetings of their multitribal governing council.[13]

Historical crises could shunt this responsibility of culture bearer onto unexpected shoulders. After the Indians of southwestern Oregon were forcibly removed to reservations in the 1850s, the only female tribal members remaining behind were married to white men. According to Coquille Indian scholar George Wasson, these women quietly assumed responsibility for safeguarding their people's oral histories and myths until those narratives could resurface in the 1990s.[14]

When Indian Histories are Used

Clearly, the old Navajo considers the moment in Tuba City all wrong for talking about such matters as the beginning of the world and his people's origins.

His wariness is in line with that of other Navajo historians, who recognized that telling complete stories or sharing powerful names could arouse the wrath of spirits and places.[15] So one might ask, when is it necessary, permissible, or culturally appropriate for Indian historicity to

[13] Among what she identifies as universal characteristics of historicity – it is highly selective, maintains multiple versions, and keeps the past and present interdependent – Emiko Ohnuki-Tierney adds the likelihood of individual historians mitigating the " 'structuration' of the past" on their own so as to legitimize aspiring chiefs (as among native Hawaiians) or to promote key national symbols (as with the Jews). "In historicity," she writes, "we see 'rich humanity' and the powerful role played by historical actors." "Introduction" to *Cultures Through Time: Anthropological Approaches*, edited by Emiko Ohnuki-Tierney (Stanford: Stanford University Press, 1990), p. 20.

[14] *The Eugene Register-Guard*, Section C, "Rediscovered tribal histories 'a gift,' " September 9, 1997, p. 3C.

[15] Concerning Navajo Coyote stories, for instance, folklorist Barre Toelken warns that "These stories should be told only in the winter, and telling of them under proper circumstances enables the Navajos to take part in the annual round of seasonal events on a cosmic level. To tell these stories out of season is to challenge the stability of this cosmic system...." *The Dynamics of Folklore* (Logan: Utah State University Press, 1996), p. 338.

come to life? As Jay Miller generalizes about Indian oral traditions:

> Many tribes have clear notions of copyright. These restrictions determine who can tell a story, what constitutes an audience (adult, child, or mixed), where a story can be told (at home around fire, at a camp site, or remote from home), when literature can be used (often winter only), and why a specific story is told at a particular time and place.[16]

For Navajos the most urgent contexts were ceremonial interludes that brought the afflicted back into accord with a timeless, holier existence. They also relished storytelling sessions about seemingly more prosaic historical events.[17] Upon closer inspection, however, we realize how often the choice of particular episodes was usually quite deliberate, as they spotlighted what Ramond D. Fogelson has called a given tribe's "epitomizing events," whose combination of notable social and religious elements and historically memorable dramas touched deep cultural nerves and rendered comprehensible to themselves a people's transformations over time.[18]

Along with formal ritual occasions, many tribes also enjoyed more relaxed moments for their histories to take center stage. In the winter lodges of the Arikara, one heard recountings of the past during family get-togethers, when delegates from different tribal societies gathered to negotiate or reminisce, or when a youth was prompted by an elder (often a grandparent) to bring food to an uncle in exchange for personal instruction.[19] Evenings were the preferred time for tale-telling, with the

---

[16] Jay Miller, *Oral Literature* (Chicago: The Newberry Library, D'Arcy McNickle Center for the History of the American Indian, 1983), Occasional Papers in Curriculum Series, No. 13, p. 13.

[17] For good examples, see *Navajo Historical Selections,* selected, translated, and edited by Robert W. Young and William Morgan (Phoenix, Ariz.: Department of the Interior, Bureau of Indian Affairs, March 1954).

[18] A strong example is found in Fogelson's "Who Were the Ani-Kutani?: An Excursion into Cherokee Historical Thought," in which he scrutinizes ethnohistorical accounts of Cherokee stories about a mysterious priesthood's demise so as to remind us that "The Cherokees, in common with most peoples of the world, do not view history in terms of abstract, disembodied, invisible, immutable laws and forces. History is generated by human action...." (*Ethnohistory* 31[4] [1984]), p. 261.

[19] Douglas R. Parks, *Traditional Narratives of the Arikara Indians: Stories of Alfred Morsette: English Translations,* V. 3, Studies in the Anthropology of North American Indians (Lincoln: University of Nebraska Press, 1991).

cold season (between first snowfall and first ice breakup) nearly always the appropriate season (lest, in many Indian traditions, you lay yourself open to poisonous snake or scorpion bites).

Among Woodland and Plains tribes as disparate as the Omaha, Ojibwa, Winnebago, Creek, and Pawnee, these last two taboos were rigidly observed. This is because over winter nights the creatures featured in these narratives are hibernating or sluggish and won't know they are being talked about or, worse, made fun of. This explanation was elaborated by the astronomically sophisticated Skidi Pawnee, as recorded by ethnographer George A. Dorsey. In the summer skies their Snake Star stood in proximity to their Coyote Star. If he whispered to the Coyote Star that humans were telling coyote stories among themselves, the Pawnee feared that Coyote might retaliate by having his celestial neighbor sick his reptiles after them.[20]

Indians also used their histories as preemptive strikes during diplomatic encounters. When Canadian Cree and whites sat down at a council, the Alberta elders first insisted on retelling folktales of their trickster, Wisakechak, which included their prophecies about the arrival of white men and their questionable character. Everyone was reminded of aboriginal warnings about alcoholic drink, coin currency, and Christianity so that the imminent negotiation might follow an open-eyed path. This establishment of an "evident sacral atmosphere" helped restore a separate but equal foundation for realistic discussion across cultural boundaries.[21]

Legends likewise enabled Indians to lay their cards on the negotiating table.[22] Before a critical trade discussion in 1735 with Georgia's colonial governor, James Oglethorpe, a Creek leader named Tomochichi made

---

[20] George A. Dorsey, *Traditions of the Skidi Pawnee*, American Folklore Society Memoir 8 (1904), p. xxiif.

[21] P. Joseph Cahill, "Aspects of Modern Cree Religious Tradition in Alberta," *Studies in Comparative Religion* 28 (November 1977), p. 211.

[22] As South Indian historian Nilakanta Sastri succinctly put it, in ancient times as well as now, "legends were arguments" (*A History of South India* [Oxford: Oxford University Press, 1975], p. 77). And as Adolph F. Bandelier commented on secondary exploitation of such "arguments" (which then become primary data about Anglo-European historicity), "All I desire to call attention to is the danger of early Indian lore having been colored, by those who gathered it, so as to support a favorite theory" ("Traditions of Precolumbian Landings on the Western Coast of South America," *American Anthropologist* 7 [1905], p. 251).

sure that his people's migration narrative was translated into English and depicted on a buffalo hide so that the British would realize that they were dealing with a legitimate, and equivalent, territorial authority.[23] Still later, at the Medicine Lodge Treaty negotiations of 1867 in Kansas, "Each speaker [first] told the history of his people and explained the Indian rapport with nature," writes historian Donald Fixico, "stating that his and his people's lives were affected by the coming of the white man."[24]

Creation stories were the preferred invocation when dissident Hopi leader Yukeoma traveled from Arizona to the nation's capital in March 1911 to dissuade the government from sending Hopi children to the white man's boarding school. Sharing his people's predestinatory myths and prophecies about a long lost "white" brother, Yukeoma also mentioned the inscribed stones given by the Red Headed Spirit to the Hopis as proof of their sacred right to their land – "and that is why he don't want the civilized way," explained the interpreter.[25] For this traditionalist, myth was the first, last, and only diplomatic discourse a Hopi could advance. If it went unheeded, it was only proper for him to pass on his people's alarm about the cosmic destruction that would ensue. Following in Yukeoma's footsteps a half-century later, Hopi and Iroquois spokespeople delivered similar mythic prophecies about the fate of the world at large from the podium of the United Nations in New York.

Sacred narratives were also the discourse of choice for a venerable Tohono O'odham speaker whom historian of religions Sam Gill heard during an Arizona seminar on Indian education. Instead of addressing teachers' salaries or student needs, for fifteen minutes the speaker delved into Earthmaker's original creation of his people and their geographical landmarks before shifting to how their culture hero I'itoi, or Elder

---

23 Albert S. Gatschet. *A Migration Legend of the Creek Indians* (New York: Kraus Reprint, [1884] 1969), p. 235.

24 Donald L. Fixico, "As Long as the Grass Grows . . . The Cultural Conflicts and Political Strategies of United States–Indian Treaties," in *Ethnicity and War*, edited by Winston A. Van Horne and Thomas V. Tonnesen (Madison: University of Wisconsin Press, 1984), p. 140.

25 Katherine C. Turner, *Red Men Calling on the Great White Father* (Norman: University of Oklahoma Press, 1951), p. 203; based upon conference between Yukeoma and Commissioner of Indian Affairs Valentine, U.S. National Archives, BIA Central Files, 1907–1939, 101559-10-Moqui-056 (RG 75).

Brother, taught his people to camp, marry, and behave properly. At first Gill was thrown for a loss. Then it struck him that the old man was "demonstrating to his audience a basic principle in education: knowledge has meaning and value only when placed within a particular view of the world" – a view that was codified within a traditionalist's sense of history.[26]

Waiting throughout all these references to chartering narratives and inherited knowledge could drive impatient whites up the wall. During hearings of the ICC, anthropologist Nancy O. Lurie recalled that Indians often frustrated lawyers when they tried to provide their people's bigger picture. One claims attorney recalled eliciting testimony from a Southwestern witness: "The old man wanted to tell the entire tribal history from the time of creation, and would respond through his interpreter to repeated interruptions to move his testimony along to points at issue, 'But I ain't been born yet!'"[27]

How Indian Histories Come Alive

The old Navajo finds the narrow band of this verbal interrogation in an impromptu setting during the middle of the day altogether confining and uncongenial for talking about his people's holy history.

The ambience is not auspicious. The almost aggressive mode of interrogatory communication has been imposed by an outsider. The elder cannot express himself in his own language. The ultimate purpose of the meeting bewilders him. It is not taking place in a "beautiful" or "harmonious" atmosphere. His words are not orchestrated within a medley of other artistic genres in order to make sure that the results are "good" and "blessed" or "satisfying."[28] If Navajos considered their

---

[26] Sam D. Gill, "The Tree Stood Deep Rooted," in *Native American Religious Action: A Performance Approach to Religion* (Columbia, S.C.: University of South Carolina Press, 1987), p. 17.

[27] Nancy O. Lurie, "Epilogue," in *Irredeemable America: The Indians' Estate and Land Claims*, edited by Imre Sutton (Albuquerque: University of New Mexico Press, 1985), p. 371.

[28] All are glosses on the Navajo term *hozho*, a core concept, key symbol, and paramount cultural value that embraces them all, and that Clyde Kluckhohn considered "of the greatest importance for the understanding of Navajo philosophy" ("The Philosophy

myths "talk about doing," the rituals that harnessed the powers that were evoked by those stories were known as "doing" – a modest term for their critical goal of obtaining reversals of negative conditions or blessings for human endeavors.[29] Clearly, this interview has neither end in mind.

For Navajos these "two sides of the same coin," as religious historian Karl W. Luckert pairs myth with ritual, work in concert to bring the tribe's deepest knowledge of its origins and history to *purposeful* life – in the way that Claude Levi-Strauss meant by his comment that this is "therefore never [just] history, but history *for*."[30] At the same time that they were chanting about their ancestral histories in ceremonial contexts, Navajo "singers" also portrayed their symbols, depicting the Tuba City man's toads, ears of corn, and "holy people" of the four sacred directions in the stylized "dry" paintings (fine sand colored with powdered minerals), which were created and destroyed during five or nine night-time "chantways."

Beginning and ending narratives often involved a conventionalized call-and-response between storyteller and audience, creating a tacit contract of almost coconspiratorial intimacy. Before launching into particularly old or holy stories, the Northern Cheyenne called for a nonverbal oath, as described by the tribe's premier raconteur, John Stands in Timber:

An old storyteller would smooth the ground in front of him with his hand and make two marks in it with his right thumb, two with his left, and a double mark with both thumbs together. Then he would

of the Navajo Indians" in *Ideological Differences and World Order*, edited by F. S. C. Northrup [New Haven: Yale University Press, 1949]); see also its centrality in Gary Witherspoon's classic work *Language and Art in the Navajo Universe* (Ann Arbor: University of Michigan Press, 1977). According to Maureen Trudelle Schwarz, the concept is also a formative criterion for Navajo historicity, as exemplified by the way tribespeople drew upon ancestral charters to explain sudden crises ("Coping with the 'Mystery Illness,' 1993," *Ethnohistory* 42(3) [Summer 1995], pp. 375–401).

29 A linguistic distinction offered in Karl W. Luckert's "An Approach to Navajo Mythology" in *Native Religious Traditions*, edited by Earle H. Waugh and K. Dad Prithipaul (Waterloo: Canadian Corporation for Studies in Religion, Wilfrid Laurier University Press, 1979), p. 117.

30 Claude Levi-Strauss, *The Savage Mind* (Chicago: University of Chicago Press, 1966 [1962]), p. 257 (emphasis mine).

rub his hands, and pass his right hand up his right leg to the waist, and touch his left hand and pass it on up his right arm to his breast. He did the same thing with his left and right hands going up the other side. Then he touched the marks on the ground with both hands and rubbed them together and passed them over his head and all over his body.... That meant the Creator had made human beings' bodies and their limbs as he made the earth, and that the Creator was witness to what was to be told.... And it was a good thing. I always trusted them, and I believe they told the truth.[31]

Most tribes also evolved "multimedia" productions for activating their narratives. Rhetorical skills provided one level of coloration: "The elements of these stories and songs," according to Navajo author Luci Tapahonso, "include the proper use of rhythm, meter, symbolism, concrete diction, and imagery.... The Navajo language lends itself well to rich, connotative allusions to time, surrounding physical conditions, and historical as well as spiritual imagery."[32] As minds were preoccupied by their plots, eyes were glued to visual media – the movements of masks, attire and regalia, colors and symbols, the occasional pictorial chart illustrating the present situation's ties to tribal cosmology and legendary actions, the mnemonic props that assisted in recounting aristocratic lineages, distant migrations, or momentous occurrences. And nervous systems were further engaged by flickering flame shadows, insinuating winds, hissing snow, coughing animals, and smoke from scented woods, grasses, and bark. This sensory ambience enabled culturally conditioned imaginations to soar and coaxed all sorts of history into present reality.

Other genres only thickened the magic – prayers, songs, spells, and dancing. While storytellers improvised on their inherited narratives, when they broke into songs that originally came from the throats of narrative characters, the verses were usually recalled word for word and keyed the entire occasion into another wavelength of supernatural intensity. According to Donald Bahr, what distinguishes verbal genres among

---

[31] John Stands in *Timber*, *Cheyenne Memories: A Folk History*, with Margot Liberty and Robert M. Utley (Lincoln: University of Nebraska Press, 1972), p. 12.

[32] Quoted in Hirschfelder, ed., *Native Heritage*, p. 153.

the Tohono O'dham of Arizona, for example, is the identity of their intended recipients. Stories, whether of the creation epic or a less sacred,
legendary variety, were intended for human ears alone. Oratory was
addressed to both humans and supernaturals; but songs were directed
solely to the spirits.[33]

Eruptions into oratory, incantation, or verse often indicated magical liftings of the past into the present. Theatrical alterations of voice
pitch, tone, and pace, sudden shifts into formal modes of address, and
mimicries of humans and animals made it seem as if a ventriloquist were
channeling the drama's personalities. Using shamanic vocabularies also
induced this sort of transformational atmosphere, antiquated terms that,
like the non-Indian's "abracadabra," few could understand but all knew
activated ancient powers merely by virtue of their utterance.

"If anthropologists, folklorists, linguists, and oral historians are interested in the full meaning of the spoken word," ethnolinguist Dennis
Tedlock warns us, concluding his analysis of the "history" he extracted
from Zuni Indian songs, speeches, and myths, "they must stop treating oral narratives as if they were reading prose when in fact they are
listening to dramatic poetry."[34] As for songs, Tedlock continues, "The
song is an attempt by them [Zuni Indian priests] to come to terms with
an historical event and at the same time reassert tradition." And the
meanings of these Pueblo songs could wrap around root metaphors that
demanded more than mere memorization in order to embody them. As
Hopi artist Michael Kabotie described one means by which his people
internalized the living essence of their past:

> The Hopi believe that if you want to teach a person the history or
> the song that is deeply connected to our history you feed them corn.
> You're planting this history into this person. You're planting your song
> into this person. That way that history will grow inside him.[35]

---

[33] Donald M. Bahr, *Pima and Papago Ritual Oratory: A Study in Three Texts* (San
Francisco: The Indian Historian Press, 1975), p. 6.

[34] Dennis Tedlock, "Learning to Listen: Oral History as Poetry," in *The Spoken Word
and the Work of Interpretation* (Philadelphia: University of Pennsylvania Press, 1983),
pp. 123, 110.

[35] Quoted from *Hopi: Songs of the Fourth World*, a film by Pat Ferraro (San Francisco:
Ferraro Films, 1982).

Multiple Pasts in Indian Histories

For our reluctant Navajo interviewee, there appears to be no strict division between the time frames of tangible evidence you can touch, like those associated with arrowheads found in dirt, and that primal realm evoked in the old man's anecdotes about cohabiting mythic entities or insect ancestors that religious historian Karl W. Luckert calls the era of "pre-human flux."

For many Navajos and scholars, the tribe's past, or *atk'idaa* ("on top of each other"), was marked by the "stacking" of former experiences or events, which could draw in, according to Kenneth J. Pratt, everything from material "particular to an individual's recall or personal opinion" to separate clan migration narratives to acquisitions of the major "sources of healing power."[36] In a diagram of these temporal accumulations that he sketched for Pratt, a Navajo named Old Age Kill differentiated between vertical and horizontal advancement. Ceremonials associated with Navajo upward movement, as they ascended through a sequence of underworlds (sometimes portrayed as superimposed hemispheres supported by pillars of precious stones and separated by lenses filled with stars), climaxed with the Emergence. But horizontal movement across the earth's surface then progressed under a "patriarchal" umbrella and featured the "separation of the sexes," the birth of the sacred twins, and creation of their central Blessingway ceremonial. At this point, history entered today's "matriarchal" period, again punctuated by the periodic appearance of new ceremonials, one major flood, and finally human creation and the Nightway ceremonial.[37]

Some scholars argue that Navajo rituals that emphasize hunting encode memories of other, less mythic migrations of Athabaskan-speaking, proto-Navaho who ventured south from western Canada into the Pueblo

[36] Kenneth J. Pratt, "Some Navajo Relations to the Past," in *Papers from the Third, Fourth, and Sixth Navajo Studies Conference*, edited by June-el Piper (Window Rock, Ariz.: Navajo Nation Historic Preservation Department, October 1993), pp. 151–157. "Concern with the way the past enters the present," writes anthropologist Nancy D. Munn, who could well be introducing connections between Navajo oral tradition and its practical applications, "foregrounds the implications of the meaningful forms and concrete media of practices for apprehension of the past" ("The Cultural Anthropology of Time: A Critical Essay," *Annual Review of Anthropolgy* 21[1992], p. 113).

[37] James C. Faris and Harry Walters, "Navajo History: Some Implications of Contrasts of Navajo Ceremonial Discourse," *History and Anthropology* 5(1990), p. 2.

Indian Southwest, from whom they acquired new cosmological concepts, ceremonial practices and gardening traditions.[38] But most fieldworkers have learned from Navajos themselves that their own key historical markers for "deep time" are indeed those named "ceremonials," whose scenarios usually include, as Franc Newcomb wrote of the Hail Chantway, "a warp of history and a woof of colorful embellishment from generations of storytellers."[39]

Even so, today's Navajo folklore about that period can seem "very close to the cultural perception of historical processes," wrote Barre Toelken after eliciting stories from Montezuma Canyon Navajos in the 1950s. But Toelken did notice that when his consultants spoke as if they had personally witnessed this arrival into the Southwest, estimated by archaeologists to have occurred well over five hundred years before, their descriptions of stealing corn and squash from the smaller-statured, timid residents they found living already there sounded suspiciously like present-day Navajo stereotypes about their neighboring Hopis.[40]

For most Indian peoples, the unpredictable "events" of human history erupted within the reassuring ceremonial cycle of a yearly round. Rituals associated with hunting, "first fruits" foraging, agriculture, or "world renewal" helped to coordinate the interdependence of the (often personalized) cosmic behaviors that affected seasons, weather, underworlds and aboveworlds, and the symbolic practices that afforded humans a degree of "participatory management" in keeping the universe on track. Among the Pueblo Indians, designated "sun watchers" kept their eyes on the distant, familiar horizon so as to anticipate arrivals and departures of the sun and to announce imminent rituals.[41]

---

[38] For an example of the more European scholarly approach, which teases out of liturgical texts clues and data about prior forms of collective existence, see Karl W. Luckert, *The Navajo Hunter Tradition*, with field assistance and translations by John Cook, Victor Beck, and Irvy Gossen, and with additional translation by Father Berard Haile (Tucson: University of Arizona Press, 1975).

[39] Franc Johnson Newcomb, *Hosteen Klah: Navajo Medicine Man and Sand Painter* (Norman: University of Oklahoma Press, 1964), p. 103.

[40] Barre Toelken, "The End of Folkore," The 1998 Archer Taylor Memorial Lecture, *Western Folklore* 57 (Winter 1998), p. 15.

[41] Florence H. Ellis, "A Thousand Years of the Pueblo Sun-Moon-Star Calendar," in *Archaeoastronomy in Pre-Columbia America*, edited by Anthony F. Aveni (Austin: University of Texas Press, 1975).

In other tribal zones, different natural cycles scheduled the collective representations enacted by men and women. Key constellations in the Nebraska sky were monitored by star-gazing specialists among the Pawnee for the ordering of camp movements, village arrangements, and major rituals. In northwestern California the First Eel and First Salmon rites practiced by the Hupa people were, as Lee Davis observes, "scheduled seasonally according to when the eel and salmon were at the height of their upriver runs in the spring."[42] For the coastal Salish of present-day Washington State, time reckoning was governed by the ebb and flow of tidal waters.[43] Compared with the Navajo conceptions just reviewed, time appears relatively less "progressive" for the plains-dwelling Arikara, according to scholar Douglas R. Parks. Among the five distinguishing features of their sense of history, Parks highlights a lessened concern with dates and historical periods and the frequent "displacement" of narrative elements, which allows actors from historical anecdotes, for example, to merge with or be projected into more mythic or sacred narratives.

From distinctions among genres of tribal narrative, we can also gain an insider's perspective on their multiple historical periods akin to those just reviewed for the Navajo. Among the Koyukan of interior Alaska, for instance, it is stories from *kk'adonts'idnee*, or the "Distant Time," that explain both the origins and behavioral patterns of all "beings" – living entities that may be biological, geologic, or even climatic in nature.[44] In some cases, temporal categories actually double as cover terms for those genres, as with the Zuni term *chimiky'ana'kowa*, or "the Beginning," referring to the genesis narratives they regard as historical truth.[45]

---

[42] Lee Davis, "The Hupa Calendar: Time in Native California," paper presented to the Department of Anthropology, University of California-Los Angeles, May 3, 1989, p. 16.

[43] See Wayne Suttles, "Time and Tide," in his *Coast Salish Essays* (Seattle: University of Washington Press, 1987), pp. 68–72.

[44] Richard K. Nelson, *Make Prayers to the Raven: A Koyukon View of the Northern Forest* (Chicago: University of Chicago Press, 1983), pp. 16–19.

[45] See Andrew Peynetsa and Walter Sanchez, *Finding the Center: Narrative Poetry of the Zuni Indians, from Performances in Zuni*, translated by Dennis Tedlock (New York: Dial Press, 1972).

Among the Tillamooks of Oregon, according to Elizabeth Jacobs, the past was divided into three broad spans of time: the "myth age," the "era of transformations," and the "period of true happenings."[46] Grouped in the first were original creation events that bestowed life on all things; this was a volatile period of dangerous processes and indeterminate identities. The second era witnessed the more entertaining stuff of re-creative drama as a "trickster-transformer" named Southwind conquered monsters, molded topography, and readied the earth for the distinct ethnic groups we know today. Only in the third period came what non-Indians consider true "history," when human beings diversified into multiple traditions and named ancestors took part in known events in specific locations. (In some respects, these epochs remind us more of the *longue durées* of the French *Annales* historians, with their appreciation for broad environmental and climatic constants, large geographical regions, and long-term social and economic structures, than they do of North American academic history's predilection for the impacts of singular events, particular ideologies, functional explanations, and evolutionary progress.)

While the same tripartite division held for the Nunamiut Eskimos studied by Nicholas J. Gubser, their time frames were even vaguer: *Ithaq amma*, the ancient, almost timeless days before any known ancestors; *Ipani*, recent times, within the memory of individuals living today; and *Ingalagaan*, the indistinct period in between.[47] Interestingly enough, the Nunamiut generally positioned their "true history" (*koliaqtuaq*) in the first, ancient era, while their "imaginative stories" (*unipquaq*) were consigned to recent times.

All of these temporal blockings were wedged between the comforting repetitions of Time's Cycle and the unpredictable and irreversible destinations of Time's Arrow.[48] When George Widengren worried about a name for the intermediate discourse between these extremes, he coined

46 Elizabeth D. Jacobs, *Nehalem Tilamook Tales*, University of Oregon, Monographs in Anthropology, No. 3, 1959, p. ix.

47 Nicholas J. Gubser, *The Nunamiut Eskimos: Hunters of Caribou* (New Haven: Yale University Press, 1965).

48 These terms are drawn, of course, from Stephen Jay Gould's *Time's Arrow, Time's Cycle: Myth and Metaphor in the Discovery of Geological Time* (Cambridge: Harvard University Press, 1987), to which Bill Cronon guided me.

the term "condensed history" to describe the "patriarchal legends" of ancient Israel that combined elements of both.[49] And to these temporalities I am tempted to add a fourth, what I will clumsily call "Time's Eternity," which sounds almost like a second cousin to what Fernand Braudel suggests with his phrase *l'histoire immobile*. By it I wish to indicate the politics of morality, identity, and persistence through which the collective imaginations of human groups strive first to impose some idealistic, existential stability on this brew of natural cycles and evolutionary progress, and then to inject that atemporal positioning into their historical representations.[50] For by now it should come as no surprise to readers how preoccupied are most Indian representations of the past with their stabilizing impact upon the unfolding present.

Multiple Accounts of Indian Pasts

Almost like teeth, the Navajo man has had these story fragments extracted from his memory by a representative of a foreign, possibly threatening culture whom he obviously feels has no right to know any more.

Nor will he leak further information about whether the larger narratives to which he alludes are the property of any particular Navajo constituency. This is not surprising. When the renowned Navajo medicine man Hosteen Klah hoped to expand his three-chant repertoire, he ran up against the code that restricted his access to available mythic narratives and their ritual applications to those belonging to his mother's, father's, or grandmother's clans. In his ceremonial system, the ownership or

---

[49] George Widengren, "Myth and History in Israelite-Jewish Thought," in *Culture in History: Essays in Honor of Paul Radin*, edited by Stanley Diamond (New York: Columbia University Press, 1960), pp. 467–495.

[50] I'm tempted to see today's vernacular notion of "Indian time" as tied to this concept as well, a way for territorially impoverished Indians to claim a last-ditch, oppositional temporality with its host of proudly ethnic associations, evoking an exclusively nativistic, relaxed zone in which, as Bentley Spang puts it, "Anglo time has been suspended indefinitely, replaced wholly by Indian Time. The hands of time hang limp and lifeless. Coup has been counted on the white man's clock" (from "On Indian Time," in *The Magazine*, August 2000, p. 33, and elaborated in Spang's summer 2000 exhibition for the Institute of American Indian Arts Museum in Santa Fe entitled "Indian Time: Art in the New Millennium").

practical application of particular historical discourses was also determined by who you're related to or where you live.

Who has what at stake in any Indian historical discourse? Where are the relevant circles of a narrative's rightful "owners" and implicated listeners? From what social constituency does it arise, how extensive are the ripples of its intended reception, and what are the widest ramifications of its perpetuation? By identifying the multiple, often quarreling interest groups within any society, and by making each of their claims the measure of any given history's intended relevance or "scale" (rather than abstract concepts of time or genres of narrative), we arrive at oral tradition's defining benefit and unending pleasure: multiple versions. Ultimates and absolutes belong to the gods; it is as hopeless to search for any single, authoritative ur-narrative as it is to look for paradise. Besides, locating any such original version would obviate the invariably messy work of human agency. It is the incessant wrangling over truth, and the sense of endless rehearsal, that are the yeasty essence of cultural reproduction, and that provide one of humankind's most creative alternatives to totalitarianism, and the delaying tactics that often minimize violence.

Among American Indians, any given narrative's radius of relevance might draw in or be owned by a particular cluster of social entities, whether immediate family, lineage, clan, moiety, phratry, subtribe, tribe, confederacy, nation, or outcast group, each with its overt and possibly covert agendas. Keeping many versions of its primordial claims and cultural experiences fluid and available for discussion enables a society to check and adjust its course through uncertain times.[51]

Any of those interest groups might provide a version that privileges its ancestral role in the account. When a Navajo storyteller starts his account with "The way I heard it was ...," as Luci Tapahonso explains, his variant "doesn't discount other versions, but rather adds to the body of knowledge being exchanged." It is the innately democratic virtue of

---

[51] This was why the Saramaka of Suriname were anxious about anthropologist Richard Price putting their historical memories into print. They feared, as George E. Marcus and Michael M. J. Fischer write, that "the tradition itself will die. The text will become canonical; knowledge will lose its power and become frozen, no longer flowing with the rhythms of particular men's skills or particular group needs, no longer allowing multiple versions." *Anthropology as Cultural Critique: An Experimental Moment in the Human Sciences* (Chicago: University of Chicago Press, 1986), p. 102.

much oral tradition that its multiple versions "enrich the listener's experience," in Tapahonso's words, and do so by providing cross-referencing native glosses and commentaries that are themselves underlain with complementary fragments or competing claims that usually require an intimate awareness of the community's different, perhaps contradictory microhistories to interpret.[52]

Within the cultural world of the Hopi Indians of Arizona, as religious historian Armin Geertz points out, one looks in vain for a single, authoritative account of their Four Worlds myth of tribal emergence "because there is no such complete version. Each clan jealously guards its own version as being autochthonous and complete in its own right. . . . These clan traditions are mutually incompatible, and accounts – even within a single clan, especially from other mesa villages – are conflicting. . . ."[53] Upon close comparison of plot variants, such a range of narratives can betray the hidden histories and knowledge hierarchies that are often part of far more involved native pasts than we find reflected in non-Indian tribal histories.

As the Omaha Indian scholar Francis La Flesche scrutinized different accounts of the legendary painful split between his people and their Osage brethren on the banks of the Mississippi, for instance, he detected two separate strains within the Osage material. In versions from the "common people," clarifying structural causes and effects was less important than emphasizing emotional consequences; the severing of ties of affection and bonds of kinship during the dispute between the fissioned tribes even preserved poignant word-for-word phrases that memorialized its human toll. But to the "ruling and priestly class" among the Osages, worries about the continuity of certain rites and ceremonies left a major impression in their accounts of the split. In later years, however, when the two peoples visited each other again, the version with which the Osages regaled the Omaha was the more personalized one that both parties then hashed over at length, sharing family traditions back and forth. This joint re-creation of an interactive past reestablished ties of

---

[52] As quoted in Hirschfelder, ed., *Native Heritage*, p. 154.

[53] Armin W. Geertz, "Reflections on the Study of Hopi Mythology," in *Religion in Native North America*, edited by Christopher Vecsey (Moscow: University of Idaho Press, 1990), p. 130.

friendship and fictional kinship that were cemented by reciprocal give-aways of gifts between hosts and guests.[54]

For our increasingly uneasy Tuba City traditionalist, internal sirens are also warning that those supernatural authorities will know if he conjures up the mythic past, as through a magical formula, without good cause. Only by appreciating the profoundly religious nature of much history-making and history-perpetuating in many Indian societies can we understand his anxiety and stubbornness. American Indian "mythistory," to borrow historian William H. McNeill's term, is often cloaked with the protective sanction of sacred utterance so as to protect it within a certain constituency, be they a kin group, a priesthood, or a nationhood.[55] To speak it promiscuously or publicly may also be perilous, since its stories often remain imbued with the powerful forces that originally created the world and that can still destroy it. Sometimes such reticence actually issues from consideration for the welfare of those *not* in the know.

Claims of Indian Histories

From the old Navajo's tone, we gather that the Doris Duke interrogator has trespassed into Navajo intellectual and spiritual space. We also catch hints of that common motivation behind any people's historical narrative – the desire to stake some sort of claim on behalf of some constituency, even if it is only to prioritize a particular brand of historical consciousness.

Personal experience or some sixth sense seems to be alerting him that at this moment at Tuba City the vested interests that underwrite the two cultures' historical points of view or collective memories stand at cross purposes. The archaeologist's privileging of temporal chronology challenges his allegiance to the persistence of Navajo religious, aesthetic, and moral symbols. And while he knows what good his people's traditions might have for them, what possible benefit might they have for a

---

54 Francis La Flesche, "Omaha and Osage Traditions of Separation," *Proceedings of the XIX International Congress of Americanists*, 1915, pp. 459–462.

55 William H. McNeill, *Mythistory and Other Essays* (Chicago: University of Chicago Press, 1986).

white guy from beyond the confines of his sacred mountains? Without a clearer purpose, the old Navajo considers the telling of his people's history irrelevant, even dangerous. This sense of history is more than academic; its activation is intended to have effects in the real world. Not by their Treaty of 1864, but rather by "keeping the secret for such a long time," we are told, has the Navajo nation become the largest reservation in the United States. At the center of that "secret" are the accounts to which he is referring that bind together Navajo origins, ancient events, distinctive identity, and unfolding destiny.[56]

While secret, this history is not the silent, written variety concocted out of archives and destined for library shelves or for exchanges between writers and readers who are strangers and lack a shared community and system of social inheritance. This is the same past that is called up, for instance, by the Tlingits of the Northwest Coast in the speeches delivered during mortuary rituals. Their rhetorical touchstones are references to physical heirlooms, especially the masks, crest symbols, and dance regalia known collectively as *at.oow*, which, in turn, evoke the *shuka*, the generations of owner-descendants – the "ones who had gone before" – as well as the unborn, those who remain "ahead." Their orations affirm the Tlingit sense of historical continuity, provide therapy for close relatives, and integrate social subsets of the community.[57]

Before Euro-Americans were on the North American scene, the stories they would dismiss as mere entertainment were central to tribal identity and continuity. Adam Hodgson was told by a half-Choctaw how, in the old days, after a cold plunge in the river, all the youngsters were gathered on its banks "to learn the manners and customs of their ancestors, and hear the old men recite the traditions of their forefathers. They were assembled again, at sunset, for the same purpose; and were taught to

---

[56] As Paul G. Zolbrod observes, the culmination of the Navajo origin myth revolves around such a claim, for "it defines the advent of a distinct Navajo identity...the manifest readiness of one band of people to assimilate another, to organize in clan groups, to set appropriate limits on which clans may intermarry, and to institutionalize agricultural and domestic procedures." *Dine bahan: The Navajo Creation Story* (Albuquerque: University of New Mexico Press, 1984), pp. 408–409.

[57] Nora Marks Dauenhauer and Richard Dauenhauer, editors, *Haa Tuwumaaqu Yis, for Healing Our Spirit: Tlingit Oratory* (Seattle: University of Washington Press, 1990).

regard as a sacred duty the transmission to their posterity of the lessons thus acquired."[58]

Pre-European evidence for this claim-staking dimension to Native history is especially compelling in Central and South America. As struggles among the feuding post-Toltec city-states of central Mexico became as much ideological as military after 1200 A.D., some groups reconstituted their own historical charters. According to archaeologists Geoffrey W. Conrad and Arthur A. Demarest, they employed "creative mythography" that traced their ancestry to "apotheosized Toltec" forbears in order to legitimize assertions of predestined authority.[59] The same hegemonic function of Native historicity obtained after Europeans crushed these Latin American empires. When the Incan artist-chronicler Poma de Ayala assumed responsibility for drawing and describing his culture's history, he maintained a pre-Columbian tradition of pictorializing history so as to make a case for the adoption by the ruling Spanish colonists of Incan concepts of record keeping, social control, communication, and political organization.[60]

From the shards of lore in the elderly Navajo's responses, we gather that nothing less than a case for Navajo land sovereignty, the threatened core of The People's survival in historical space and time, is at issue here. In tightening circles of geographic specificity, as if he were zooming in through a satellite's camera, he suggests that the narrative he is so uncomfortable about airing without a clearer purpose legitimizes not only his people's sense of time but also their sense of space: we get a long shot of "this world," then a medium shot of "this land here," and finally his close-up on "the reservation."

But his tribe's multifaceted historicity could also zero in on more pressing emergencies. When the deadly disease that biomedical experts dubbed "hantavirus" struck Navajo country in 1993, tribal traditions

---

[58] Adam Hodgson, *Remarks During a Journey Through North America* (New York: Samuel Whiting, 1823), p. 278.

[59] Geoffrey W. Conrad and Arthur A. Demarest, "The Aztec Imperial Expansion," in *Religion and Empire: The Dynamics of Aztec and Inca Expansionism* (Cambridge: Cambridge University Press, 1984), pp. 11–151.

[60] See Felipe Guaman Poma de Ayala, *La nueva Coronica y Buen Gobierno*, edited by L. Bustios Galvez, 3 vols. (Lima: Tallers del Servico de Prensa, Propaganda y Publicaciones Militares, 1956–1966).

helped medical investigators track its source. Their stories pointed to a correspondence between instances of killing illnesses earlier in the century and winters with heavy snowfall that yielded especially fecund pinon trees, which, in turn, produced a rise in rodent populations. But the scientific explanation that mice excreta infected dust that, when breathed, could be lethal satisfied Navajos only up to a point. They also needed to know *why* the epidemic had occurred, and they explained this, according to ethnohistorian Maureen Trudelle Schwarz, by citing the "improper, disharmonious behavior of contemporary Navajo," such as telling myths out of season, defiling the earth with toxic waste dumping and coal mining, and disrespecting the elders.[61] Only by placing breaking events into such a framework could the Navajos reorient themselves in a culturally congruent fashion so as to right the imbalances, restore *hozho*, and take charge of their own history.

How Indian Histories are Validated

The Navajo from Tuba City is dead certain what is true about his people's past and what isn't.

The white man's picture book of tribal origins he dismisses as the product of irrelevant "thinking" and "theorizing." Everyone should know that the horny toads chipped those stone arrowheads; he is positive about this in much the same way that Navajos once told folklorist Barre Toelken that it wasn't any old ants that visited illness upon someone who inadvertently kicked apart one of their anthills, but ANTS – by which they meant the undying, precursor supernatural entities from ancient times that were extremely sensitive to any slight.[62] Our old Navajo is sure of this because of the testimony of "these old men," by which he seems to mean the echelon of trained ritualists whose business it is to draw the powers of those stories into the present.

[61] Maureen Trudelle Schwarz, "The Explanatory and Predictive Power of History: Coping with the 'Mystery Illness,' 1993," *Ethnohistory* 442(3) (1995), p. 395.

[62] Barre Toelken, "Poetic Retranslation and the 'Pretty Languages' of Yellowman," in *Traditional American Indian Literatures: Texts and Interpretations*, edited by Karl Kroeber (Lincoln: University of Nebraska Press, 1981), p. 90.

And when a Navajo storyteller launched his narrative with the phrase *"alk'idaa'jini"* ("a long time ago, they said . . ."), his audience was alerted that he was preparing them to join in the escapades of those sacred beings. The phrase also erased any doubts that his account was not absolutely so – and not another "just-so" story.[63] And Paul Zolbrod, a scholar of Navajo mythology, adds that by employing the distributive plural, "they said," the storyteller implies that "many others have formerly told the story," further nailing down its authority.[64] When the Navajo storyteller Claus Chee Sonny gave religious historian Karl W. Luckert his version of the Deer Huntingway myth, he verified it with his particular chain of narrators: "I learned the Deer Huntingway from my father, the Very Tall One. He learned it from his father, the Stick-dice Player – my grandfather. My grandfather learned it from Mister Rope." But three generations exhausted his memory, so then he leapt backward to mythic times: "The first people who taught the Deer Huntingway were the gods."[65]

One often hears Indian old-timers and intellectuals grumbling that characterizing their indigenous histories as "mythology" or "folklore" suggests fabrication or simple-mindedness, and furthers the stereotype that they had no sense of history or that they made things up. "I want you to know that this is not one of the fairy stories I am telling you, but a fact, " insisted a Kutenai elder named Abraham Wolf Robe to Harry Holbert Turney-High in 1930 before relating a legend. "It is real history, " he reiterated.[66] Despite these demands to have their narratives taken at face value, there were also circumstances when strict accuracy backed up by eyewitnesses was indigenous practice. Stereotypical recitations of battlefield exploits among certain Plains tribes, for instance, which indexed a warrior's claims to advancement to a scale of specific "coups" or war honors, usually called for corroboration. Only then were the war deeds credited and the claimant's new status approved.

[63] Luci Tapahonso, as quoted in Hirschfelder, ed., *Native Heritage*, p. 153.
[64] Paul G. Zolbrod, *Dine bahane: The Navajo Creation Story* (Albuquerque: University of New Mexico Press, 1984), p. 347.
[65] Karl W. Luckert, "An Approach to Navajo Mythology," in *Native Religious Traditions*, edited by Earle H. Waugh and K. Dad Prithipaul (Waterloo, Ontario: Wilfrid Laurier University Press, 1979), p. 129.
[66] Harry Holbert Turney-High, "Two Kutenai Stories," *Journal of American Folklore* 54(213–214) (1941), p. 191.

But these public confirmations of a Plains Indian warrior's "How-I-Earned-My-Honors" form of personal testimony were, simultaneously, verifications of a parallel genre that H. David Brumble characterizes as the warriors' "How-I- Came-By-My-Powers" narratives. He is speaking of accounts of supernatural encounters that had been pursued through vision questing, usually on one's own and with physical suffering, in order to gain a guardian spirit "helper" who lent warriors their critical edge during raids for horses, scalps, and war honors. Nobody else could substantiate these deeply private narratives. In their otherworldly vividness, these out-of-body experiences were regarded as perhaps more "real" than everyday occurrences. Validations for battlefield achievement in "this world" authenticated these claims of success in gaining favors from the "spirit world." Their historical impact was to inspire confidence in prospective followers who rushed to join the supernaturally gifted war leader on his next foray or a prophet in his new crusade.[67]

For other sorts of chronological declarations, such as oratorical citations of a clan's accumulations of prestigious crests in the Northwest Coast or recitations of the original fifty chiefs of the Iroquois League during their Condolence Ritual, accuracy was usually mandated, and knowledgeable listeners could be counted on letting you know if your recollection was askew. Another common Indian turn for validating a historical recitation was for narrators to position themselves within a storytelling lineage. Crow and Kiowa Indians, in my experience, carefully preface their remarks about anything of mytho-historical significance by noting the narrative's transfers through at least two previous owners before it was bequeathed to them. But one might also find such lineal citations at the close of a narrative, less to validate the accuracy of its contents than to put the stamp of approval on its consequences. Thus a Winnebago storyteller concluded his rendition of the mission to his people by Tenskwatawa, the famous "Shawnee Prophet" of the early nineteenth century, with a list of their religious leaders who were influenced by him. Like other Winnebago who cited this prophet, he was

---

[67] Notable vision quest accounts charted communitywide rituals and key symbols that assisted tribal coalescence, such as is related in *The Seven Visions of Bull Lodge*, edited by George Horse Capture (Lincoln: University of Nebraska Press, 1992), a narrative that originated the Fort Belknap Gros Ventre institution of the Feathered Pipe.

doing so to justify current religious innovations, in his particular case the adoption of peyote.[68]

Then there are the material exchanges that can function as a sort of dialogical contract to ensure a story's pedigree. When Paul Radin heard a trickster cycle from the Winnebago Sam Blowsnake, for example, he assured readers that it had been obtained under "proper conditions":

> By proper conditions I mean that adequate offerings of tobacco were presented to the narrator and gifts commensurate with the traditionally accepted value of the myth given to him. That Sam Blowsnake recorded it as he heard it, I am certain for a number of reasons. It would never occur to a Winnebago to alter, in any appreciable manner, a narrative told to him by one who had the traditional right to tell it and for which he was paying.[69]

And finally, as the interviewer at Tuba City has learned to his probable discomfort, an assertive dimension of Indian historicity today is its protective shell. The tendency of outsiders to minimize Indian expressions of how the past went and what it meant is a major reason why Native Americans have grown wary of sharing their narratives. As the Tuscarora writer Elias Johnson wrote in 1881, "They will fear your ridicule and suppress their humor and pathos . . . so thoroughly have they learned to distrust pale faces that [even] when they know that he who is present is a friend, they will shrink from admitting him within the secret portals of their heart."[70] That such apprehension persists is clear when an elder Cree spoke more recently from personal experience: "To make a man tell a story or to recount legends of the past that are discredited as lies later on or made like fairy tales, really does something to a man's

---

[68] This observation is from Jay Miller, *Oral Literature*, Occasional Papers in Curriculum Series, N. 13 (Chicago: D'Arcy McNickle Center for History of the American Indian, Newberry Library, 1992), p. 85, and draws upon Paul Radin's "Winnebago Hero Cycles: A Study in Aboriginal Literature," Supplement to the *International Journal of American Linguistics*, 14(3) (1948), 168 pages.

[69] Paul Radin, *The Trickster: A Study in American Indian Mythology* (New York: Schocken Books, 1956), p. 112.

[70] Quoted in Ella Elizabeth Clark, *Indian Legends of Canada* (Toronto: McClelland and Stewart, 1983), p. xii.

pride."[71] Anna Walters enumerates less self-defensive reasons why her people often feel ambivalent about seeing their histories put into written English:

> First is the suspicion that they will be appropriated by the larger society like so much other cultural appropriation that has already occurred. Second, the material is often considered sacred and not for the knowledge of outsiders. Third, the "fixed" quality of written histories carries with it some very complex ideas about how this will affect the "living" state of the people and their continuity. Fourth, tribes often fear distortions of their histories. Concerns go on and on.[72]

Perhaps history itself should also be added to that list of scarce "limited goods" whose unequal distribution in face-to-face societies, says anthropologist George Foster, produces cycles of envy and envy-deflecting practices – and in multicultural contexts, one might add, xenophobia and a craving for secrecy.[73] Not sharing history as a form of active persistence, because it contains crucial guidelines for group survival, and not revealing it as a form of passive resistance, because it has become a token in psychological tussles between whites and Indians, are often merged motivations. The shifts from "you'll make fun of what we tell you" to "what you don't know won't hurt us" to "what we don't tell you makes you crazy" reflect the ever-changing and always subtle interplay of intercultural relations.

In the more defiant posture of some American Indian cultural leaders, increasingly anxious over their people's shrinking and appropriated intellectual heritage, the history that on its face seems social, political, and safe for public recounting often gets formally reglossed as "religious property." This alerts outsiders that centuries of being taken for granted are over. It safeguards history from usurpation by prying outsiders. It reaffirms history's origins in myth, its unfolding through

[71] Regna Darnell, "Correlates of Cree Narrative Performance," in *Explorations in the Ethnography of Speaking*, edited by Richard Bauman and Joel Sherzer (New York: Cambridge University Press, 1974), p. 325.
[72] Anna Lee Walters, "History," in *Talking Indian: Reflections on Survival and Writing* (Ithaca, N.Y.: Firebrand Books, 1992), p. 80.
[73] George Foster, "Peasant Society and the Image of Limited Good ," *American Anthropologist.* 67(2) (1965), pp. 293–313.

constant renegotiations of identity, and its outcomes as ordained by prophecy.

This chapter's list of dynamics is only one individual's first pass; others will add or consolidate their preferred dimensions of Indian historicity. But parsing the exchange with the old Navajo from Tuba City and setting it in his cultural context should have revealed enough disconnects between non-Indian and Native historical practices and priorities so that we can better appreciate why it has taken so long for outsiders to explore the forms of remembering to be surveyed throughout the rest of this book.

TWO

———◄◦►———

Within Reach of Memory

Oral Traditions, Legends, and History

A legend is a story passed by word of mouth from generation to generation. Legends live because of the truths in them. They are important parts of the culture of a people, perhaps because they help us understand the questions and concerns of related communities. American writer Stephen Vincent Benet said, "It always seems to me that legends and yarns and folk tales are as much a part of the real history of a country as proclamations, provisos, and constitutional amendments."[1]

Mary Galloway, Cherokee

Many years back, after hunting buffalo with Crow Indians as part of my government job, I hauled one old bull's head to an Indian friend's backyard, where it sat under the sun and the seasons for about sixteen years. When I finally retrieved the bleached skull, it was in mint condition; dried cartilage still held the fragile nose bones in place. Then I learned that an elderly acquaintance, keeper of one of the tribe's last medicine-pipe bundles, was unable to activate its powers without such a skull. He knew nothing of my redeemed possession, but I recognized my duty and drove over to his place. When he saw me at the door, he threw out a warning hand and hastily stepped outside, shutting it behind him. Gripping one horn, he lugged the skull around the house to a shed in back, and I never saw it again. Over coffee he explained that his

---

[1] Mary Regina Ulmer Galloway, *Aunt Mary, Tell Me a Story: A Collection of Cherokee Legends and Tales as Told by Mary Ulmer Chiltoskey* (Cherokee, N.C.: Cherokee Communications, 1990), p. 3.

guardian powers forbade him from ever bringing the head of a buffalo into his house or eating its tongue; this was a matter of personal sacrifice and respect. That incident tucked itself away until recently, when it helped me defend a piece of oral history against the same government I worked for then.

For newcomers to American Indian narratives, the forms that best approximate their expectations for historical documentation usually arrive in English under the cover terms "oral tradition" or "legend." But can we be confident that these events, described in different forms and under various circumstances, credibly happened at a given time with all the places, personnel, sequences, and particulars found in these stories? Since one rarely gets one's dinner served up from a menu one brings to the restaurant, keen disappointment can ensue when the facts of these stories don't add up or seem "softer" than hard facts should be. This attitude can mushroom into blanket repudiation, as with anthropologist Robert Lowie's notorious pronouncement in 1915, "I cannot attach to oral traditions any historical value whatsoever under any conditions whatsoever."[2] Once again, the natives haven't behaved like civilized folks, their sense of time is retrograde, or they're simply "reinventing" their history as they go along. This chapter takes a more positive look at the contributions of oral materials to both Indian cultures and anyone else interested in the American past.

My most recent reminder of these benefits and that skull came when I was wrapping up a coauthored study of American Indian links to our country's inaugural national park. Among the flash points that challenge Yellowstone National Park's contradictory mandate as a multiple-use sanctuary for both endangered wild animals and city-drained recreationists has been corraling its buffalo, which have minds and habits (and, Indians might add, societies) of their own. Disturbing any key symbol,

---

[2] Lowie's comment is in "Oral Tradition and History," his opening salvo in the famous debate with John R. Swanton and Roland B. Dixon over the persistent question of how accurately Indian narratives might record precontact migrations. *American Anthropologist* n.s. 17 (1915), pp. 596–599. Two years later, Lowie expanded on his conviction in "Oral Tradition and History," *Journal of American Folklore* 30 (1917), pp. 161–167, in which he stated more simply, "Indian tradition is historically worthless" (p. 165).

like national flags, painted madonnas, or totemic buffalo always arouses strong sentiments. Here is an American icon par excellence, profiled both on the nickel (one side) and on the National Park Service seal, a root metaphor for the Wild West, for its bygone free Indian way of life (the nickel's other side), and for our nostalgic sense of the trans-Mississippi America as Paradise Lost. Even deeper, it might be argued, lies their resonance to American Indians hailing from virtually anywhere – although the Plains, Plateau, and even Pueblo peoples who once hunted the buffalo feel special affinity for these melancholy reminders of another day, as still expressed in religious and social practices. What were the relationships between these creatures and the Indian peoples who traversed the greater Yellowstone Park region?

In mid-1992, when archaeologist Larry Loendorf and I were researching the park's "ethnographic resources," a fight was raging over local ranchers shooting buffalo that strayed out of the park, in the fear that they might contaminate cattle with brucellosis. A coalition of Indians protested the park administrators' approval of these killings and decried the slipshod, brutal way they were carried out. At the same time, park officials were resisting claims by neighboring Indians of ancestral connections to Yellowstone, maintaining that there was no evidence of Indians hunting in the park and encouraged by conservative historians who dismissed as a "noble savage" stereotype the proposition that Indians possessed anything equivalent to a conservation ethic.

In its handouts and museum displays on buffalo ecology, Yellowstone Park refused to allow that early Indians may have hunted animals within its boundaries. The park also ignored hints that some members of the founder herd that it took credit for safeguarding after 1894, when Congress passed a bill to save the species, were first rescued by Indians. Early wildlife writer Ernest Thompson Seton maintained that some animals that replenished Yellowstone's herd of fewer than twenty-five surviving buffalo in 1902 originated from a bunch bred by two mixed-blood Indian ranchers, Michael Pablo and Charles Allard, whose spread adjoined the Kutenai–Salish reservation in northern Montana. Seton furthermore traced these animals to wild buffalo that were cut out by a member of the neighboring Pend d'Oreille tribe named (Sam) Walking Coyote in 1873 after he had joined some Blackfoot buffalo hunters along the U.S.–Canadian border. Saving two bulls, four cows, and six calves,

Walking Coyote protected them near his home in the Jocko Valley, and around 1884 sold ten to Pablo and Allard.[3] After a few other transfers, as we wrote in our Yellowstone Report, "In this roundabout way, then, even the Anglo-American version of the hybridized Yellowstone National Park buffalo herd has some Indian roots."[4] What could we possibly add to this well-researched topic?

Like most ethnohistorians, we first turned to the written record. To investigate Indian hunting in the park, we dug into the underused Wyoming Workers Project Administration (WPA) files in Bozeman, Montana, archived just outside the park's northern boundary. This yielded a one-page memoir from the Crow chief, Plenty Coups, which had been transcribed in the 1930s.[5] Chatting with other old-timers, the chief was fairly specific about pursuing buffalo with his father across the park's present-day boundaries. Plenty Coups was about twelve, and the Crow hunters had scared a herd of two or three hundred animals into a killing cul-de-sac on Buffalo Flat – a grazing and sunning area near today's Northeast Entrance Road, between two Yellowstone feeder streams, and not far from an older buffalo-hunting site known as the Slough Creek Compound. The date, around 1860, fell within the period we know as the tribe's final free-hunting years. Plenty Coups's offhand recollection was about as hard as the facts of oral tradition ever get. So at least some Indians hunted buffalo in the park. What about any intentional Native conservation of the species?

For that we visited Indians. At the Kutenai–Salish reservation in northern Montana, we learned that in early 1977 a blind Salish elder named Moses Chouteh, born in 1890, tape-recorded some stories that the tribe's Culture Committee began the time-consuming process of translating in 1992. Among the earliest put into English happened to be four linked narratives that tracked the family ties between buffalo and a historical medicine man named Blanket Hawk.

---

[3] Ernest Thompson Seton, *Lives of Game Animals* (Garden City, N.Y.: Doubleday, Doran and Company, 1929), p. 658. See also Judith Hebbring Wood, "The Origin of Public Bison Herds in the United States," *Wicazo Sa Review* 15(1) (Spring 2000), pp. 167–168.

[4] Peter Nabokov and Larry Loendorf, *American Indians and Yellowstone National Park* (Yellowstone, Wyoming: Yellowstone National Park Press, 2001).

[5] Our project botanist, Jan Nixon, should be credited with this find.

As a young man in the first, seemingly abbreviated story, Blanket Hawk is magically able to lure buffalo directly into the camp when his people are dying from starvation. Clearly, he possesses some sort of "buffalo medicine."

The second narrative finds Blanket Hawk up north, in Blackfeet country. He plans to herd some buffalo back south in the hope that having animals close by will avoid the risks to hunters of seeking food in enemy territory. When other elders veto his idea, the buffalo still sidle strangely close to Buffalo Hawk and his friends, refusing to leave. In a drawn-out goodbye, as if parting from their own relatives, the men find themselves crying when they must finally bid farewell to the animals.

Before the third story, Moses provides a forecast of Blanket Hawk's premature death: his wife will break a taboo. He is never supposed to take a buffalo's head into his house as a sign of respect for the animal. But she ignores him and butchers a buffalo's head in the kitchen, probably to separate the horns for shaping into spoons and the brains to use for tanning hides, as well as to slice out that delicacy, the tongue. Before her eyes, Blanket Hawk suffers a nosebleed, vomits blood, and writhes on the floor until he expires.

In the fourth account, Blanket Hawk's son takes over. We never learn his name or if he is conceivably the same Walking Coyote of Seton's account. There is a suggestion that he may have inherited his father's affinities, however, for the story opens with him herding two wild buffalo from the plains and allowing them to breed. One day while he is away, his stepfather sells his small herd to two ranchers named Michael Pablo and Charles Allard. The story ends as the boy returns home to find his animals gone. He sits down and weeps.

When we presented these stories to Yellowstone Park officials as a possible context for contemporary Indian claims of ancestral associations with buffalo, one of the park's cultural personnel responded, "I get no 'deep sense' of personal or cultural ties to bison from these stories." Then that memory of my buffalo skull came back as support for the story's taboo. Given such regulations prohibiting certain uses by Indians of creatures with which they were supernaturally allied by means of vision quest "adoptions" or other symbolic mechanisms, we replied, one might infer that the link between Blanket Hawk and buffalo was, like that of my elderly Crow acquaintance, symbiotic and sacred. This was no invention of an Indian tradition by a sentimental ecologist. This was what the French sociologist Emile Durkheim meant by a "social fact."

To claim that all Salish were animal conservationists based upon a single family's multigenerational tradition would be a stretch. The only suggestion we have that Blanket Hawk's affinities with buffalo reflected a tribal ethos is the circumstantial fact that in 1977 a respected culture bearer selected these narratives from his wide repertoire for subsequent generations of his own people to learn about in their own language. Here the stories provided more than corroboration for the proposition that Indians contributed indirectly to Yellowstone Park's early buffalo herd. They made religious, ethical, and dramatic sense of what otherwise sounded like the random act of an Indian who kept oversized pets. Moses Chouteh did not hammer home any lessons; his string of stories left us free to witness a particular human–animal relationship unfold *over time*. As with the animals protected by Blanket Hawk and Walking Coyote, we sense that he intended them as a legacy, perhaps even a synthesis, of some of his people's core values.

But they also open up further questions. Was Moses Chouteh himself a descendant of this family, how did he come by their narratives, and what did they mean to him? Did this set of multigenerational stories represent an indigenous genre, some sort of "legend cycle" perhaps? Indeed, we would like to learn more about a host of already archived but poorly understood American Indian examples of history-transmitting genres. Why, for instance, does the "migration legend" appear so predominant in the southeastern and adjacent Plains regions?[6] Why did "war epics" play such a central role in Colorado River tribal traditions?[7] How did the covert genre of "shaman's" feats and "duel" narratives,

---

[6] For citations see Alexander Veschenko, "Oral Historical Epic Narratives," in *Handbook of Native American Literature*, edited by Andrew Wiget (New York: Garland Publishing, 1966), pp. 91–97, and Elizabeth A. H. John, "A Wichita Migration Tale," *American Indian Quarterly* (Fall 1983), pp. 57–63.

[7] See A. L. Kroeber and G. B. Kroeber, *A Mohave War Reminiscence*, V. 10, University of California Publications in Anthropology Series (Berkeley: University of California Press, 1973).

found among the Abenaki and other cultures farther north, survive the colonial years when other forms clearly went under?[8] What historical content is still preserved through public oratory among the Iroquois, Tohono O'odham, Tlingit, and nativistic movements like the Ketoowah Cherokee?[9] Why are women invariably the heroines in patterned sagas of band formation and family tribulations among Great Basin peoples?[10] Why do some Northwest traditions allow indigenous forms of personal history, intermeshing chronicles of the individual, group, and environment in discernible, repetitive ways and other don't?[11] And which emphases or regularities in collections of Indian folklore actually reflect the vagaries of ethnographic fashion among non-Indians or are the

[8] As Maine historian Fanny Hardy Ekstrom recalled in a 1919 speech ("Maine Indian Folk-Lore," Fanny Hardy Ekstrom Papers, University of Maine Special Collections, Orono, Maine), only when she uttered the loaded word *m'teoulin* ("shaman" in Penobscot) did native consultants suddenly unlock the store of hidden historical episodes that constituted her *Old John Nepture and Other Maine Indian Shamans* (Portland, Maine: Southworth-Anthoensen Press, 1945). Although I have turned up examples in many culture areas, this seemingly "covert genre" of shamans' careers and contest narratives is exceptionally prevalent in the Northeast up to the Arctic; see, for example, *The Things That Were Said of Them: Shaman Stories and Oral Histories of the Tikigaq*, told by the Asatchaq, Introduction by Tom Lowenstein (Berkeley: University of California Press, 1992).

[9] For the Iroquois, see Michael K. Foster, "Another Look at the Function of Wampum in Iroquois–White Councils," in *The History and Culture of Iroquois Diplomacy*, edited by Francis Jennings (Syracuse, N.Y.: Syracuse University Press, 1985); for the Tlingit, see Nora Marks Dauenhauer and Richard Dauenhauer, editors, *Haa Tuwunaaqu Yis, for Healing Our Spirit: Tlingit Oratory* (Seattle: University of Washington Press, 1990); for the Tohono O'odham, see Donald Bahr, *Pima–Papago Ritual Oratory: A Study of Three Texts* (San Francisco: Indian Historian Press, 1975); for the Keetowah Cherokee, see Robert K. Thomas, "The Redbird Smith Movement," in *Symposium on Cherokee and Iroquois Culture*, edited by W. N. Fenton and J. Gulick, Bureau of American Ethnology Bulletin 180 (Washington, D.C.: U.S. Government Printing Office, 1961), pp. 159–166.

[10] Sven Liljeblad, "Oral Tradition: Content and Style of Verbal Arts," in *Great Basin*, edited by Warren I. D'Azevedo, V. 11, *Handbook of North American Indians* (Washington, D.C.: Smithsonian Institution Press, 1986), p. 652.

[11] Amid the growing critical literature on Indian autobiography, see H. David Brumble's discussion of "preliterate traditions" in *American Indian Autobiography* (Berkeley: University of California Press, 1988); for a study of narrative conventions and recurrent themes whereby life history, family history, and a collective sense of the past are braided together, see Julia Cruikshank, in collaboration with Angela Sidney, Kitty Smith, and Annie Ned, *Life Lived Like a Story: Life Stories of Three Yukon Native Elders* (Lincoln: University of Nebraska Press, 1990).

repertoire that astute tale-tellers felt their white listeners were eager or simply able to hear? Addressing such questions can remind us that all of America's cultural regions are deeply compacted with the strata of humans making sense of events, their contexts and consequences, and of other cultures entering that discourse as well.

The term "legend" is commonly employed to lump together any Indian stories bearing content that is vaguely historical. Like the "culture area" concept in American Indian social anthropology that parcels the continent into broad ecological domains occupied by culturally similar peoples, the generic myth/legend/folktale trinity of "etic" narrative forms (meaning categories imposed by outsiders, as contrasted with "emic" or Native categories) remains a clumsy but helpful outsider's tool for distinguishing traditional narratives. To me, these gross categories still seem an improvement over looser wording that sweeps virtually all Indian narratives into the legend bin, or turns all three terms into euphemisms for distortion or falsehood, rather than treating them as separate repositories for some brand of historicity.

Not all scholars concur. In Tlingit folklore from southwestern Alaska, as analyzed by Catherine McClellan, externally imposed categories sound so permeable as to be analytically useless. In their clan traditions she found "mythlike action" blended with the behaviors of relatively recent clan ancestors. And while she certainly recorded some "long ago" stories with the solemn cosmological teachings one expects from myths, they could also contain the vulgar, hilarious episodes one normally finds in folktales.[12] In George R. Hamell's search for symbolic categories and recurrent themes in Indian narratives that can illuminate the archaeological, ethnological, and historical records of the early fur trade, he found that genre distinctions

within northeastern Woodland Indian oral traditions are difficult, if not impossible to make. More to the point, they are irrelevant to

[12] Catherine McClellan, "Indian Stories about the First Whites in Northwestern America," in *Ethnohistory in Southwestern Alaska and Southern Yukon: Method and Content*, edited by Margaret Lantis (Lexington: University Press of Kentucky, 1970), pp. 118–119.

my interests in these traditions, which is in their shared repertoire of concepts, themes, and dramatis personae, and not in the distinctions in their social contexts and functions. In my understanding and use of the term *myth*, legend and folktale are only special cases of myth. They are "secularized" myth, but no less cognitively and behaviorally motivating.[13]

With such exceptions duly noted, for the moment I will stick with folklorist William Bascom's digest of their formal distinctions. The *legendary* narratives to be discussed later are generally regarded as secular or sacred, transpiring in today's world and featuring human characters, and are considered factual and often historical; the *myths* to be examined in Chapter 3 are usually sacred narratives that involve nonhuman characters, take place in a different or earlier world, and are treasured by the societies that hold them as absolute truth; and the *folktales* of Chapter 4 are considered secular narratives, commonly occurring outside of any specific place or time, involving human and nonhuman characters, and are regarded as fictional stories with high entertainment (and educational) value.[14]

Applying this scheme to specific traditional expressions of American Indian historical consciousness always calls for fine-tuning, and leaves much to be desired when one tries to understand why and when this or that genre is being employed. From tradition to tradition, region to region, and language to language, different standards and categories quite often obtain. Some tribal traditions have produced fewer types of folklore, others more, and Indian communities are always coming up with surprisingly creative hybrids. Localizing Bascom's genres also calls for a cautionary second look at the functional roles of different narrative styles in Indian culture in their own changeable historical frames. For when tough times made Indians draw upon any of their oral traditions for support and reassurance, the former properties of almost any genre could bend to the task.

---

[13] George R. Hamell, "Mythical Realities and European Contact in the Northeast During the Sixteenth and Seventeenth Centuries," *Man in the Northeast* N. 33 (Spring 1987), p. 65.

[14] William Bascom, "The Forms of Folklore," *Journal of American Folklore* 78 (1965), pp. 3–20.

Generally, "legend" covers stories about the era of named people and remembered events that move much closer in reality and time to the present day than myth. We expect them to represent past times that a linkage of named human ancestors, perhaps three or four generations back, can almost touch and make believable. As William S. Simmons nicely characterizes this category:

> Legend conveys one generation to the next. Through legend people select some experiences and not others for retelling. They depict these experiences in terms of motifs and symbols that are available to them at that time. These may come from ancestral tradition or from external sources to which one has been exposed. Legends float through a twilight between what may really have happened and what people believe to have happened. Although they are a collective phenomenon, no two individuals tell them in the same way. Through legend, place names and events are pressed into stories that have a life of their own.[15]

When scholars seem to talk past each other in their arguments about the time depths into which such narratives can reliably reach, we often note a deeper disagreement about the very nature of history: should its priority be facts and chronologies or themes and attitudes? Exemplifying the more conservative position, when ethnohistorian Harold Hickerson looked to oral traditions for reconstructing the growth of the Great Lakes Midewiwin ritual, for instance, he felt that normal memory capability plus "European introduced ways of behaving" made it impossible to obtain trustworthy data beyond "two or three generations ago, perhaps at most 70–100 years."[16] Folklorist Tom Lowenstein

---

[15] William S. Simmons, "The Mystic Voice: Pequot Folklore from the Seventeenth Century to the Present," paper prepared for the Mashantucket Pequot Historical Conference, October 23–24, 1987, Norwich and Ledyard, Connecticut, p. 2.

[16] Harold Hickerson, *The Chippewa and Their Neighbors: A Study in Ethnohistory* (New York: Holt, Rinehart and Winston, 1970), pp. 32–33. Equally conservative was the archaeologist Albert H. Schroeder, who maintained that "Any [Pueblo Indian] ties to the past are based on oral traditions which basically reflect the memories of several generations. The chronological and historical relationships of events, or even their order and details, become more vague with the passing of each generation as details and correlations are forgotten or altered according to Pueblo traditional readjustment or the whims and frailties of the storyteller" ("Rio Grande Ethnohistory," in *New Perspectives on the Pueblos*, edited by Alfonso Ortiz [Albuquerque: University of New Mexico Press, 1972], p. 42).

became convinced that local "ancestor stories" (*uqaluktuaqs*) recalled by his Arctic consultants provided fairly accurate information for as far back as five generations, after which "a history would usually merge with others of its kind, slip into *unipkaaaq* [myths, or narratives from the indefinite past], or be forgotten."[17] But even older memories were attributed to the folk traditions of the Paiute of Utah, according to David M. Pendergast and Clement W. Meighan, who cross-referenced comments in their traditional histories pertaining to migrations, physical appearances, subsistence patterns, and material culture of nearby Hopi Indians with archaeological and ethnohistorical data, and hypothesized that their secular stories, at least, "may preserve historical information for several hundred years with a relatively high degree of accuracy."[18]

Rather than fragments of recollected data, the investigations of anthropologist William S. Simmons into New England Indian narratives emphasized persistent themes and pushed further into the past. After he spent the 1970s analyzing a corpus of stories from library research, his own tale-collecting commenced in 1981 among remnant Wampanoag, Mohegan, and Narragansett families still living in Connecticut, Rhode Island, and Massachusetts. "Such fieldwork," Simmons reflected later, "can be like interviewing 350-year-old persons with whose earlier experiences one is already familiar."[19] Matching their narratives against those he culled from colonial diaries, newspapers, and folklore collections, Simmons realized that where scary protagonists were ghosts, giants, the devil, and little people, he was facing evidence of over three centuries of narrative continuity, of situations, as he put it, when "past generations communicate with their living descendants" through folklore. Already aware, for instance, of seventeenth-century European accounts of a Gay Head Wampanoag Indian belief in Maushop, the giant who resided on

---

[17] Lowenstein, *The Things That Were Said of Them*, pp. 182–183.

[18] David M. Pendergast and Clement W. Meighan, "Folk Traditions as Historical Fact: A Paiute Example," *Journal of American Folklore* 72 (1959), p. 132. See also their even-handed response to Lord Raglan's critique of their claims, "Notes & Queries," *Journal of American Folklore* 73 (1960), pp. 58–60.

[19] William S. Simmons, "Culture Theory in Contemporary Ethnohistory," *Ethnohistory* 35(1) (Winter 1988), p. 10.

Martha's Vineyard and created its topography, Simmons's ears perked up when an elderly widow from the island told him how that same giant formed the "Devil's Bridge" in a failed attempt to link his Gay Head people to the mainland (yet another instance of old Indian spirits and sacred places getting tagged with negative nomenclature derived from Christian cosmology).

Legend by legend, variant by variant, Simmons pieced together his own "bridge" of narratives, spanning 1643 to 1983, which told and retold Maushop's deeds on behalf of his Wampanoag constituency. Like skeletal presences revealed through the comparative folklorist's X-ray lens, Simmons studied the thematic superstructures within these typically New England tales of the spectral vintage popularized by Washington Irving. Beneath their Europeanized outerwear he detected the unmistakable signs of Algonquian Indian *manitos* (spirits) and *powwows* (shamans, diviners, and sorcerers), as well as underlying storylines originating from old Indian curing and weather-controlling rituals, dances, and folk beliefs. Behind closed doors and over kitchen tables, their motifs and themes remained native to the core. Or in the analogy Simmons preferred for this remarkable example of historicity's persistence:

> In the words of the "Old Indian hymn" that the Narragansett and other tribes "heard in the air" years before the arrival of whites, and despite the many pronouncements about the disappearance of New England Indian cultures, "There is a stream that issues forth." The stream bed is shaped by the racial, economic, and political terrain of the larger society. The stream is the Indian people themselves. Their folklore, which follows them like a mist, is a key into understanding their course through history and the primary domain where an Indian spirit still survives.[20]

Along with searching for fixed genres or enduring themes, another avenue into a different culture's historical consciousness is to look for what anthropologist A. Irving Hallowell has called the "temporal guide posts" by which peoples blaze their way through the forests of their

---

[20] William S. Simmons, *Spirit of the New England Tribes: Indian History and Folklore, 1620–1984* (Hanover: University Press of New England, 1986), p. 270.

times. Where and how one locates them differs in scale and genre. As already mentioned in the previous chapter, for the Iroquois along the St. Lawrence River in upper New York State, official markers of the past correlate with their three successive mythic charters. But according to Michael Lupow, historical episodes among the Koniaq people of Alaska frequently "fall into two groups: 1) eras that become defined by the use and abuse of natural resources, and, 2) disasters – natural and manmade, personal and collective – that have altered the shape of the culture."[21] For the Ojibwa bands that Hallowell studied just east of Canada's Lake Winnepeg, however, former events were nailed in memory by more mundane guide posts, such as (1) correlation with external happenings, including treaty signing, the arrival of missionaries, or tenure of Hudson Bay Managers, (2) significant markers in one's personal history, marriage, major travels, and the like, or (3) or the life spans of deceased relatives.

But Hallowell concluded that "One hundred and fifty years is the outside limit of any genuine historic fact," and investigating any "long ago" events and (usually immortal) characters beyond that "plunged [one] into a bottomless mythological epoch that lacks temporal guide posts of any conventional sort."[22] On the *near* side of this temporal expanse, one hits the wall that Sven Liljeblad describes from his experience with Great Basin Indian oral literature as "the ultimate horizon of personal history [that] coincides with the time-depth of known genealogy,"[23] usually indicating "the grand parental generation of the speaker," and that about squares with Hallowell's estimation.

On its *far* side, however, writes Donald Bahr in an analysis of the extreme time depth of a Piman origin epic (which he has no problem characterizing as *chronicles*), "one finds a final zone rich in tales about how the world was created and how the tribe's constituent social groups came

[21] Michael Lupow, "Tsunamis and Sea Otter Days: Toward an Understanding of Koniaq Historical Consciousness," seminar paper, Anthropology 940, December 1995, University of Wisonsin-Madison, p. 4.
[22] A. Irving Hallowell, "Temporal Orientation in Western Civilization and in a Pre-Literate Society," *American Anthropologist* 39 (1937), p. 667.
[23] Sven Liljeblad, "Oral Tradition: Content and Style of Verbal Arts," in *Handbook of North American Indians, Great Basin*, V. 11 (Washington, D.C.: Smithsonian Institution Press, 1986), p. 651.

into existence."[24] As for the murky, expanding, and contracting span of time in between, what African historian Jan Vansina has characterized as the "floating gap," Bahr says that it "does not float as a space between discernible points of past time but *is floated toward*, as one travels back through the relatively confidently held zones of personal and group history."[25]

But the validity claims of Native American narratives can be more unfettered than Bahr suggests. In the case of Europe, as novelist Milan Kundera once wrote, history may well be the thinnest thread of what's remembered, stretching across an ocean of what's been forgotten. But many American Indian oral traditions would maintain that it is really more like a thick rope, a long ladder, or a wide corridor, which also allows for two-way traffic. The Pawnee/Otoe writer Anna Lee Walters says that she

> discovered two principal sequences of tribal history. The first starts at the beginning and works its way toward the present. The second starts with the present and work its way back to the beginning. Although there may be discussions on the history of the people moving to a particular place, for example – isolated events – often these historical notes seem to be just that until they are pinned down in this large framework.[26]

---

[24] This remarkable document was first transcribed by archaeologist Julian Hayden from two Pima Indian members of his work crew at the Snaketown excavation site in Arizona in 1935. It purports to chronicle events before the Spanish conquest of the Tohono O'odham (Pima–Papago), through the turbulent rise and fall of their Hohokam ancestors who built south-central Arizona's multistory adobe "great houses," and mythic-origin times well before that. Donald Bahr divided Hayden's transcript into thirty-six stories to suggest natural storytelling breaks and for easier reading, in Donald Bahr, Juan Smith, William Smith Allison, and Julian Hayden, *The Short Swift Time of Gods on Earth: The Hohokam Chronicles* (Berkeley: University of California Press, 1994), p. 3. For a test of the accuracy of such old Tohono O'odham narratives see Lynn S. Teague, "Prehistory and the Traditions of the O'odham and Hopi," *Kiva* 58(4) (1993), pp. 435–454.

[25] Bahr et al., *Short Swift Time*, p. 3, emphasis mine.

[26] Anna Lee Walters, "History," in *Talking Indian: Reflections on Survival and Writing* (Ithaca, N.Y.: Firebrand Books, 1992), p. 77. To illustrate this two-way movement: while Canadian Cree elders might have established their narrative authority by hopping from personal biography *backward* through a five-step process until they reached the zone of mythological time (Regna Darnell, "Correlates of Cree Narrative Performance," in *Explorations in the Ethnography of Speaking*, edited by Richard Bauman

Varying by cultural tradition and storytelling techniques, Indians claim the ability to dredge up all sorts of "true" information from the depths of deep time. When these stories remain within the Indian community, few pay their assertions any mind, no matter how temporally wild and revised they are. But let any scholar suggest that legends might shed accurate light on older events than those accessible to Hallowell's Ojibwa or found in Simmons's thematic continuities of Native New England, and watch the debates over the authenticity and utility of Indian historical narratives boil over.

The three (often interrelated) "guide post" categories of what can be called "deep time" to which some American Indian oral traditions claim access are (1) biological (2) climatological, and (3) cataclysmal. In the first category, for instance, after Naskapi Indian hunters of northeastern Labrador told archaeologist W. D. Strong about large-headed, long-trunked, big-toothed monsters that were eventually slain by their trickster hero, he gave their accounts a second thought.

Normally an evidence-demanding scientist who was more comfortable with timelines for bygone Indian eras that he concocted from hard data dug out of the ground, Strong took pains to distinguish these "historical traditions" from other "myths of observation" he found in the literature, which were the result, he believed, of Indians "rationalizing" into story format their exposure to huge fossil bones. But Strong credited those accounts he personally heard from Indian lips as being possibly "a dim but actual tradition of the time when the mammoth lived in North America."[27] Nine years later, the eminent physical anthropologist Loren C. Eisley argued that while Indian hunting of extinct megafauna surely took place, such legends could not reach that far back.

and Joel Sherzer [New York: Cambridge University Press, 1974], p. 324), some Interior Salish narrators from Washington State took the reverse tack, beginning with a family's mythological origins before moving steadily *forward* so as to validate their contemporary social and political prominence (Clifford E. Trafzer, "First History of the Americas," in *New Voices in Native American Literary Criticism*, edited by Arnold Krupat [Washington, D.C.: Smithsonian Institution Press, 1993], pp. 482–483).

[27] William Duncan Strong, "North American Indian Traditions Suggesting a Knowledge of the Mammoth," *American Anthropologist* 36 (1934), p. 87. For a compilation of folkloristic and other representations of cryptozoological monster studies, see Michel Meurger, with Claude Gagnon, *Lake Monster Traditions: A Cross Cultural Analysis* (London: Fortean Tomes, 1988).

Legends might provide data on the "upper archaeological horizons," but older origins were "ghostly, disembodied, and unverifiable." In fact, Eisley surmised, these stories were really evidence of Indians trying to please or dupe their white listeners, or were tainted by African – derived descriptions of elephants.[28]

This debate over the reliability of formalized Indian memories brings us to one of American Indian folklore's most controversial cases: the authenticity of Tuscarora and Delaware "crossing the ice" migration epics. Despite a Tuscorara version championed by the Native anthropologist J. B. Hewitt as recording just such a transcontinental passage, revelations of the theme's appearance among other tribes suggest a more recent, less monumental origin.[29] Few Native annals have aroused scholars so much as a purported Delaware Indian verse narrative that also contained the ice-crossing theme. Acquired in 1820 by an eccentric scholar named Constantine Samuel Rafinesque, the epic was mnemonically summarized in 183 pictographs that were carved into a bundle of red sticks known as the Wallam-Olum.[30] Rafinesque's "reading" of their pictographs and associated songs told of Delaware tribal origins, ordeals with an evil serpent and a great flood, their migration across frozen water, social fissions, the adoption of agriculture, and more migrations that led them to their historic-period Atlantic seaboard habitat and the early-sixteenth-century arrival of Europeans. If many non-Indian academic scholars remain dubious about anything such accounts can

---

[28] Loren C. Eisley, "Archaeological Observations on the Problem of Post-Glacial Extinctions." *American Antiquity* 8(3) (1943), pp. 209–217.

[29] Anthony F. C. Wallace and William D. Reburn, "Crossing the Ice: A Migration Legend of the Tuscarora Indians," *International Journal of American Linguistics* 17 (1951), pp. 42–47.

[30] This work is included with commentary in Daniel G. Brinton's *The Lenape and Their Legends* (Philadelphia: D. G. Brinton, 1885), which also includes intriguing early references to tribal historicity turned up by Brinton, and more recently appears in *The Red Record, The Wallam Olum: The Oldest Native North American History*, *trams.* by David McCutchen (Garden City Park, N.Y.: Avery Publishing Group, 1993). A doubting opinion is Stephen Williams's "The Wallam Olum: Where Did the Delaware Go?" in his *Fantastic Archaeology* (Philadelphia: University of Pennsylvania Press, 1991), pp. 98–115). Williams is unaware of some ethnographic corroboration for such red-painted stick records, known as *maxkwe' laksu*, among the Delaware (see Frank G. Speck, *The Celestial Bear Comes Down to Earth* [Reading, Pa.: Reading Public Museum and Art Gallery], n. 7, 1945, pp. 90–91).

relay of such early times, Indians are more open. Writes the Pawnee lawyer and activist Roger C. Echo-Hawk:

> Many Native American oral traditions refer to the existence of danger-ous "monsters" and giant animals in ancient times, and other stories are set in a period when animals and birds ruled the world. Paleontolo-gists describe Ice Age America as a realm dominated by giant animals, or "megafauna.... In many Indian traditions, a great flood covered the earth in ancient times, and some stories associate this event with the age of monsters.... If Native American origin traditions shed light on the lifeways of people who settled in North America during the last Ice Age, then Indian literature preserves a remarkable legacy of documents about ancient history in the New World.[31]

When Indian memory-culture focuses on natural cataclysms for which there is datable evidence, advocates for the depth of Indian history may have their strongest case. Scientific records of volcanic eruptions, mete-oric showers, major floods, or earthquakes are unambiguous; one might also expect their psychological impact to carve themselves deeply into Indian oral tradition.[32] But the Native discourses regarding those catas-trophes are often more interested in explicating them as the cost of past violations of acceptable behavior between species than through any sci-entific hypotheses by which outsiders dated them.

This was what cultural anthropologist Frederica de Laguna surmised after collecting narratives from the west side of Icy Bay in southern Alaska. One told about some disrespectful young men who jokingly in-vited the ice to a feast. To their horror, the ice obliged, and they lost the

---

[31] Roger C. Echo-Hawk, "Oral Traditions and Indian Origins: A Native Perspective," in *Exploring Ancient Native America*, edited by David Hurst Thomas (New York: Macmillan, 1994), pp. 41–42.

[32] For more on geofolklore, see Dorothy B. Vitaliano, *Legends of the Earth: Their Geologic Origins* (Bloomington: Indiana University Press, 1973); from Papua New Guinea, R. J. Blong, *The Time of Darkness: Local Legends and Volcanic Reality in Papua New Guinea* (Seattle: University of Washington Press, 1982); and for evidence of seven centuries of Hopi Indian oral accounts of an Arizona eruption, Ekkehart Malotki with Michael Lomatuway'ma's bilingual *Earth Fire: A Hopi Legend of the Sunset Crater Eruption* (Flagstaff: Northland Press, 1987). For an argument that Alaskan Indian narratives may memorialize events that extend back twelve hundred years, see D. Wayne Moodie, A. J. W. Catchpole, and Kerry Abel, "Northern Athapaskan Oral Traditions and the White River Volcano," *Ethnohistory* 39(2) (Spring 1992), pp. 148–171.

frozen ground that supported the rest of their dwellings. Other villagers said that the receding icebergs resulted from Indians throwing a dog's carcass into a crevasse. From the Native perspective, these explanations dramatized human arrogance toward a personified force of nature and impropriety toward a fellow animal. Then de Laguna learned that radiocarbon dating of wood from the "endmoraines" had fixed the date of one glacial retreat at about 1400 A.D. Gathering more stories throughout region, she concluded, "Other Natives' statements about the stages in the retreat of the ice in Yakutat Bay during the eighteenth and nineteenth centuries are in complete accord with geological evidence."[33]

The prolific American Indian intellectual Vine Deloria, Jr. reactivated the debate over Indian eyewitnessing of deep time events with his *Red Earth, White Lies*,[34] a book-length brief against the "myth of scientific fact." Previously, in *God Is Red*, Deloria proposed that, like certain trickster stories that were referenced to accounts of megafauna, many legendary Indian comments about ancient cataclysms, supernovas, and volcanic eruptions had literal, almost eyewitness truth. Might they not simply be, he stated, "the collective memories of a great and catastrophic event through which people came to understand themselves and the universe they inhabited"?[35] Incensed over archaeology's orthodoxy about the Bering Strait hypothesis, infuriated by its smear campaign suggesting that the extinction of Pleistocene big game was due to Indian "hit men," and irritated by its bias against Indian stories about volcanic eruptions and floods that offer alternative explanations for the pre–Bering Strait presence of Indians in the New World, Deloria's new book elaborated his impassioned case for reconsidering the cold truths relayed through Indian oral traditions.[36]

---

[33] Frederica de Laguna, "Geological Confirmation of Native Traditions, Yakutat, Alaska," *American Antiquity* 23 (1958), p. 434.

[34] Vine Deloria, Jr., *Red Earth, White Lies* (New York: Scribners, 1995).

[35] Vine Deloria, Jr., *God Is Red* (New York: Grosset and Dunlap, 1973), p. 138.

[36] This debate made headlines in September 2000 in the controversy over the cultural affiliations of a 9,000-year-old skeleton found four years earlier on the banks of the Columbia River near Kennewick, Washington. While anthropologist Richard Jantz maintained that "I don't think anybody's ever shown that oral tradition has 9,000 years of historical depth – and that it's accurate for that long," U.S. Secretary of the Interior Bruce Babbitt was persuaded by "the geographic data [regarding glacial melting in Montana] and oral histories of the five tribes that collectively assert they are the

Most of today's non-Indian ethnohistorians are less inclined to ask oral traditions to clinch any literalist reconstructions than to explore how this material can complement, contextualize, or provide reinterpretations for written constructions of shallower pasts. The following sample of case studies, drawn from places ranging from the East Coast to the West Coast, all employ Indian oral traditions to present and interpret more multistranded North American histories.

Fieldwork Recovers Historical Facts and Reveals Cultural Priorities

In 1959, after ethnohistorian Gordon M. Day gathered stories from St. Francis Abenakis in northern New England concerning the destruction of their village by Rogers' Rangers in 1759, he felt confident in pinpointing exactly where the houses stood in which named individuals were killed, explaining why the Abenaki casualties were far fewer than reported, and hypothesizing on the identity and personal motivations behind the informer of the impending attack.[37] What preserved the accurate details in this Abenaki oral history, according to Day, were not any "fixed form" procedures, whereby information is scrupulously transmitted via memorized speeches or genealogical recitations of the sort delivered during public performances, chiefly investitures or funerary rituals. Instead, he concluded, something about the social precision and intrinsic importance of their content to the Abenaki's sense of cultural identity had apparently safeguarded their details for two hundred years.

Indian History Delivers the Rest of the Story

The dramatic split within Arizona's Hopi village of Oraibi in 1906 that led to the establishment of a brand new pueblo named Bacavi was caused by a fractious dispute between Hopi factions that were either friendly

descendants of people who have been in the region of the Upper Columbia Plateau for a very long time," and returned the remains of the skeleton to contemporary Columbia Basin Indians (*Los Angeles Times*, September 26, 2000, pp. A3, A17).

[37] Gordon M. Day, "Oral Tradition as Complement," *Ethnohistory* 19(2) (1972), pp. 99–108.

or hostile to two decades of harsh American assault on their cultural and political practices. That, at least, was the non-Indians' official story. After fieldwork with contemporary Hopi people, however, the British ethnographer Peter Whiteley felt he had uncovered a deeper explanation. Rather than a mere reaction to external conditions, the break followed collusion by the entire community's religious elite to restore harmony and rectitude to Hopi ethos and ritual processes, and to remove at least some of their people to a new, unpolluted locale.[38] The significance of Whiteley's argument, which remains controversial, was twofold. It liberated the Hopi life philosophy and belief system from their romantic, sainted, and apolitical portrayal in popular literature. It also provided a complicated case for returning what contemporary historians call "agency" to Indian people, putting them in the driver's seat, and showing them capable of ulterior and unifyingly conservative motives.

Native Categories Subvert Historical Clichés

Even when fieldwork seems impossible and new data out of the question, the past may be revisited by the innovative ethno-ethnohistorian. Reexamining an iconic historical episode – that of the "Indian princess" Pocahontas saving the life of colonist Captain John Smith – Margaret

[38] To his credit, Peter Whiteley produced two accounts from his early Hopi work. In *Deliberate Acts: Changing Hopi Culture Through the Oraibi Split* (Tucson: University of Arizona Press, 1988), he focused on this argument for a clandestine Hopi historical initiative, while in *Bacavi: Journey to Reed Springs* (Flagstaff, Ariz.: Northland Press, 1988) he provided general readers with an overview of Hopi turn-of-the-century history, including photos. A similar division between official and unofficial explanations was uncovered in Hopiland by ethnolinguist Paul V. Kroskrity, only it involved Indian versus Indian accounts. Rather than appearing as helpless refugees dragging themselves west after the All-Pueblo revolts of 1680 and 1696, in their own songs and stories the Arizona Tewa explain their arrival at First Mesa (where they live today) as a forthright response to four repeated invitations by Hopi Bear and Snake clan chiefs to protect them from Ute Indian pillagers. For this service the newcomers were promised land and food if they succeeded, recompense they never received for a job well done – thus positioning themselves in Tewa memory as ethically *and* militarily superior to their Hopi "hosts," who sometimes denigrated them as second-class, uninvited guests (*Language, History, and Identity: Ethnolinguistic Studies of the Arizona Tewa* [Tucson: University of Arizona Press, 1993], pp. 182–183).

Williamson teased out a plausible picture of two cultures actually vying to assimilate each other.[39] She suggests that this was an example of events that are, as anthropologist Marshal Sahlins has put it, "externally induced but indigenously orchestrated." Perhaps the Powhatan Indians conceived of Smith as a *werowance*, or sacred being, from a faraway people. And perhaps, using customary Native strategies such as adoption and arranged marriage, their chief manipulated his daughter's union with Smith so as to bring the powerful, auspicious Europeans under his confederacy's fold for its own political and economic gain.

Indian Histories Perpetuate Social Claims

Scrutinizing Winnebago stories from the Great Lakes region that were collected about a century later, anthropologist Paul Radin realized that Indian "legends" could weld together dissynchronous elements.[40] His test case, a Native version of the French "discovery" of the Winnebagos, opened with a curiously objective profile of traditional Winnebago society's defining characteristics, the good and not so good, which Radin considered the more recently composed portion of the narrative (although, from his excerpt, even it appears cobbled together from disparate mythic elements). From external evidence, however, Radin judged the narrative's second, more historical portion, which dealt with the founding of the mixed-blood Decora dynasty, to transmit historical data over two centuries old with considerable accuracy. His conclusion alluded to the narrative's underlying vested interest, which was less one of chronological accountability than, in essence, charting the Decoras as

---

[39] Margaret Holmes Williamson, "Pocahontas and Captain John Smith: Examining a Historical Myth," *History and Anthropology* 5(3–4) (1992), pp. 365–402, but so indifferent (or theoretically distracted by deconstructing their own society's politics of representation) are many historians to the possibility that there might be another cultural perspective that Robert S. Tilton's *Pocahontas: The Evolution of an American Narrative* (New York: Cambridge University Press, 1994) appears totally unaware of the Williamson argument.

[40] Paul Radin, "Reconstruction from Internal Evidence and the Role of the Individual," in *The Method and Theory of Ethnology: An Essay in Cricitism* (South Hadley, Mass.: Bergin & Garvey, 1987), pp. 183–252.

a quasi-mythic lineage and celebrating the compounded French–Siouan benefits they bequeathed upon generations of Winnebago people.

Lessons of Indian History Hide in Stylistics

To illustrate his quarrel with rewritings of American Indian narratives for trade book anthologies, the ethno-linguist Dell Hymes chose a text by a tale-teller from the Kalapuya, a small hunting and fishing tribe in western Oregon. Called "Our People after the Whites Came," the first part of the narrative, describing a time when "everything was good long ago," conformed to an alternating three-line, five-line sequence that Hymes found common to Kalapuya rhetorical patterning. Viewing such texts as oral poetry, and organizing them into stanzas on the page, clarified this patterning. As the narrative unfolded, it became clearer how repeated figures of speech and recurrent topics were constantly evaluating Native (when "We took care of our hearts") and white (when "Everything has vanished") lifeways. From attitudes toward nudity to ways of doctoring the sick, the cross-cultural comparisons mounted in intensity through subtle patterning and parallelism. To Hymes, "texts are not shards one can paste into whatever pattern one pleases. Their narrators were skilled, economical users of language.... The stories draw upon ways of marking such things. Put most broadly, any way of putting such a story on the page implies a claim that the relations on the page represent the relations of the telling."[41]

41 Dell Hymes, "Our People After the Whites Came," in *Dialectical Anthropology: Essays in Honor of Stanley Diamond* (Gainesville: University Press of Florida, 1992), p. 285. When one does detect a shardlike breaking apart in Native stories, as did folklorist Tom Lowenstein for the fur-trading period when Alaskan oral traditions started to lapse, he felt that the stylistic shift reflected history, a depressing "time of fragmentation" (Lowenstein, *The Things That Were Said of Them*, p. 163). Andrew Wiget not only noticed the same process when comparing what he calls "Golden Age" and more "recent" Zuni Indian testimonies, but paradoxically he assessed the latter as more persuasive for the tribe's land claims case since their lack of well-oiled coherence suggested that the pieces were more accurate in non-Indian terms ("Recovering the Remembered Past: Folklore and Oral History in the Zuni Trust Lands Damages Case," in *Zuni and the Courts: A Struggle for Sovereign Land Rights*, edited by E. Richard Hart [Lawrence: University Press of Kansas, 1995], pp. 182–183). It was also attentiveness to verbal forms and episodic patterning in a Chilcotin narrative from southwestern Canada that

Oral Traditions Personalize and Mythologize the Written Record

When their story of first contact with the French in 1715 is related by Chipewyans of Fort Chipewyan, Alberta, the protagonist is not the anonymous "slave woman" of Western accounts. She is identified by name – Fallen Marten. As sociolinguists Ronald Scollon and Suzanne Scollon point out, the two storylines underscore contrasting frames of value.[42] In its impersonal voice, the English version stresses the economic and historical benefits of contact. The more intimate Indian account stresses the argument between the Crees and Chipewyans over credit for first discovering the possessions-bearing French (a switch on the European race to claim the New World's natural resources). The Native story also highlights the Indian woman's alienation as she trades her knowledge of terrain for access to alluring goods and then undergoes a stressful homecoming. This is almost a new subgenre – an Indian's "reintegration ordeal" among her own kind; later generations might identify with this bitter foretaste of divided loyalties. The European story focused on frontier riches and courageous European traders facing the frozen wilderness; Crees emphasized how Fallen Marten's bravery "found the Frenchman" and how she imperiled her identity to bring her people "knives, pails, and everything."

To Understand Indian–White Relations, Look at Native Historicity

After examining Alaskan Indian and European contact through Indian memories, Catherine McClellan detoured from her simple search for

---

enabled ethnolinguist David W. Dinwoodie to detect what he calls the "didactic history" embedded within it. The subtext of their story of a white storekeeper named Spence who disregarded Indian warnings about proper regard for a personified mountain was to remind Native listeners that white society offered two contradictory resources: it supplied economic benefits at the same time that it provided "a model of how not to act, or how to act humorously." "Obviation and Textual Organization in a Chilcotin History Lesson," paper presented in the session "Genre and Discourse" at the 31st. Conference on American Indian Languages, December 3, 1992, San Francisco, p. 16.

[42] Ronald Scollon and Suzanne B. K. Scollon, *Linguistic Convergence: An Ethnography of Speaking at Fort Chipewyan, Alberta* (New York: Academic Press, 1979).

verification of non-Indian accounts to explore their underlying historical consciousness.[43] Where she found discrepancies between Indian and white accounts – as with Indians asserting that the famous explorer Robert Campbell had an Indian wife – she let them stand, leaving open the possibility that Indian recollections often yielded behind-the-scenes exposés of historical figures. She was also struck by the fact that "both the Tlingit and the Athabaskans have what appears to be a high tolerance for discontinuity in time"; their myth-time could coexist with either the present or the recent past. That explained how some Indian accounts of the 1898 gold rush credited a European prospector and his Indian associate with finding the precious mineral, while others had gold originating from an Indian encounter with the mythic Wealth Woman, thus conjoining their separate indigenous genres, which McClellan learned were usually distinguished as "long ago stories" and "true stories."

Indian Versions of the Past Hold Their Own

When literary scholar Andrew O. Wiget compared Hopi Indian stories about the Pueblo Revolt against their foreign colonizers in 1680 and Spanish documents concerning the same momentous event, he subdivided his evaluative criteria into the relative accuracy of motivation, detail, and sequencing of events.[44] First, he concluded that the Native oral

43 Catherine McClellan, "Indian Stories about the First Whites in Northwestern America," in *Ethnohistory in Southwestern Alaska and the Southern Yukon*, edited by Margaret Lantis (Lexington, Ky.: The University Press of Kentucky, 1970), pp. 103–133. McClellan also observes that Indian plots often "patterned" certain story elements: when the white discovery of gold was recalled (practically its own genre in native Alaska and California), they frequently reiterated the consequent Indian loss of wealth and abuse of Indian labor, and drew fairly identical cultural contrasts (see Julie Cruikshank, "Images of Society in Klondike Gold Rush Narratives: Skookum Jim and the Discovery of Gold," *Ethnohistory* 39(1) [Winter 1992], pp. 20–41). Ubiquitous Indian stories of "firsts" – sighting or meeting whites, obtaining horses, shooting firearms, drinking coffee, etc. – often feature similar patterning.

44 Andrew O. Wiget, "Truth and the Hopi: An Historiographic Study of Documented Oral Tradition Concerning the Coming of the Spanish," *Ethnohistory* 29(3) (1982), pp. 181–199. With considerable sophistication, Wiget subsequently evaluted multiple Zuni Indian narratives of the 1680 revolt to argue for the probable veracity of their

testimony preserved with emotional specificity Hopi resentment of the cruel and capricious behavior of the Spanish priests. Second, in such details as the architectural shape of the Spanish friary, the number of priests killed, the uprising's actual date, the stories of the priests' arrival and early authoritarianism, the forced-labor construction of Oraibi, Awatovi, and Schungopavi missions, and the string of indignities that climaxed with the surprise attack, Hopi accounts also matched the Spanish versions. Along with this high degree of durability and reliability, the Indian narratives were interlarded with "a statement of shared values, represented by shared symbols." Admitting that some historical details were clearly collapsed, Wiget resisted giving priority to the search for factual accuracy over that for historical meanings. For him it remained crucial to avoid reducing some narrative elements to literalness and elevating others to myth if the "truth of the Hopi" were to be rescued from the "distortion of Western categories."[45]

---

account of a spared priest ("Father Juan Greyrobe: Reconstructing Tradition Histories, and the Reliability and Validity of Uncorroborated Oral Tradition," *Ethnohistory* 43(3) [Summer 1996], pp. 459–482).

[45] Comparing Indian and white interpretations of the same cultural predicaments or episodes is a frequent narrative strategy in case studies on American Indian historicity. In his analysis of legal claims by the Mashpee Indians of Massachusetts that constituted an exhaustive chapter in his *The Predicament of Culture*, scholar James Clifford concluded, in the words of Melissa L. Meyer and Kerwin Lee Klein, that "the Mashpee suffered from the law's reliance on modern western notions of historical identity that preclude the sort of social improvisation that has characterized Mashpee lives. Ultimately, the state's historicity (linear chronologies anchored by written documents) defeated the Mashpee's historicity (complex genealogies encoded in oral tradition and local practices)" ("Native American Studies and the End of Ethnohistory" in *Studying Native America* [Madison: University of Wisconsin Press, 1998], p. 188). In Richard A. Gould's comparision of "Indian and White Versions of 'The Burnt Ranch Massacre: A Study in Comparative Ethnohistory,'" which contrasted accounts of citizens' revenge assault on a Tolowa Indian camp in northwestern California in 1853, objectivity seemed of such secondary importance when it came to selecting key elements in both representations that Gould suggested, "It may then be as important a part of the ethnohistorian's task to determine the cultural attitudes which have caused certain events and impressions to be selected and emphasized in favour of others in both the written and oral records, as it is for him to determine what we usually refer to as 'history'" (*Journal of the Folklore Institute* 3 [1966], p. 42). And when state educators in northern New York State commissioned in 1987 a new resource guide on Indians, according to Gail Landsman and Sara Ciborski, "the restless, impermanent quality of the foundation of [Iroquois Indian] historical discourse" collided with an "objectivist

Citing Indian Forms of History Affect that History

When British Columbia extinguished aboriginal land rights in 1871, setting aside a few Indian reserves, it made a big mistake. For prior to joining the Canadian commonwealth, it never legally acquired those rights. This was what the Gitksan and Wet'suwet'en tribes, close neighbors of each other, argued in 1983 in their landmark case *Delgamuukw versus the Queen*. As legal evidence of titles held by their 120 major "houses" and nine matrilineal clans to as much as 22,000 square miles in the Skeena and Bulkley River watersheds, they cited narratives that traced their collective experiences over thousands of years, from the mythic days of great birds saving the tribes from melting glaciers to ancient gatherings hosted by mountain goat people to the destruction of a founding village by a giant grizzly bear and a terrible flood.[46] Although a provincial judge dismissed the Indian case, Canada's Supreme Court sustained it in 1997, declaring that "The law of evidence must be adapted in order that this type of evidence can be accommodated and placed on an equal footing with the types of historical evidence the courts are familiar with." Said one tribal leader afterward, "What evidence did we have to show them this land was ours? There are the names of the territory, the names of the streams, the names of the mountain peaks. This took thousands and thousands of years. These are our boundaries. You could not fake them."[47]

---

history" that traded in "fixed rules and eternal verities," leaving no room whatsoever for "the concept of negotiated representation of history" ("Representation and Politics: Contesting Histories of the Iroquois," *Cultural Anthropology* 7(4) [November 1992], p. 443).

46 Among the numerous "books of claims" that assemble such Northwest Coast clan and house narratives are *Visitors Who Never Left*, edited by Frances Robinson (Vancouver: University of British Columbia Press, 1974), and *Histories, Territories, and Laws of the Kitwancool*, edited by Wilson Duff, Anthropology in British Columbia Memorial N. 4 (Victoria: British Columbia Provincial Museum, 1959).

47 Anthony DePalma, "Canadian Indians Win a Ruling Vindicating Their Oral History," *The New York Times*, February 9, 1998, pp. A1–A8. Also see Terry Glavin's book-length treatment of the case, *A Death Feast in Dimlahamid* (Vancouver: New Star Books, 1998), and Jay Miller's "Tsimshian Ethno-Ethnohistory: A 'Real' Indigenous Chronology," *Ethnohistory* 45(4) (Fall 1998), pp. 657–674, which argues that this Native nation's own sense of its successive historical sagas (*adawx*) provides "a sequence of at least fifteen episodic overlays across ten thousand years."

Indian Narratives Turn Shared Pasts into Richer Histories

A pleasure of Indian versions of history is how they educate, explain, and entertain at the same time. What, for instance, did the Washoe Indians make of the first nineteen wagons of white pioneers to cross the Sierra foothills near Lake Tahoe in midwinter 1846? How did they explain their consequent harassment, beating, and lynching at white hands? The gift to Washoe imagination from the Donner Party, which was trapped for months in snow drifts, came when whites cut up, cooked, and ate each other. The Washoe found it easier to slot them after that. One of their prose genres features stories about creatures eating creatures, either "true" accounts of grizzly bears and mountain lions that pounce on hunters or wayward girls and boys, or "monster" stories about one-eyed giants or huge cannibal birds that drag humans to their lairs. When the Washoe, in one version, spied on the Donner members cannibalizing each other or, in another when they discovered severed human skulls with hair on them the following spring, they simply tacked this worst-case scenario to the corpus. As anthropologist Barrik Van Winkle says, "White men became the most extreme, frightening, ferocious members of this series – not animals, not monsters – but humans who act like animals and monsters toward their own kind (and kin)." The grotesquerie was also prophetic of the inhuman treatment that whites shortly thereafter visited on them. "The worst cannibals were men," one old Washoe woman told him, tapping the anthropologist's knee with her finger to make sure she had his attention, "men like you."[48]

[48] Barrik Van Winkle, "Cannibals in the Mountains: Washoe Teratology and the Donner Party," in *Native North Americans: Cultures, Histories, Representations*, edited by Sergei Kan and Pauline T. Strong (Lincoln: University of Nebraska Press, in press).

THREE

───◄o►───

Almost Timeless Truths

Myth and History

The [Osage] personal name had as well its tribal history, and family history, and gentile history, into which it placed its bearer.... The "wild" Indian was tied to land, to people, to origins and way of life by every kind of human ordering we can imagine. "History" and "Myth" and "Identity" are not three separate matters, here, but three aspects of one human being.[1]

Carter Revard, Osage

Heading for the post office in Redding, California, one mid-October morning in 1884, the folklorist Jeremiah Curtin struck up a conversation with a homeless Indian. Already an eminent linguist – by the end of his life Curtin was reputedly proficient in over fifty languages – and a tireless collector of folklore in Europe and Mexico, the forty-nine-year-old scholar was keeping his ears open for Indian stories. During that season, Curtin's new acquaintance, Mike Reed, and his half-Northern Yana, half-McLoud Wintu uncle were occupying canvas tents pitched near the upper Sacramento River. The Indians accepted his invitation to visit him at Mrs. Smith's boarding house, and soon Curtin was paying close attention to a "tall" and "fine-looking" old man of about ninety years of age.[2]

---

[1] Carter Revard, "History, Myth, and Identity Among Osages and Other Peoples," *Denver Quarterly* 14(4) (Winter 1980), p. 97.

[2] Background on Norelputus, the Yana-Wintu elder, and Curtin among the Wintu is in Jeremiah Curtin, *Memoirs of Jeremiah Curtin*, edited by Joseph Schafer

85

An itinerant singer and dancer, and welcomed by every Indian community where he sojourned, Reed's uncle turned out to be "one of the most remarkable persons I have ever met," Curtin later wrote. He possessed a "mental power of the first quality," with storytelling gifts "not only of narrative but of unusual mythological combination." After interviewing him intermittently over the next five years, with the nephew as translator, Curtin credited the elder with granting him "a world of knowledge of their traditions, religion and myths . . . the only man in the tribe capable of doing this."

He was known as Norelputus. That meant "South Indian Summer," but one of his earlier names, perhaps his prophetic one, was "Spirit of the West." Born in the mid-1790s, Norelputus had witnessed his people's holocaust of disease, murder, and displacement, when they plummeted in size from an estimated 14,200 Wintu in his infancy to fewer than 1,000 members by the time of his meeting with Curtin.[3] From his interactions with Norelputus and the Wintu people, Curtin took away two assignments. He would carry the fight for his landless friends to Washington. Sadly, the petition he personally handed to President Benjamin Harrison in May 1890 only received the president's lip service about Wintu recovering portions of their old homeland, but no concrete boundaries or protections. However, he made good on his vow to analyze nine of Norelputus's myths and prepare them for publication.

Some of the kinds of history they contained Curtin did perceive. But at least one, I believe, escaped him. He recognized that within Norelputus's narratives lay implications of social practices, descriptions of hunting and practical life, and other cultural data that Curtin could have inventoried through the "myth as mirror" approach by which oral folklore was milked for its reflection of cultural lifeways (and ignored for any

(Madison: State Historical Society of Wisconsin, 1940), Jeremiah Curtin, *Creative Myths of Primitive America* (London: Williams & Norgate, 1899), and Cora Du Bois, *The 1870 Ghost Dance*, Anthropological Records 3(1) (Berkeley: University of California Press, 1939), pp. 13, 14, 40, 43–45, 52–55.

3 Background on Wintu in *Papers on Wintu Ethnography*, N. 1, Occasional Papers of the Redding Museum (Redding, Calif.: Redding Museum and Art Center, December 1980), and Frank R. Lapena, "Wintu," in V. 8, *California*, in *Handbook of North American Indians* (Washington, D.C.: Smithsonian Institution Press, 1978), pp. 324–340.

historical data) by Franz Boas for the Kwakiutl,[4] Clara Ehrlich for the Crow,[5] and Ruth Benedict for the Zuni.[6]

Curtin also realized that indigenous concepts of chronology informed these narratives. In his 1898 introduction to the collection, he outlined three prehuman "periods of duration." First was a temporal realm in which nonhuman and nonanimal spirits known as the "first people" lived in a state "of complete and perfect harmony." Following came its terrifying flip side, an era "of violence, collision and conflict." As a consequence of this cataclysmic interim, those original inhabitants "were turned into the various kinds of living creatures that are on earth now or have ever been on earth, except man." In the third epoch humans entered the scene, whose stage was today's flora, fauna, and geology – the ecological features into which those previous spirit-occupants had transformed, "all kinds of beasts, birds, reptiles, fish, worms, and insects, as well as trees, plants, grasses, rocks and some mountains. . . ."[7]

Some of those conflict-ridden myths evoked actual times gone by, as if they preserved, as Carobeth Laird wrote of southern California Chemehuevi mythology, "in disguised form much that has long faded from tribal memory."[8] According to Curtin, "The myth-maker looked at the universe around him . . . and gave a detailed account and *history* of how this world arose."[9] But Curtin also identified an overlapping subset with more durable motifs, which echo the binary oppositions identified by French structuralists. For they contained "accounts of conflicts which are ever recurrent, which began before all the first people were metamorphosed, conflicts which are going on at present and which will go on

4 Franz Boas, *Kwakiutl Culture as Reflected in Mythology*, Memoirs of the American Folk-lore Society, N. 28 (New York: The American Folk-lore Society, G. E. Stechert and Co., 1935).

5 Clara Ehrlich, "Tribal Culture in Crow Mythology," *Journal of American Folklore* 50 (1937), pp. 307–408.

6 Ruth Benedict, *Zuni Mythology*, 2 vols. (New York: Columbia University Press, 1935).

7 Jeremiah Curtin, *Creation Myths of Primitive America in Relation to the Religious History and Mental Development of Mankind* (Boston: Little, Brown, and Company, 1898), pp. xi–xii.

8 Carobeth Laird, *"Mirror and Pattern": George Laird's World of Chemehuevi Mythology* (Banning, Calif.: Malki Museum Press, 1984), p. 244.

9 Curtin, *Creation Myths* (emphasis mine). p. xxiv.

forever; struggles between light and darkness, heat and cold, summer and winter, struggles between winds that blow in opposite directions," and which included the birth of culture heroes who would become the benefactors of human beings yet to come. From all this he generalized that "Every ethnic religion gives us documentary evidence. It gives us positive facts which, *in their own sphere*, are as true as are facts of geology in the history of the earth's crust and surface"[10]

Not only did Curtin identify successions of deep time similar to those isolated by later folklorists such as Melville Jacobs and Jarold Ramsay in Far Western Indian mythic narratives, his interpretation also anticipated classic statements on myth made by Bronsilaw Malinowski twenty-five years later. For Curtin saw how these Wintu myths served as totalizing "charters" for human behavior:

> The lives of the first people are described in creation myths, and presented as models upon which faithful Indians are to fashion their lives at all times and places. All institutions of primitive man in America were patterned after those of "the first people." Every act of an Indian in peace or in war, as an individual or as a member of a tribe, had its only sanction in the world of the first people....[11]

Many scholars have tussled with mediating between the apparent poles of myth and history. Curtin's unsophisticated but prescient, proto-functional observations grew out of a respectful appreciation of cultural myths that attempted an analysis from an insider's perspective. Curtin also implied a more congenial symbiosis between myth and history than would be allowed by many later interpreters of mythology, notably the influential religious historian Mircea Eliade, who emphasized myth's timelessness and even its antagonism to history. One also detects this emphasis upon the ahistorical essence of American Indian myth in the writings of folklorist Anna Birgitta Rooth, in the search for their universal symbols by religious historian Joseph Campbell and psychologist Carl Jung, and, to some extent, in the structural analyses of the anthropologist Claude Levi-Strauss. Only Rooth and Levi-Strauss, however, invited much history into their schemata.

[10] Curtin, *Creation Myths*, pp. xxxi–xxxii (emphasis mine).
[11] Curtin, *Creative Myths*, p. xx.

Compiling and analyzing 300 of these American Indian creation myths, Rooth, for example, subdivided them thematically into eight subtypes and mapped their geographical range. Her only bow to temporal change lies in hesitant conjectures about how "genetically related" themes and motifs may have diffused through "channels of cultural contact" from continent to continent in a conjectural past.[12] For Levi-Strauss, time can drip through seams in the "closed" binary structures that underlie myth, whose narratives may thus be exposed to the "open system" of historical change. At the same time, Levi-Strauss also warned fellow scholars about dismissing Indian-written histories as "fanciful," since an argument could be made that they occupied an "intermediary level" between oral myth and written history. Moreover, he challenged academics, "When we try to do scientific history, do we really do something scientific, or do we too remain astride our own mythology in what we are trying to make as pure history?"[13]

In their search for myth's abiding archetypes – and their often romantic identification with its underlying "truths" – more mystically inclined scholars like Eliade and Jung at least displayed an affinity for the reverence felt by most Indians for their ancient or origin stories. Rather than regarding myths as human hand-me-downs, Native people esteemed them as seemingly autonomous, untouchably sacred accounts that bypassed the need for factual verification. Any proposal that they encoded the functional or historical "just thinking" processes that the

---

[12] Anna Birgitta Rooth, "The Creation Myths of the North American Indians," in *Sacred Narrative: Readings in the Theory of Myth* (Berkeley: University of California Press, 1984), p. 181.

[13] Claude Levi-Strauss, "When Myth Becomes History," in *Myth and Meaning* (New York: Schocken Books, 1978), p. 41. Jonathan D. Hill goes further in his comment that structuralism's "disengagement of mythic 'structure' from historical 'event' " has been trivialized into a false dichotomy between fiction and fact. Instead, Hill maintains, "neither myth nor history is reducible to a text, thing, fact or event. Both history and myth are modes of social consciousness through which people construct shared interpretative frameworks." And Hill further proposes that "Through careful study of the full range of genres that give expression to mythic and historical (or mythic-historical) consciousness, researchers can begin to study how indigenous peoples have constructed shared interpretive frameworks for understanding the social situations of contact and the historical process of coping with a dominant, external society" ("Myth and History," in *Rethinking History and Myth: Indigenous South American Perspectives on the Past*, edited by Jonathan Hill [Urbana: University of Illinois Press, 1988], pp. 5, 9).

old Navajo from Tuba City of my Introduction disdained as the Western way of making sense would be considered irrelevant and impious. For traditional Indians as well as these sympathetic outsiders, who often share a nostalgia for golden ages, mythic narratives were mysteriously (supernaturally, psychologically, or biologically) determined and, at root, humanely unquestioned. However much generations of Indian story-tellers might reformulate myths "behind the scenes," as it were, their truths were represented as if inscribed on the stars (or in the human psyche or brain), on firmaments beyond the fictions and nonfictions created by human agency.[14]

In this inclusive and nonscientific sense of myth, anything old and everything new can – indeed, *must* – be absorbed into its all-knowing, omnipotent purview. For a strong statement on what one might term this "encompassing reflex" of mythic thought, by which it cannot help but extend its proprietary reach over multiple time frames, let anthropologist Frederica de Laguna explain the Tlingit Indian term *cagun*, a key concept in the historical thought of this Northwest Coast nation:

> It has been claimed with justice that every people live their own myths, that is, that their conduct in the present reflects what they believe their past to have been, since that past, as well as the present and the future, are aspects of the "destiny" in which they exhibit themselves as they think they really are. The Tlingit themselves sense this and use the term "ha (our) cagun" for the origin and destiny of their sib [or, of their clan, both terms meaning all descendants through the male or female line of a single human or supernatural ancestor], including the totemic animal or bird encountered by their ancestors and the powers

[14] As Yankton Sioux educator Leonard Bruguier testifies to this contrast between ways of knowledge: "I come from two different cultures. As a person in a university, I have to practice the method they taught me: be skeptical and use detective work to confirm what I'm told versus what I read in books and papers. In a white world, myth is on a fictional plane, and oral history is acceptable as long as you check it out. In the Indian world, it's all true. You accept it for what it is." Quoted in Maryjane Ambler, "History in the First Person." *Winds of Change* 10(4) (Autumn 1995), p. 85. Moreover, from the Sioux perspective, adds Raymond J. DeMallie, myth "is the only true history because it explains the moral framework within which Lakota culture developed and flourished. It can best be characterized as sacred history." *The Sixth Grandfather: Black Elk's Teachings Given to John G. Meihardt*, edited and with an Introduction by Raymond J. DeMallie (Lincoln: University of Nebraska Press, 1984), p. 69.

and prerogatives obtained from it, as well as their own place in the universe and the ultimate fate of their unborn descendants.[15]

Despite this instinct for inclusiveness, myth may find room for some coordination with alien explanatory paradigms, as we have just heard from Claude Lévi-Strauss and Jonathan D. Hill. Such a prospect is shared by anthropologist Robin Ridington, who, while certainly unwilling for his Dunne-Za Indian friends from northeastern British Columbia to relinquish any of the wisdom they shared in mythic stories they exchanged each summer at the gathering place known as Where Happiness Dwells, also envisions some coexistence between contrasting epistemologies:

> There is no documentary or scientific evidence to indicate that frogs really sing and dance and gamble beneath the waters of a pond, but the old man said he experienced this, too. There is no documentary evidence of foxes who live like people. Because we lack documentary evidence, we are compelled to class his second story as myth.... Unless we can find some way to understand the reality of mythic thinking, we remain prisoners of our language, our own thoughtworld.... The language of Western social science assumes an object world independent of individual experience. The language of Indian stories assumes that objectivity that can *only* be approached through experience.... Their truths are complementary.[16]

Mythic thought can enter this more "complementary" and contemporary multicultural (and semihistorical) discourse probably because it has been doing so for ages. Its narrative embodiments have always proven more responsive and malleable than either its Native constituencies or academic interpreters readily admit. Appreciating the formidable attributes of mythic thought need not minimize our appreciation for human creativity when it confronts the vagaries of history. Along with the requirement that such narratives encompass through patterning all events of the past, present, and future comes the survival mechanism for

---

15 Frederica de Laguna, *The Story of a Tlingit Community: A Problem in the Relationship between Archeological, Ethnological, and Historical Methods*, Bulletin 172, Bureau of American Ethnology (Washington, D.C.: Government Printing Office, 1960), p. 202.

16 Robin Ridington, "Myth and History," in *Trail to Heaven: Knowledge and Narrative in a Northern Native Community* (Iowa City: University of Iowa Press, 1988), p. 71.

doing that, known as "adaptation." Rather than being closed systems of fixed symbols, if myths are to remain relevant and recited, they must be susceptible to internal tinkerings and updatings. Reminding us of the pragmatics of Indian mythology, literary scholar Karl Kroeber writes:

> Western commentators on myth from Max Muller to Lévi-Strauss have been unwilling to recognize that myths are invented and adapted through diverse enactments to provide practical assistance for people in confronting actual problems, even unexampled social catastrophes. By refusing to admit that "primitive" people in fact live lives as "historical" as our own, Western experts have denied to those they pretend to admire the terrible honor of tragic experience and the imaginative strength to face boldly the realities of defeat and irreparable loss.[17]

Investigating what Raymond Firth has called this "plasticity of myth" entails appreciating the "created" and "contingent" factors embodied in a dynamic comprehension of what culture does for participants who, like it or not, cannot help but live in time. What governs the force of myths in real life, observes Morton Klass, is less their "accuracy" than their "acceptability."[18] Loosening up old attitudes about the relative conservatism of myths does not necessarily mean that these narratives become impoverished through their responsiveness to changing historical circumstances, nor, as P. van Baaren has noted, that they automatically "become secularized when a certain myth is in the process of losing its [original] function."[19] On the contrary, myth in this proactive mode, while betraying "adaptability to new situations and challenges," enriches its power as a sacrilizing, truth-decreeing strategy.

A striking range of mythic revisionings is found across Native North America. That the gradual mythologizing of history may be a precontact practice, at least in the central plains, is suggested by Douglas R. Parks's study of a corpus of Pawnee and Arikara narratives that feature survivors of scalping ordeals during intertribal fighting. As

[17] Karl Kroeber, *Artistry in Native American Myths* (Lincoln: University of Nebraska Press, 1998), p. 86.

[18] Morton Klass, *Ordered Universes: Approaches to the Anthropology of Religion* (Boulder: Westview Press, 1998), p. 125.

[19] P. van Baaren, "The Flexibility of Myth," *Studies in the History of Religions* 22 (1972), p. 199.

disfigured oddities, existing in some nether zone between the living and the dead, the "scalped men" were ridiculed, feared, and ostracized, yet remembered by name. Once they joined the ranks of bygone heroes, however, legendary stories enshrined these walking wounded as gifted medicine men whose special powers helped warriors steal horses and heal the injured.

Over time they were even on their way to joining the Pawnees' mythic pantheon, as their scarred presences were already instrumental – before white society truncated the tribe's normative evolution – in enabling cosmological narratives to explain the origins of summer and death.[20] The temporal trajectory traced by these liminal Pawnee personalities is thus reminiscent of the legend-to-myth continuum discerned by William W. Elmendorf in Pacific Coast (Salish) narratives. They dwell from the present day back to the "Semihistoric," with their exclusively human characters and historically known peoples at the cusp of eyewitness memory. They are also found deeper in the "Semimythic," joining its human characters who are endowed with transformative and magical powers. And they are among the animal-human "Myth-time" personalities who appear during the universe's first stirrings.[21]

In the majority of mythic materials covered in this chapter, however, Indian reflections of and observations about historical change come more modestly, obliquely, piecemeal, and, dare one say it, "recently." Like transformations of the scalped man's supporting role across the spectrum of Pawnee folk forms, myths of the Chiricahua Apache center on a star player named Child of the Water, whose various roles were

---

[20] Douglas R. Parks, "An Historical Character Mythologized: The Scalped Man in Arikara and Pawnee Folklore," in *Plains Indian Studies: A Collection of Essays in Honor of John C. Ewers and Waldo R. Wedel*, edited by Douglas H. Ubelaker and Herman J. Viola (Washington, DC: Smithsonian Institution Press, 1982), pp. 47–57. Upstreaming these disfigured historical personages into origin stories would seem another instance that refutes anthropologist Carobeth Laird's proposition in *Mirror and Pattern*, p. 17, that the road between mythic and present eras is one-way or, in her words, that "The mythic era spills into the human era, but the reverse is not true." This exception may be due to the fact that the Pawnees possibly saw these scalped men as confounding cultural categories; as ambulatory humans who have lost their souls. And perhaps they could travel both ways because, Laird adds, "Mythic persons have breath and minds, but they do not have souls" (p. 18).

[21] William W. Elmendorf, *Twana Narratives: Native Historical Accounts of a Coast Salish Culture* (Seattle: University of Washington Press, 1993), pp. lii–liv.

introduced into their folklore at different times. But unlike the stories assembled by Parks, these Apache narratives were personally collected by Morris E. Opler during a single field season (1935) from seven different storytellers.

Opler's first grouping of stories focused on this culture hero's slaying of monsters. What nonconformities occurred in this set Opler attributed to "elaborations" and natural extensions of "elements and ideas" already built into the narratives; they tightened or lengthened episodes but added nothing significant. An etiological emphasis ran through his second cluster of stories; they did attach elements that sought to rationalize the origins of ceremonies, ritual procedures, and social customs. As for the subtle idiosyncracies that characterized the third group of narratives, Opler attributed those more to biographical context – the careers and preoccupations of his individual shaman storytellers – than to any internal rearrangements or cultural agendas.

In inevitably unflattering ways, however, virtually all of Opler's storytellers inserted episodes that accounted for the presence of Euro-Americans, their murderous behavior, lust for riches, preference for domesticated plants and animals, and ultimate irreconcilability with the Chiricahua Apache way of life – which always emerged triumphant. But one wonders whether an even subtler form of cultural critique informed these texts. As Opler ends by noting that what he has paraded before us is less narrative "change" than its Apache alternative, "variation," we are struck again by oral tradition's central strength: the coexistence of *multiple versions*, whose preservation of options often stands in philosophical and political opposition to the monopolizing inclinations of the non-Indian's print medium.[22]

As for more overt censure, one finds it folded into origin narratives from other cultural regions as well. Among the Three Affiliated Tribes of North Dakota, the Mandan tale-teller John Brave's account of how Lone Man and First Creator first made the world makes reference to Euro-American society through scattered moralistic explanatory motifs.

---

[22] Morris Edward Opler, "Three Types of Variation and Their Relation to Culture Change," in *Language, Culture, and Personality: Essays in Memory of Edward Sapir*, edited by Leslie Spier, A. Irving Hallowell, and Stanley S. Newman (Menasha, Wisc.: Sapir Memorial Publication Fund, 1941), pp. 146–157.

When First Creator, the omnipotent, initially makes "white man's cattle," their horns are so crooked that their vision is obstructed, and their testicles are so heavy that they must walk bow-legged. Save those ridiculous beasts for later, advises Lone Man; for now, create buffalo for the Indians.

When he and First Creator discover red-headed maggots in a wolf carcass, neither will take responsibility, and Lone Man removes them to the opposite side of a lake. "In the days to come," Lone Man decrees, "they'll have intelligence." Here narrator Brave comments, "when you see white men, some of whom have red heads, they are descendants of those maggots. And today these white men are very intelligent, as it was promised. Today they are doing everything which seems impossible [such as building the world's largest rolled-fill dam, Garrison Dam, on the middle Missouri River, which may be Brave's timely reference here]."

The selection ends with a digression on the pair's relative powers. Long ago, Brave points out, Lone Man *was* God. Then he provides a tender glimpse of why he is so sure: "Whenever he saw some children around the village, he always wiped their noses. For Lone Man was kind-hearted." But First Creator seemed in Brave's imagination more akin to the Euro-American's God, "always the one who fooled people."[23]

According to Fred Eggan, writing in 1967, "The Hopi Indians [of Arizona] are still creating myths."[24] To illustrate, he compared two accounts of a bloody clash between Hopis and Navajos in the mid-1850s, narrated over forty years apart. For the older rendition, which Eggan comments is deficient in chronological specifics – "always a weak point in Pueblo accounts" – the observed events were remarkably detailed and "accurate," as if brought close through a telescope. In the later version, the telling fell into a seemingly earlier, more mythic narrative canon, as if seen far away through a telescope turned the wrong way. New

---

23 Douglas R. Parks, A. Wesley Jones, and Robert C. Hollow, *Earth Lodge Tales from the Upper Missouri: Traditional Tales of the Arikara, Hidatsa, and Mandan* (Bismark, N.D.: Mary College Press, 1978), pp. 67–71. The dynamic ways that the Judeo-Christian God and his transformer-like Son have been incorporated into American Indian mythologies remains understudied.

24 Fred Eggan, "From History to Myth: A Hopi Example," reprinted in *Essays in Social Anthropology and Ethnology*, University of Chicago Studies in Anthropology, Series in Social, Cultural, and Linguistic Anthropology, N. 1 (Chicago: University of Chicago Press, 1975), p. 297.

motivations for triggering events were attributed, generalized ways of Hopi behavior were sanctioned, and the story enunciated basic cultural divides between Hopis and Navajos (in much the reverse fashion that the Navajo's Beautyway myth and ceremony, David Brugge has proposed, served as a Navajo way to make the same distinction on behalf of retaining Navajo identity in their new Pueblo-dominated environs).[25]

In Eggan's example, what sounded at first more like a historical legend was "on its way to becoming tradition and myth." His test case was designed to persuade other American Indian scholars that the cautious sieving of mythologizing narratives and their controlled comparison – separating generic affirmations of cultural themes from "the historical events embedded in them" – could reveal "a good deal about Hopi [or American Indian] history and character, and help us to understand the changes they have undergone."

But the critical factors behind mythological change vary widely and are best revealed through specific cases. When Greg Keyes compared the "ball game myths" recorded by the Spanish from the hierarchical Apalachee in the 1670s or by the French from Natchez Indian elites in the early eighteenth century, to those collected in the mid-twentieth century among the Tunica of Louisiana, he found curious omissions. The origins of ceremonies remained constant in all of them, but the variants still circulating within marginalized, impoverished Indian enclaves around Marksville, Louisiana, dropped out any reference to heaven-sent chiefs and proscribed rules of divine right. In his warning against imprudently speculating about earlier ancestors based upon features in present myths, Keyes suggested that while some motifs "might appear to resist the ravages of time like granite building blocks," one should remain vigilant that "the castles and towers those blocks are used to build may tumble and be rearranged into humbler – or perhaps more different – structures."[26]

---

[25] This idea is broached in David M. Brugge's *Navajo Pottery and Ethnohistory* (Window Rock, Ariz.: Navajo Tribal Museum, Navajoland Publications, October 1963), pp. 22–23.

[26] Greg Keyes, "Myth and Social History in the Early Southeast," in *Perspectives on the Southeast: Linguistics, Archaeology and Ethnohistory*, edited by Patricia B. Kwachka, Southern Anthropological Society Proceedings, N. 27 (Athens: University of Georgia Press, 1994), p. 114.

A variety of motivations drove these reformulations. Under more or less ordinary circumstances, the Indians strove to bring the historically contingent into conformity with cosmic reliability. They reflected adaptations to new social climates. They adjusted to "internal" upheavals such as takeovers from within or usurpations by neighbors, to technological or economic revolutions, and to the "external" causes emphasized in conventional histories of Indian–white relations.

Where they address multiracial realities, one again might expect mythic narratives to fulfill their exegetical mandate to account for the very existence, relative status, and defining proclivities of all shades of human beings. Yet in almost all of the American Indian etiological accounts of racial or ethnic diversity – even when Indians have explained the presence of African-Americans by borrowing from African storytelling motifs – an unapologetic ethnocentrism is the norm.[27] Where comparisons are drawn between Indian and white societies, mythic narratives deliver frontal attacks of the unsugared sort we have already witnessed among the Mandan; among the Copper Eskimo, for instance, the birth of Europeans is described as the consequence of a woman who copulated with dogs.[28]

Indeed, deep readings of many myths disclose them as riddled with subtle detonations of the "reverse cultural critiques" to be described in the following chapter, wherein one society measures itself against another, generally giving itself the upper hand or casting itself in the better light but also expressing amazement at the other's technological (often interpreted as supernatural) superiority. For users only, these absolutist renditions of the preordained history of Native–European relations frequently strive to negate or coopt change. Their claims to community credulity buy time while they attempt to balance the retooling of plots and transformations of characters with their resistance to anything implied by their own cultural "disappearance."

---

[27] Adding his comment on the long debate over possible African influence on Indian myths and tales is William G. McLoughlin's interesting "A Note on African Sources of American Indian Racial Myths," *Journal of American Folklore* 89 (353) (July–September 1976), pp. 331–335.

[28] Knud Rasmussen, "Those Who Became White Men," in *Intellectual Culture of the Copper Eskimo*, Report of the 5th Thule Expedition, 1921–1924, V. 9 (Copenhagen: Gyldenal, 1932), pp. 240–241.

When such narratives show Indians improvising on traditional plot lines to incorporate historical events, they also demonstrate how mythic recomposition can loop its revisionist reach backward in time, so as to embrace an approximation of those broad epochs that the French historian Fernand Braudel termed the *longue durée*. One Indian technique for doing this is by absorbing new events within the cosmological time frame of mythic narratives. Among the Tewa people of northern New Mexico, writes Alfonso Ortiz, "an expression frequently used in Tewa oral tradition is 'when it has been four times,' which is used to convey both a sense of time and sense of space simultaneously. . . . There is so much of this four of this, and four of that [spans of days or travels] that this is obviously not history in the sense that we as scholars understand it."[29]

When events took place outside the landscape demarcated by their four sacred mountains, units of twelve were the norm because, Ortiz went on, "in the Tewa genesis the migration from the northern boundary of the Tewa world to the present Tewa villages took place in twelve steps." Similarly, in Plains Indian accounts of vision quests, battle forays, and getting sacred medicines to work, one usually had to go through three unsuccessful tries before the goal was reached on the fourth. For the Navajos, however, their relative sense of security was reflected in whether the preferable numbers were even or odd: in their myth, "Growth of the Navajo Nation," scholar Gladys Reichard points out that early Navajo journeys and clan migrations into dangerous foreign territory featured objects and events happening in odd numbers, but when Navajos described their ancestors coming under the familiar, protective sway of their sacred Changing Woman, everything unfolded in twos or fours.[30]

Here we return to Jeremiah Curtin and the third strand of Wintu Indian history-in-myth that I believe escaped him or that, perhaps, he was not meant to see. A radical way in which myths respond to historical change is via the prophetic doctrines that flower during periods of extreme crisis. Their chartering narratives range from intensified reformulations of the

[29] Alfonso Ortiz, "Some Concerns Central to the Writing of 'Indian' History, *The Indian Historian* 10(1) (1977), p. 19.
[30] Gladys A. Reichard, *Navaho Religion: A Study in Symbolism* (New York: Bollingen, 1963), pp. 246–247.

sort already described, to new epilogues that are spliced onto a tribe's cumulative corpus of guiding narratives, or to replacement myths that supplant earlier doctrines and are promoted as newly revealed sources (or syntheses) of mythic history and future orientation. Behind Norelputus's narratives we have documentary hints that some such reformulation was staring Curtin in the face. What the British folklorist learned about the old California Indian's personal history suggests that human intervention, and myth's responsiveness to trying times, influenced the Wintu narratives that Curtin wrote down in the 1880s.

The terrible events that swirled around the McLeod River region in the 1850s drove a stake through Norelputus's heart. The depredations suffered by his Wintu friends and kinfolk were great; the toll on the Yana side of his family was even worse. From their estimated precontact population of between 2,000 and 3,000 when Norelputus was a boy, by the time of his conversations with Curtin only an estimated 35 Yana individuals were scrambling to survive in the hills between the southern Sacramento River Valley and San Pablo Bay. As gold miners and ordinary citizens thought nothing of annihilating Indian families and rancherias on their weekends, one of these rampages struck his own camp on Cow Creek in 1864 when he way away in Casper City. Upon his return home, Norelputus found the murdered bodies of his two wives.

About six years later, his name surfaces as a leader of a localized rendition of the California Ghost Dance, which more accurately might be characterized as a great wave of religious fervor that rolled in from Nevada across the dispersed, remnant Indian hamlets of north-central California after 1870. True to their dispersed, autonomous nature, each Indian hamlet's resident shamans developed their particular take on its core ideology, whose generic plot held that the world would be destroyed by fire or flood, and that the Indians would survive to find the earth carpeted by wild flowers and dead ancestors returned to life.

The spin that Norelputus put on this general doctrine may have derived from some mystical revelation of his own. A well-known headman of his Clikapudi Creek village and widely respected storyteller, the vision he adopted seems to have instructed people to commence construction of oversized dance halls, circular lodges framed with timbers, featuring sunken floors and sacred center poles and roofed with earth. And after the spring of 1872, for a full year community after community joined this building campaign. As the chosen huddled inside these large chambers, went the prophecy, the world outside would be obliterated (in what sounds like a reprise of Norelputus's tumultuous second mythic "duration"). When the flooding waters ebbed or the raging fires subsided (both were possible causes of this destruction), the Indians would emerge to discover the white man gone, their ancestors brought back to life, and the world renewed. From its origins among the northern Yana, the Earth Lodge doctrine was taken up by the Hill Patwin, the Lake and Coast Miwok, the Cahto, the Wintu, the Shasta, the Achumawi, the Wappo, the Coast Yuki, the Sinkyone, the Pomo and the Nomlaki, and even some small Oregon tribes. Native accounts identify Norelputus as personally responsible for transmitting the message to the Wintu and Hill Patwin, who eagerly embraced it.

But when this promised New Day failed to come, we can assume that the general faith in Norelputus's adventist message waned. From scanty accounts of his "earth lodge cult," however, we never hear that the failure turned into a repudiation of his sincerity or any slurs that he was a false prophet. Most likely his people considered him just another shaman whose heart was in the right place but against whose dreams the odds were overwhelming. How could this legacy not have shaped the way Norelputus injected some degree of persistent relevance into the cosmic myths that explained and controlled his world?

Had Curtin been aware of the man's role in the California Ghost Dance, he might have discerned from the unusual prominence his stories gave to a monotheistic, almighty creator ("Oleibus") and their emphasis on Armageddon or Noah's floodlike apocalyptic upheavals that here was yet another major way that myth and history intersected throughout Native America. I am speaking of that string of instances, erupting not long after 1500 and lasting right through 2000, when social stress, population loss, economic deprivation, or other terrifying uncertainties called forth the creative impulses and revised guidelines for magical transformation or some kind of alternative, fulfilling identity that sprang from the religious imagination.

I am speaking of what anthropologists call "revitalization movements." From the Eastern Seaboard to the West, prophetic individuals and their urgent visions, hopeful forecasts, revitalized mythologies, and associations with armed struggle or more quiescent accommodations were a major force for tribal resistance and continuity across Native America. Had we any data on Wintu mythology around 1800, we might compare the degree to which Curtin's narratives actually amounted to a revised ideology of the sort that was cobbled together by other tribes caught in similar straits.[31]

Often whipping Christian symbols and imported themes into old storylines, the richness of expressive culture that developed out of this collision of cultures remains understudied.[32] Across North America these extraordinary movements produced a visionary literature, and a wide range of performative traditions, that amounted to a foundation, built *in extremis* and from the bottom up, that enabled Indians and their old spirits to hang on. The new prophets produced out of such revitalization narratives include Sweet Medicine of the Cheyenne, Tailfeather Woman of the Santee, White Buffalo Calf Woman of the Lakota, and Redbird Smith of the Cherokee, to name but a few.[33]

Iroquois auto-history offers one of the clearest summarizing examples of the different shades of myth covered in this chapter. As mentioned in the Introduction, the doctrinal evolution of the Iroquois six-tribe confederacy is exceedingly well documented. Three epic narratives structure

[31] I am bypassing the debate over whether such "revitalization movements" result from postcontact depredations and deprivations or are a consequence of intertribal adaptations or internal religious crises; for this discussion see Wayne Suttles, "The Plateau Prophet Dance among the Coast Salish," *Southwestern Journal of Anthropology* 13 (1957), pp. 352–393, and Elizabeth Vibert, " 'The Natives Were Strong to Live': Reinterpreting Early-Nineteenth-Century Prophetic Movements in the Columbia Plateau," *Ethnohistory* 42(2) (1995), pp. 197–223.

[32] Lee Brumbaugh agrees that "American anthropologists have paid little attention to the oral traditions surrounding the various Ghost Dances, or Native American revitalization movements," and after his own comparative survey he finds an "Orpheus" ur-plot underlying many of their memorats in which a shaman-hero seeks power in the land of the dead: "Quest for Survival: The Native American Ghost-Pursuit Tradition ('Orpheus') and the Origins of the Ghost Dance," in *Folklore Interpreted: Essays in Honor of Alan Dundes*, edited by Regina Bendix and Rosemary Levy Zumwalt (New York: Garland Publishing, 1995), pp. 183–198.

[33] For radical philosopher Walter Benjamin, it was precisely such redemptive religious revolutions that shattered gradualist, unsystematic, and insignificant "homogeneous time," replacing it with a utopian, messianic visionary perspective that allowed the disenfranchised or marginalized to "seize the inner truth of their historical moment," to paraphrase reviewer Michael Andre Bernstein ("Walter Benjamin's Long, Limited View: One-Way Street," *The New Republic*, December 8, 1997, p. 39).

their national past along the St. Lawrence River in upper New York State.[34] Their foundational cosmology is established through the "Earth Grasper" epic, a genesis drama demonstrating many of the elements that Birgitta Rooth isolated for her comparative work on Indian creation stories: this earth is created on a turtle's back, a pregnant woman falls through a hole in the sky from a prototypical above-world, and a pair of twins prepare the earth for the first Iroquois to practice the system of gender division and social practice that reflect the practices of their "elder brothers" in the sky-world.

The second Iroquois narrative of epic proportions is more political. It narrates the efforts of a "more historical" pair of legendary culture heros, Deganawidah and Hiawatha, to establish the Iroquois League, a confederacy of initially five and later six tribes. Replete with the intricacies of establishing decision-making protocols based upon the rules of their matrilineal kinship system, this story charters a more strategic, rule-bound way of negotiating in a human world. It also underwrites the Iroquois' seventeenth- and eighteenth-century profile as an American Indian imperium with which Europe had to reckon.

Like the Wintu of California in the mid-nineteenth century, however, about seventy years earlier the Iroquois underwent brutalization at white hands. In revenge for their alliances with the British, in 1790 American troops imposed a scorched earth policy on their farms and forests. In its aftermath the New York Iroquois were a beaten, impoverished, and depressed people. But in their case, a single change agent appeared: a former drunk named Handsome Lake began preaching his "good word" from community to community. As scholars differentiate between revitalization movements, his was less apocalyptic – like those of Norelputus and his kind – than redemptive. Its teachings and rituals, a blend of Quaker tenets and selected Iroquois traditions, were prefaced by a new

---

[34] For comprehensive treatments of these sequential narratives, see "This Island, the World on the Turtle's Back" (Chapter 2), "Early Versions of the League Legend" (Chapter 3), and "The Good Message of Handsome Lake" (Chapter 7) in William N. Fenton, *The Great Law and the Longhouse* (Norman: University of Oklahoma Press, 1998). A nativistic take on the second "myth" is Anthony F. C. Wallace's "The Dekanawideh Myth Analyzed as the Record of a Revitalization Movement," *Ethnohistory* 5(2) (Spring 1958), pp. 118–130, while his classic, *The Death and Rebirth of the Seneca* (New York: Alfred A. Knopf, 1970) documents the development of the Handsome Lake or "Longhouse" Religion.

chartering narrative. This was his personal conversion testimony, which is still preached, along with his code of conduct, whenever Handsome Lake's followers convene for congregations of what is still known as the Longhouse Religion.

The lucidity and magnitude of this long Iroquois marriage between myth and history are unusual; its fruit is a formidable ideology. None of the Iroquois "grand narratives" entirely eclipsed their predecessor. As these sequential charters for cosmic, social, political, and ethnic identity built upon each other, the Iroquois cumulative theory of history only reinforced itself.

Even today, many of the narrative conventions discussed earlier are imposed by Indian people on breaking events so as to shift their accounts into the mythical and hence unassailably superhuman and predestined domain. As already noted, it is not uncommon for Pueblo or Plains Indians to reconstruct things happening in fours, in the way that a Crow Indian friend of mine who fought in World War II struck his requisite quartet of "coups" against the Germans near the Maginot Line. Other tendencies toward "mythological structuring" were noticed by the Dauenhauers during their study of Tlingit Indian life histories from southern Alaska, alterations in oral folklore that ranged from simple exaggerations that stretched community yarns into proto-epics to ways that Alaskan native fishing brotherhoods evolved from Native versions of labor unions into "a kind of secular religion, with its scripture and saints, and cultural traditions."[35]

Their public reputation of ultimate conservatism where existential questions are concerned, together with their mysteriously autonomous ability to elaborate their basic structures when adding or reshuffling elements, make myths very durable. And their universal storylines that express supremely human yearnings through the actions of prototypical characters certainly don't hurt. When I was hunting around for those Native stories about Yellowstone Park, I located two Vietnam veterans, one a Kiowa and another a Crow, whose family ties to certified storytellers gave me access to hefty myths about the primordial monsters and

---

[35] *Haa Kusteeyi, Our Culture: Tlingit Life Stories*, edited by Nora Marks Dauenhauer and Richard Dauenhauer (Seattle: University of Washington Press, 1994), p. xx.

culture heroes whose battles and death throes gave birth to the thermal wonders of Mud Volcano and Geyser Basin. Neither of their stories may be typically historical, but as Sam Gill writes about the false distinction between myth and chronicle, "history is behind and within" both of them.[36]

At the same time, the consequences of potential disenchantment or worse, pervasive indifference, should not be underestimated. Cosmogenic myths can never wholly be transformed into historical manifestos, nor can their truth claims metamorphose into matters of personal opinion. Tragic as it may seem, many if not most of the language structures that originally carried the myths mentioned in this chapter from one generation to another have become functionally extinct. In this process of language loss, an unknown number of aesthetic devices and nuances of a culture's propelling narratives can become lost for good. Finally, irreversible upheavals in a society's economic or ecological underpinnings can render traditional myths largely irrelevant as charters for a people's most characteristic or necessary institutions. Many Indians, too, want their histories on the Discovery Channel and not around fires in the darkening night. Romantic yearnings to the contrary, some old cultural lifeways, together with their unique senses of the past, can drift away in the smoke.

This chapter opened with discussions of the deep time durations that mythic thought takes for granted as its temporal habitat. It then tried to explore some of the internal ways that myth can shape-shift so as to extend its claim over historical eventualities. Lastly, it showed how myth rallies during cataclysmic shocks to the cultural system. But outsiders' tidy distinctions of genre notwithstanding, the great figures and creative forces of myth may also inhabit the world of the classic folktale, and adjust their behavior in the light of historical contingency in that entertaining sphere as well, as we shall see in the next chapter.

[36] Sam D. Gill, " 'And he took away their wings': Story and History in American Folk Traditions," lecture presented at the University of Kansas, March 19, 1984, p. 11.

FOUR

Commentaries and Subversions

Memorates, Jokes, Tales, and History

There was a white man who was such a sharp trader that nobody ever got the better of him. Or so people said, until one day a man told this *wasichu*: "There's somebody who can outcheat you anytime, anywhere."

"That's not possible," said the *wasichu*. "I've had a trading post for many years, and I've cheated all the Indians around here."

"Even so, Coyote can beat you in any deal."

"Let's see whether he can. Where is Coyote?"

"Over there, that tricky-looking guy. . . ."[1]

Brule Sioux

In the early 1970s, I was working as an adult education consultant and living on Indian Island in southern Maine. It was the last of 146 tribally owned islands strung up the Penobscot River that was still occupied by Algonquian-speaking people of the same name – Penobscots. Near my single-lane street was the cabin site of Joseph Polis, who was Henry David Thoreau's guide in 1857. And even older Native presences still hung around the island's woods, attics, and darker crannies, as I discovered one day after a neighbor knocked on my door.

My memory has him as the only other white man living on the island, an educator married to a Penobscot woman from the place. He'd been excavating out his root cellar when his spade bit into a clump of iron oxide. Wedged into the red-colored clay were dozens of the smooth

[1] Quoted from "Coyote and Wasichu," in *American Indian Myths and Legends*, edited by Richard Erdoes and Alfonso Ortiz (New York: Pantheon Books, 1984), p. 342.

stone axe heads that archaeologists call "celts." Dashing back to the house behind him, I knelt to inspect the treasure in a cardboard box. Damp chunks of brick-red dirt clung to their lovingly worked curves, which converged at sharp, straight edges. Come back tomorrow, he said; I could buy some. To archaeologists these caches of axe heads are clear evidence of what they call the Maritime Archaic period, when Indians were harpooning seals and porpoise from ocean-going dugouts and driving caribou onto thin ice for easier spearing eight to twelve thousand years ago.

At the time, the Penobscot Indians were embroiled in the biggest land claim case in Eastern Indian history. A dedicated lawyer named Tom Tureen was reactivating some clauses of the Indian Trade and Intercourse Act of 1790 to argue that the tribe still owned two-thirds of the state of Maine. There was agitation against church as well as state: quietly circulating throughout the island's homes was a delegation from Iroquois country, the White Roots of Peace, bearing nativistic messages of religious revitalization and exciting the island's traditionally Catholic elders. Ignored for decades, the residents of Indian Island were shaking off a long slumber.

When I knocked on my neighbor's house the following morning, I got no response. Finally, his door cracked open. "Forget about it," he muttered. Why? Had I done something wrong? He just couldn't sell them, he said, avoiding my eyes. When I didn't budge he looked trapped, then whispered, "My wife had a dream last night. This big Indian was standing at the end of our bed. He told her he wanted his tools back. I reburied them."

Had I not seen those mud-caked celts with my own eyes, I would have had good reason to consider his words an abbreviated example of the verbal genre known to folklorists as *memorate* – narratives of personal encounters with the supernatural that become part of family or even community folklore. Had I only heard the story, I might also have read it as a disguised commentary on Penobscot–white relations spruced up with timely references. The island's own typescript journal, *Maine Indian Newsletter*, often republished old Indian barbs, recorded by scholarly visitors like Fr. Eugene Vetromile and Frank Speck for over a hundred years, in which Indian Island residents proved they were smarter or turned the tables on abusive or arrogant whites. Viewed as a historical metaphor, my "story" also keyed into the island's current rejuvenation of its deep aboriginal past. And it seemed a fitting allegory, as well, for the theme of repatriation that was so vital to Penobscot solidarity behind their present land claims case.

That the celts' discoverer was a white man willing to sell, and the dream against doing so coming to his Indian wife with more to lose than gain, only added a telling wrinkle about relationship priorities from an Indian perspective: in a crunch, tribe, kinship, and culture over husband. As a *memorate*, my story also bore a subtheme that crops up across Native American folklore: Indian foreknowledge of some form of "buried treasure," often the gold coveted by whites, which the Natives either disregard or lose, only to suffer from the white man's greedy hunger for it later on (which they, in turn, often enslave Indians to mine, only salting the historical wound).

But the irony in this anecdote lay in the fact that it was ordinary rocks and not precious metals whose refinement *by Indians* had transformed them into alluring goods that could command high prices in today's Indian artifact black market. Perhaps that proprietary transformation, turning "raw" into "cooked," as a French structuralist might put it, is what made the story's denouement the opposite of most buried treasure *memorates*. For here the Indians won. Their "acculturated" raw materials were returned to their hands to be reburied in their lands, safeguarded like an auspicious forecast for the pending restoration of Penobscot territories.

Two caveats. Since I haven't returned to Indian Island since then, I have no way of knowing if this episode made it into the evolving body of Penobscot folklore, whether of the printed or house-to-house gossip variety. Also, my memory may have played tricks on me. For I can't swear to the mixed-ethnic couple angle. Perhaps it was just my Indian neighbor who found the stuff. But then, I tell myself, those are precisely the kinds of culturally enabled tricks of memory that for people from any society often turn good anecdotes into meaningful and memorable stories. Why should I be exempt?

Apart from the *durées* of time that are so *longue* that they are untouchable by any narrative category but myth, and those that are a little more reachable through legends and oral traditions, there are in-between genres like these *memorates*, in-jokes, and remodeled folktales, which allow people to ponder and editorialize about the histories they have suffered through. In my introduction to an anthology on Indian–white relations, I called these kinds of reflections and evaluations, for want of a better phrase, "attitudinal history," but "historical commentary" or "projective dramatization" will also do.[2] While some Indian traditions could be quite didactic when it came to instructing pubescent girls and boys in proper adult behavior, the historical "lessons" and "oral editorials" to which I am referring usually got slipped into other genres less obtrusively, in encoded or offhand ways, as if to make sure that only intended listeners got the point and the reassuring pleasure of the jibe or joke, or to identify the true target of the ploy of insincere self-depreciation. But, "we jus' pour dumb Ind' ins," the older generation would say, self-protective, highly suspicious and deeply amused behind their unreadable faces.

I enter this bastion of Indian psychological privacy with some trepidation, for as one Indian says in a famous reservation joke about a white man admiring his wolfing down a meal, "First you stole my land, now you want my appetite." God forbid I might weaken with disclosure any of those imaginative defenses of the politically powerless: parable, humor, satire, allegory, irony, mockery, and parody.

The American Indian genre known as the "folktale" is customarily the vehicle for fanciful or ribald yarns featuring randy animal tricksters who get their comeuppance and yet straggle on to entertain us for another day. It seems an unlikely conveyor for contemplations of historical experience. But let us combine two observations. First, of all folk genres, the

---

[2] Folklorists have been more comfortable with the historical contributions of such material: William A. Wilson extols his discipline for giving "a view of 'cultural fact' (values and attitudes) and of the peoples' own beliefs about what happened in the past" ("Folklore and History: Facts Amid the Legends," in *Readings in American Folklore*, edited by Jan Harold Brunvand [New York: W. W. Norton & Company, 1979], p. 449), and of Tigua Indian chronicles Thomas A. Green cautions, "Whether these oral traditions are truth or fictions or some combination of the two, there can be no doubt as to the fact that they express the feelings of these people about themselves and, thus, if not a history of the deed these traditions may at least be seen as a history of the Tigua self-concept" ("Folk History and Cultural Reorganization: A Tigua Example," *Journal of American Folklore* 89 (353) [July–September 1976], p. 312).

tale, or *marchen*, allows for the imagination's readiest responsiveness to shifting socioeconomic conditions. Second, ninety percent of the published stories in American Indian folklore were elicited during decades (1880–1940) of dizzying change, the terrors of population loss, the anxieties of land loss, political powerlessness, cultural disparagement, and religious suppression, all dumped on a bed of abject poverty. Now the suggestion that Indian reflections, value judgments, and pent-up fury about conditions of everyday life might be folded into this body of oral literature does not seem farfetched.

Often couched in seemingly apolitical, amusing forms, and featuring culture heroes, evil monsters, and other familiar characters whose fantastic antics seem outside historical time, the "hidden transcripts" encoded within these stories, as political anthropologist James C. Scott might characterize them, could remain subversive, retain their pragmatic, real-life references, and yet be discounted as harmless jokes by the unwary outsider watching as Indians chuckled among themselves. But Native listeners might take them on many levels, relishing the improvisations on traditional plots, absorbing their parablelike lessons regarding ethically and *ethnically* appropriate behavior and cross-cultural comparison, and experiencing a modicum of relief by this affirmation of their personal takes on sociopolitical reality.

For Scott these hidden transcripts constitute a dominated population's repertoire of resistance to their historical predicament. They are expressed in "anonymous" actions such as poaching, shunning, and other forms of passive resistance, as well as through the secretly insubordinate speech acts discussed here. Late in his book, Scott takes an indirect swipe at the blind eyes of folklorists when, in discussing "the arts of political disguise," he recognizes that "It doesn't take a great deal of subtle analysis to notice that the structural position of the trickster hero and the stratagems he deploys bear a marked resemblance to the existential dilemma of subordinate groups."[3]

Legions of non-Indian readers, creative writers, and scholars may adore the American Indian Trickster in all his lecherous glory and

---

[3] James C. Scott, *Domination and the Arts of Resistance: Hidden Transcripts* (New Haven: Yale University Press, 1990), pp. 162–163.

hilarious just deserts, and boundary-violating poets and anarchists may even claim him as their own. But they have demonstrated how little they appreciate the Trickster who doesn't return their affections when, in their numerous anthologies and catalogs of his multiple personalities, white writers have mostly ignored his keen awareness of the political and historical facts of life.[4] They may chortle over Coyote as glutton, thief, clown, and mischief maker and think they know him. But that is because they have not put themselves into those episodes in which he rises to the occasion as their direct antagonist – as the Indian's saboteur, samurai, Zapata, or, better yet, Scarlet Pimpernel, scheming and grinning not to get fed or laid this time, but to ridicule, subvert, and even overthrow everything they represent.[5]

True, these sightings take some close listening and careful reading. As if safeguarding his skills at besting us through his smarts and duplicity, Trickster doesn't readily expose his subversive side, almost hiding it behind his more entertaining persona as transparent egoist and eternal bumbler. For the most part, folklorists who collected his stories unwittingly aided and abetted his evasiveness by burying these insurrectionary episodes here and there and failing to apply the "unsubtle" analyses that might identify them as such. But whether he is known as Coyote, Old Man, Raven, Turtle, Sendeh (Kiowa), Gluskabe (Abenaki), Blue Jay, Rabbit, Manabozho (Algonquian), Iktomi (Sioux), or a host of other incarnations, in all Native American homelands one eventually runs into this subset of the Trickster tale. It casts him less as buffoon or transgressor than as culture hero or insurrectionary protector, a guerrilla fighter

---

[4] An exception – among others I will surely be hearing about – is Galen Buller, who discusses "Coyote and the White Man: The Newest Function" in his "Comanche and Coyote, the Culture Maker," in *Smoothing the Ground: Essays on Native American Oral Literature*, edited by Brian Swann (Berkeley: University of California Press, 1983), pp. 255–257.

[5] As Indian historian R. David Edmunds has written, "Indian humor often has followed such a pattern, and psychologists argue that humor of this type may have a dual role. It may indicate feelings of superiority, or it can serve as a defense mechanism against oppression. If humor is used against oppression, it is often a powerful weapon, and may, in itself, become an agent for social change" ("Indian Humor: Can the Red Man Laugh?" in *Red Men and Hat Wearers: Viewpoints in Indian History* [Fort Collins: Colorado State University Press, 1976], p. 145).

of the spirit and the imagination, helping his tribal children to survive the legacies of invasion and occupation.

My Penobscot Indian neighbors on Indian Island and their regional northeastern Algonquian Indian brethren certainly had their quota of such covertly loaded tales. According to religious historian Kenneth Morrison, "a seemingly 'lost' dimension of colonial history emerges from the evolution of stories as they gradually accommodated selective elements of Christian cosmology."[6] His examples come from folk literatures of the Penobscot, Passamaquoddy, Maliseet, and Micmac peoples of northern New England and eastern Canada. Foremost among their traditional characters were Gluskabe, a Trickster hero, and cannibal giants known as "Windigo," frightening entities of devilish, humanoid, and beastlike appearance, who were actually possessed human beings. In one Windigo tale the man who becomes a cannibal giant is "healed" not by his own people but by a Catholic priest. To explain the transformation, Morrison draws a structural comparison between the Indians' admiration for French Jesuits and the traditional function of the benevolent Gluskabe – whom some Algonquians came to consider Jesus Christ's first created being. Morrison's deep reading of the interplay of Christian and Algonquian religious symbols explicates the "subtle gives and takes of a mutual spiritual acculturation" that, he argues, has been "largely underexplored because of a long-standing devaluation of folkloric sources."[7]

Because its emissaries were Europe's earliest and most intrusive representatives, Christianity receives particularly harsh treatment in Trickster stories, and usually more directly than Morrison's examples suggest. One darkly amusing plotline, turning up from California to Canada, has the Trickster exploiting the Catholic rites of baptism and communion to the satisfaction of his own bottomless stomach. In a Kumeway example from southern California, Coyote promises a hen that if she loans him her chicks, he will embrace them in the Christian fold. But instead of

---

6 Kenneth M. Morrison, "Towards a History of Intimate Encounters: Algonkian Folklore, Jesuit Missionaries, and Kiwakwe, the Cannibal Giant," *American Indian Culture and Research Journal* 3(4) (1979), p. 53.

7 Morrison, "Towards a History of Intimate Encounters," p. 63.

baptizing them, one by one he pops them into his mouth, and tops off the sacrament by crunching down mother hen and father rooster to boot.[8]

When the Trickster cannot nip Christianity in the bud before baptism, he has another shot after the gullible have undergone their Catholic confirmation rituals. In a story recorded by Leonard Bloomfield from a Sweet Grass Cree storyteller from Saskatchewan, Canada, their Trickster Wisahketchahk combines jibes at French economic, medical, and religious institutions. First, he wheedles goods out of a trading post on credit. When he can't pay, he gets the French trader to advance him "some medicine, poison." Injecting it into balls of fat, he arranges foxes and wolves in a circle around him "exactly as if he were a missionary." Promising long life if they eat his offerings, and "having taught the wolves religion, he killed them all," and simultaneously gets the furs to pay off his debt.[9] (Another subarctic variant has the balls of fat containing bent splinters of bone, a common trapping lure. Once the wolf "missionary" feeds his obedient fox "communicants" these stand-ins for communion wafers, the fat dissolves, the bone slivers spring open to pierce their stomach walls, and they die painfully.)

What seems to be occurring in these stories, of course, is a transformation of the references to Trickster's customary behavior. In the orbit of normative tribal practice, he represents an example of precisely how *not* to behave or an opportunity, argue psychological interpreters, for people to experience vicariously the transgressions that their society prohibits. Here, however, his performance does not dramatize infractions of regular rules of social (and sexual) intercourse. Instead, he enacts a new set of unwelcome cultural actions and values that have been introduced by alien historical actors. "It is definitely not [in the Indian's] best interest to antagonize these [Euro-American] individuals and agencies," writes Gary H. Gossen in his analysis of a Potawatomi cycle of Trickster stories, "but at the same time, these very persons and institutions may have consistently exploited, cheated and deprived him of

---

[8] Alejandrina Murillo Melendres, "Coyote Baptizes the Chickens," in *Coyote Stories*, edited by William Bright and translated by Maria Aldama and Leanne Hinton, *International Journal of American Linguistics*, Native American Text Series, Monograph 1 (Chicago: University of Chicago Press, 1978), pp. 117–120.

[9] Leonard Bloomfield, *Sacred Stories of the Sweet Grass Cree*, National Museum of Canada, Bulletin 60 (Ottawa: F. A. Acland, King's Printer, 1930), pp. 29–32.

the social and economic means to better his minority situation. Injustice will seek expression and resolution – even if the only available vent is a traditional animal fantasy."[10] In the case of these religious spoofs, Trickster's misbehavior displays not his own infamous improprieties but those of the antisocial forces for which he is a stand-in. By allowing himself to "play the part" of Europeans, so to speak, he dramatizes the dire consequences of their way of life to any Indian participants in their institutions. Like the Savior he often personifies in order to make fun of, in a sense he sacrifices his customary ethnic standing for them (not that he has much of a reputation to start with).

Both religious and economic commentary also underlay a body of Coast Salish tales from the Pacific Northwest, according to folklorist Madronna Holden. These "most traditional" forms were flexible enough to enable Indians to share their negative reflections of Euro-American society and also depicted "Native mythical figures being used to respond to particular historical situations." Holden's interpretation of these Trickster and Transformer tales revealed hidden messages that lampooned overbearing missionaries and bossy employers. Here it was the traditional Transformer protagonist who was equated with Jesus Christ, the one who arrogantly set about to "make people straight."

When he found Indians walking on their hands, he set them right side up and proudly announced from village to village, "I am the one who is straightening everybody out." His busybody behavior becomes cumulatively funnier, and the irony thickens like smoke. Other Salish tales stated more didactically the clear superiority of Indian lifeways: "Though white people overwhelm us, it is Moon that has placed us here, and the laws we are bound to obey are those established by Moon in the ancient time."[11]

From debunkings of missionaries to excoriations of the Euro-American's obsession with material possessions, it is these indirect, loaded critiques that delight Holden. She shows how the Transformer tales dramatize an alien work ethic that produces tools so "hungry for

---

10 Gary H. Gossen, "A Version of the Potawatomi Coon-Wolf Cycle: A Traditional Projection Screen for Acculturative Stress," *Search: Selected Studies by Undergraduate Honors Students at the University of Kansas* 4 (Spring 1964), p. 14.
11 Madronna Holden, "Making All the Crooked Ways Straight: The Satirical Portrait of Whites in Coast Salish Folklore," *Journal of American Folklore* 89 (1926), p. 276.

work" that they must constantly be fed "wood chips and meat," and these tales call attention to a kind of mass production that dehumanizes people by turning them into cogs in a capitalist machine. After a new boss, Raven, extends a fish trap across a river using linked-together human beings instead of lashed poles, Moon, the protector of Indians (and humanity in general), frees the exhausted, drenched Indians and warns Raven, "Never do this again.... These people here are human beings."

While anthropologist Robert Lowie's eyebrow would have arched at William Bascom's suggestion that myths were regarded as factual, and although he always remained scornful of any contribution legends might offer to reconstructing chronology, he would have applauded Bascom's denial of any truth value to the narratives reviewed by Morrison and Holden or those directly elicited by Bloomfield and Hall. Yet a closer look at examples that Lowie highlighted from his own fieldwork, in order to substantiate his strident opposition to the historical value of Indian lore, suggests that he had little interest in or eye for Indian historicity.

In these stories the Trickster or other culture heroes confront the agents of colonialism more pointedly and defiantly. Dismayed that the Lemhi Shoshones of Idaho, whom he visited in 1906, failed to recollect an important event in white history such as Lewis and Clark's visit in 1805, Lowie complained that he could only turn up two versions of "a purely mythical story" involving a contest between an Iron Man, "father of the white people," whose home was on the water, and Wolf, "father of the Indians," who lived underground. They competed over who was faster at making guns. To begin, Wolf used the pungent fumes from Indian tobacco to stupefy his opponent, after which came the actual gun-making race, of course won by Wolf. Other versions climax with Wolf showing Iron Man that he can take away the sun and plunge the world into darkness as well, or the smoke causes Iron Man to choke to death on his own vomit.[12]

When Shoshones related these stories to Lowie, we should not forget, it was just after the turn of the twentieth century. Labeled "vicious and immoral" by government officials, Shoshone religious and social practices were banned, every year armed police rounded up their young for

[12] Robert Lowie, *The Northern Shoshone, Anthropological Papers of the American Museum of Natural History*, 2 (pt. 2) (New York: The Trustees, 1909).

the Fort Hall boarding school, the buffalo were long gone, and their population strength and collective sense of confidence had hit rock bottom. What conceivable interest had they in contributing to the archives of Lowie's disinterested fact-finding? In their creative imaginations, at least, their contender, Wolf, could use their traditional source of power, sacred smoke, to best the Euro-American at his own game, which was making metal things that killed.

This gladiatorial side of Coyote's personality seems as far from his disreputable role as does his not infrequent promotion to the status of cocreator of the universe. (But the scholarly emphasis on Coyote as asocial scoundrel and transgressor often minimizes these roles; indeed, sorting out Coyote's mutually contradictory range of personalities often exposes outsiders' deepest fantasies of escape from convention or institutionalization – simply proving, once again, his persistent power to outfox our psyches.) One attempt to get a firmer grip on Nez Perce Coyote stories, however, by anthropologists Deward E. Walker, Jr., and Daniel N. Matthews may also give us a more culturally congruent handle on the oral editorials I am stressing here.

For Walker and Matthews draw a distinction between Coyote's presence of mind in "formulaic and nonformulaic monster myths," respectively. In the latter category, he is ignorant of the monsters' threat; rather, it is the venal side of his nature that draws him into encounters with them, which initially end with his own death. But then he is resuscitated and advised how to annihilate his foes. In the former category, however, which Walker and Matthews find "more heroic" because Coyote is not killed and the selfish motivation of his personal revenge seems absent, he enters the fray fully aware of the monsters' peril to the people, "either as killers or as threats to their resources," and he "explicitly acts to benefit everyone...."[13] When we read of how whites and their ways are likened in other Indian stories to "rattlesnakes"[14] and

[13] Deward E. Walker, Jr., with Daniel N. Matthews, *Blood of the Monster: The Nez Perce Coyote Cycle* (Worland, Wyo.: High Plains Publishing Company, 1994), p. 188.

[14] "White Men Are Snakes," in *Coyote Was Going There: Indian Literature of the Oregon Country*, compiled and edited by Jarold Ramsey (Seattle: University of Washington Press, 1977), p. 258. A Paiute version of the Old Testament story of the apple in the tree of knowledge gives Indians credit for planting the tree in the first place and condemns a white man for being the rattlesnake who bit them, stole their land, and drove them into

"monsters"[15] whose large-toothed, merciless presence posed a threat to ancestral "mythic people" and their historical descendants, we cannot deny the consistency of his behavior here. In stories of more contemporary times, the deathless Trickster, one might conclude, remains effective as his people's benefactor.

As with deadly inversions of Christian rituals, the Wolf versus Iron Man narrative collected by Lowie partakes of another story type for dramatizing these wishful projections concerning confrontations between Indian and white society. This is the "shamans' duel," whose scenario of public competitions between opposing "technicians of the sacred" probably derives from a widespread precontact cultural practice and is found in both legendary and folktale narratives. In our case, it becomes elevated to the order of a cross-cultural contest, a mano-a-mano between life philosophies, as if each society had offered its contender and then been absorbed into the general audience, watching and waiting for the decisive outcome.

On the Salinas River in central California, a local Indian named Pedro Encinales told about a time when the winter rains had failed and the river was bone dry. The priest from San Antonio Mission heard about a famed Salinan rainmaker and ordered the old man brought before him, seizing on the chance to show him up. If the rain barrels were not filled, he would hog-tie the man and flog him. After the rainmaker's incantations, the skies opened up until the priest had to beg him to stop the downpour.[16]

---

the mountains. Isabel T. Kelly, "Northern Paiute Tales," *Journal of American Folklore* 5(202) (1938), p. 437. Neighbors of the Nez Perce, the Coeur d'Alene who talked with folklorist Gladys Reichard were explicit about such symbolism in their tale "The Grizzly Is Thought of as Washington" ("An Analysis of Coeur d'Alene Indian Myths," *Memoirs of the American Folklore Society* 41, [1947], p. 32).

[15] "The First White Men" (Hare Indian) in *Northern Tales: Traditional Stories of Eskimo and Indian Peoples*, selected and edited by Howard Norman (New York: Pantheon Books, 1990), pp. 97–98.

[16] J. Alden Mason, *The Language of the Salinan Indians*, University of California Publications in American Archeology and Ethnology 14(1) (Berkeley: University of California Press, 1918). The "Eye Juggler" tale is frequently converted into such an Indian–white competition; a good one is told by John Stands in Timber (and Margot Liberty) in *Cheyenne Memories* (Lincoln: University of Nebraska Press, 1967, pp. 24–26). Conceiving of missionaries as opposing shamans is a theme found in more legendary narratives as well; see Rebecca Kugel, "Of Missionaries and Their Cattle: Ojibwa Perceptions

So effective has the "shamans' duel" theme proved for personifying oppositional world views that we even find it among those informal, half-humorous stories that members of the Native American Church still tell in the languid morning hours between the ritual's completion at dawn and the formal noon feast. In a delightful collection of these peyote texts, anthropologist Warren d'Azevedo includes a reported exchange between a peyote "Roadchief" and a preacher. Instead of a spectacle of power display, however, the story turns on the Indian's verbal response to a high-voiced, grasshopper-eyed preacher, who stares at heaven when he talks and harangues Indians about his church's "solid foundation," which promised them "harmony" and "unity."

After waiting patiently and allowing some silence, the Roadchief responds in a "quiet," "slow," "easy," tone of voice that the preacher just has to listen to. One by one, he tackles each of the terms: "foundation" worries him as perhaps too rigid – "you got to make room for things." As for "harmony," it usurps the individuality of peyote songs when someone has the chance to sing his songs by himself. "Unity" denies folks the chance to choose what religious "meetings" they prefer, and perhaps "if we get too unified maybe somebody begins to think he is Jesus and tries to tell everybody how to get unity his way. We got just enough unity now. All we got to do is treat each other right."[17]

Sometimes it is actually invasive social scientists like Lowie, Bloomfield, and d'Azevedo, instead of meddlesome missionaries, who represent a questionable institution from the non-Indian world with which Indians must cope by means of these cultural contests. The Hopi tell of the residency of Dr. J. Walter Fewkes on their First Mesa in the 1890s, when he was collecting narratives and artifacts. While the government's explanation for his sudden departure from Arizona in 1898 tells of a smallpox outbreak, the Hopi have a different story. One night

of a Missionary as Evil Shaman," *Ethnohistory* (41)2(Spring 1994), pp. 227–244, while Fray Angelico Chavez reports such a Pueblo contest between their supernatural being, Pohe-yemo, and the Catholic God that ends in a draw ("Pohe-yemo's Representative and the Pueblo Revolt of 1680," in *What Caused the Pueblo Revolt of 1680*, edited by David J. Weber [Boston: Bedford/St. Martin's, 1999]).

17 Warren d'Azevedo, "The Road Chief and the Preacher," in an expanded version of his *Straight with the Medicine: Narratives of the Washoe Followers of the Peyote Way* (Berkeley, Calif.: Heyday Books, 1985), to be entitled *These People Got a Chance Yet* (forthcoming).

while working in his study, Fewkes was confronted by a handsome young man who promised to "entertain" the anthropologist. But when Fewkes shooed him away, the visitor displayed a horrid visage: he was the great Hopi creator and destroyer deity, Masauwu. Fewkes was terrified into vowing that he would "become a Hopi and believe in Masauwu" (presumably dropping his studies of Hopi ritual in the process). Shortly thereafter, say the Hopi, Fewkes departed and never returned to Hopi country again.[18]

Another anthropologist received a warmer welcome from the spirits in a tale passed on by the Mohegan Indians of Connecticut. The genre this time was a *memorate* concerning scholar Frank Speck, who conducted fieldwork intermittently with the tribe from around 1900 to 1925. Late one night Speck left some Indian friends on Mohegan Hill to walk to his lodging, despite their warning that since it was full moon, the ghostly spirit known as the "old Indian Stone Cutter," (who resembles the ancient spirit on Indian Island who wanted his tools back, as described at the beginning of this chapter), would be roaming about. Strolling past the old stone quarry, Speck could not ignore the increasingly loud "chink, chink, chink" sounds and sped back to the security of his friends' house. There he found his sheets turned down and a note welcoming him. Unlike Fewkes, Speck stayed on to work with the local Indians, but he also promised to follow their advice about when and where to move about, and they remembered that he "never made light of their superstitions."[19]

Sometimes these metahistorical commentaries focus on the almost animistic physical products of Euro-American technology. Just as Robert Lowie dismissed the Lemhi Shoshone contest between Wolf and Iron Man as a historically worthless account, he disdained the Assiniboine narratives of Indian–white encounters that he received shortly thereafter from the Assiniboine on the same trip. The Indians told him how their mythic culture hero, Iktumni, sailed on a boat made from five moose

---

[18] Edmund Nequatewa, *Truth of a Hopi*, Bulletin of the Museum of Northern Arizona, N. 8 (Flagstaff: Museum of Northern Arizona, 1936).

[19] William S. Simmons, "Frank Speck and 'The Old Mohegan Indian Stone Cutter,'" *Ethnohistory* 32(2) (1985), p. 158.

hides down the Saskatchewan River to trade with Europeans on an island. From them he received horses and cloth garments. In the Indian account, the entire story was rendered as a meaningful action that was initiated by the Indians and controlled by them from start to finish. As the Indians assimilate the first foreign wares, they are careful to keep the white men on the island, as if in quarantine. This seems like a wishful projection into the past of their present knowledge about the fuller consequences of accepting those commodities. This must have been a comforting narrative for a presently powerless people and constitutes a vital record of Assiniboine historical thought.[20]

A subtler form of cross-cultural admonition is found in European tale types reworked by generations of Indian tale-tellers. A Potawatomi example collected by folklorist Alan Dundes has an Indian boy named P'teejah ("petit Jean") exploiting the Old World motif of the "magic tablecloth" for a novel spin on the power of material culture. Meeting a starving European soldier, the boy's tablecloth miraculously produces food for him. Then the soldier exhibits his magic hat, which creates more soldiers on command, and he offers to trade it for the tablecloth. At first the boy resists but then he capitulates, calls forth the soldiers, and orders them to retrieve his tablecloth. According to Dundes, who elicited this tale from a Kansas storyteller named Bill Mzechteno, the story shows the Indian wielding control over the Euro-American's artifacts for a change, offering him whiskey when the magic tablecloth unfurls and then using his own possession to defeat him in a variation on the traditional Indian shamans' duel. The tale might not be chronologically situated, but it is historically incisive where power relations are concerned, and its aim is practically to reverse history, which, we may recall, is also what Mircea Eliade claimed to be the express design of mythic consciousness.[21]

---

[20] Robert H. Lowie, *The Assiniboine*, Anthropological Papers of the American Museum of Natural History 4 (New York: The Trustees, 1910).

[21] Alan Dundes, "The Study of Folklore in Literature and Culture: Identification and Interpretation," *Journal of American Folklore* 78 (1965), pp. 136–142; for more on this Indianized European Trickster hero, see "Ti-Jean and the Seven-Headed Dragon: Instances of Native American Assimilation of European Folklore," by Jarold Ramsey in his revised and expanded *Reading the Fire: The Traditional Indian Literatures of America* (Seattle: University of Washington Press, 1999), pp. 222–236.

In narratives of this liberated nature, unburdened by any need to reference events or notable figures that punctuate formal occasions or genres for historical recollection, the historical freight, borne by familiar metaphors, motifs, and plot lines, makes no bones about its subjective function: the restoration to conceptual equivalence, if not preferability or even supremacy, of Indian world views. From the Native perspective, history is no more an objective property than is status or charisma. The playing field of these stories, to which Lowie seemed willfully oblivious, is the contest for cultural hegemony. For Indians the symbols highlighted in them are their subversive weapons of last resort, by means of which power relations fight for the high stakes of cultural prestige and self-esteem. Tobacco, horses, iron, waters, and cosmic undergrounds become counters in a game of who's on top – politically, territorially, ethically, spiritually, psychologically.[22]

Not all of these allegorical accounts of clashes between belief systems wind up with Indians victorious. Some dramatize the reverse, as folklorist Edwin S. Hall discovered when he collected the biography of Inupiat storyteller Paul Monroe in northwestern Alaska. First, the old man spoke positively about the demise of shamanism that occurred after Christianity was introduced at the end of the nineteenth century; then he told Hall about a Cape Prince of Wales boat crew that illustrated how the new practice of prayer replaced the old-fashioned powers of shamanic invocation. The crew was surrounded in their boat by so many killer whales that they could not move. First, the shaman leader tried using his magical powers to drive them away, but nothing worked. Then one crew member, recollecting "the way they taught me long ago," lay

---

[22] Perhaps I should not let my underscoring of the historical references and psychological rebalancing in these stories overshadow those narratives or anecdotes in which Indians portray themselves as hilariously inept at incorporating the white man's goods – boiling whole coffee beans and trying to eat them, consuming raw bacon, using dried peaches for shamanistic healing. If, as Catherine McClellan suggests, these stories – in the same way that selected white goods were absorbed into ritual and social spheres – actually enriched the Alaskan Natives' preexisting humorous genres, they also reveal a people so confident in their own cultural skins that they have no problem laughing at themselves or employing what I have called "insincere self-depreciation" as a technique for keeping white intrusiveness at bay ("Indian Stories about the First Whites in Northwestern America," *Ethnohistory in Southwestern Alaska and Southern Yukon*, edited by Margaret Lantis. [Lexington: University of Kentucky Press, 1970], p. 126).

down in the boat with his mittens still on and successfully prayed in Christian style for the killer whales to leave.[23]

Aside from their interest as social commentary, the Indian "memories" of distant times that are encased in folktales can yield Native theories of cultural, even evolutionary, change. What intrigued Robert Brightman about the Missinippi Cree historical lore he collected during fieldwork in northwestern Manitoba was its apparent depiction of earlier, autochthonous "races." These included the crude "ancient people," also known as "hairy-heart beings" (*mimiditihisiwak*), and another group of territorial precursors whom Brightman described as the "xenophobic dwarves" (*mimikwsiwak*). In the Cree stories featuring these mysterious beings, Brightman detected an evolutionary bias. For the "hairy ancients" were associated, in Cree eyes, with a retrograde primitivism; they were regarded as technologically inferior, stupid, and monstrous. To Brightman they indicated "a characteristically [Cree] progressivist conception of human history" that defies glib stereotypes about primitive man's cyclical, ahistorical view of the world.

On the other hand, the prophetic gifts of the dwarves filled Crees with awe, admiration, and gratitude. If the mere mention of hairy ancients constituted the negative assessment of earlier ages, the stories of dwarves, keepers of the old ways who are said to withdraw from today's noisy, overcrowded, and polluted environment, identified with invasive Euro-American society, constituted a negative critique of modernity, overpopulation, and development. To Brightman, Cree historical consciousness seemed to be juggling three separate discourses for contrasting the past with the present. The first dramatized the growing improvement of human society over its cruder antecedents; the second, which Brightman drew from ethnohistorical sources preserving Cree accounts of the introduction of trade goods, stressed the duplicity of traders and suggested that original Cree technology was equally efficient, and that Indians before the trade period were also healthier and more vigorous. The third scenario, in which the dwarves took center stage, constituted a more emphatic indictment of the ills of modern life and affirmed the superiority of traditional Cree lifeways. "Cree historical thought," writes

[23] Edwin S. Hall, Jr., *The Eskimo Storyteller: Folktales from Noatak, Alaska* (Knoxville: University of Tennessee Press, 1975), pp. 352–353.

Brightman, "explores both the virtues and the defects of the past and the present.... From one perspective the past is vanishing, while from the other it advances to encompass the present."[24]

In this respect, we find congruities within the context of American Indian narrative forms that the outsider's etic categorizations, with their formulaic definitions of content, mostly overlook. Whether they be legends or *memorates*, myths or folktales, it turns out to be the underlying agenda of maintaining tribal autonomy, thematic integrity, and cultural survival that in the final analysis determines how these forms change and the changes they record.

How do the spirits of Indian resistance, satire, and historical commentary fare today? None of your business, respond an increasing number of tribespeople. But some outsiders have penetrated these private zones of psychological self-respect and survival, and report the ingenious sorts of joking genres such as those Keith Basso collected among the Cibique Apache, in which characteristic traits of "the whiteman" are performatively derided, based upon a checklist for how *not* to behave.[25] Nor were such observations derived overnight. Until they had the opportunity to acculturate any receptive Euro-Americans into the etiquettes that *they* considered civilized, from their earliest encounters with explorers, missionaries, diplomats, traders, scholars, and neighbors, Indians had to withstand the loud, grating voices of whites, their terror of silence and down time, their intimidatingly direct stares, chronic impatience, jerky and impetuous physical movements, preoccupation with possessions, coercive demands, verbal manipulation, unchecked greed, and other Euro-American traits that they often consider bad manners.[26] Sometimes they

---

[24] Robert Brightman, "Primitivism in Missinippi Cree Historical Consciousness," *Man* 25 (1990), p. 119. Evolutionary ideas also informed Zuni Indian descriptions of human origins, according to Arthur Woodward, curator of history at the Los Angeles Museum. As part of what religion scholar Ake Hultkrantz calls the Zuni "emanation myth," their "Drying of the World" narrative relates "the evolution of the Zuni from small reptile-like forms to men who walked upright and and lived as men." "Belief of Indians in Evolution," *SCIENCE* 74 (1908) (July 24, 1931), p. 12.

[25] Keith H. Basso, *Portraits of "the Whiteman": Linguistic Play and Cultural Symbols Among the Western Apache* (New York: Cambridge University Press, 1979).

[26] For some cross-cultural comparison, see George Devereux, "Mohave Etiquette," *Southwest Museum Leaflets* N. 22 (Los Angeles: Southwest Museum, 1948). For one of many

directly targeted their humor against these affronts, as Vine Deloria, Jr., and Gerald Vizenor have done with their writings, carrying on Trickster's mandate of protecting his people against external threats and fending off their internalized consequences – self-loathing, powerlessness, and corrosive despair. The late Zuni artist Phil Hughte accomplished much the same with a wry, cartooned chronicle of his people's relations with the nineteenth-century anthropologist Frank Hamilton Cushing.[27] And one might mention the legions of lesser-known Indian humorists, and dialect poets who communicate through the hundreds of local newspapers, periodicals, and e-mails by which Indians still share their experiences.

Beyond these modern examples of Indians biting back, where might one locate those original heros of the *memorates* and tales reviewed in this chapter? In their literary residences, I have only scratched the surface on this neglected topic of the political, economic, and social critiques that the venturesome reader can find embedded throughout the vast archives of American Indian folktale. As for their real and present lairs, I presume the Mohegan and Penobscot "Stone Cutters" still inhabit the landscape where Speck and I brushed against them – in the dark nights of Connecticut's New London County or the dense soil of Maine's Indian Island.

Since the Trickster is likewise considered an immortal, what do the tales say about his present whereabouts? Often his withdrawals from modern times are indirectly or directly attributed to his replacement by Euro-American society and its symbols. To the New England tribes, he (Maushop) either retired when Christianity took over, metamorphosed his inner circle into whales so that they might survive, or transformed himself and his followers into the waves, dunes, cliffs, and fogs that will preserve their presence in their land.[28] In British Columbia the Tsimshian people concluded one cycle of Raven stories (Tkamshim, their Trickster)

contemporary examples of how Coyote stories compare cultures today, see "Coyote and the White Man," told by Lawrence Aripa, Coeur d'Alene, in *Stories That Make the World: Oral Literature of the Indian Peoples of the Inland Northwest*, edited by Rodney Frey (Norman: University of Oklahoma Press, 1995), pp. 81–91.

27 Phil Hughte, *A Zuni Artist Looks at Frank Hamilton Cushing* (Zuni, N.M.: Pueblo of Zuni Arts & Crafts, A:shiwi A:wan Museum and Heritage Center, 1994).

28 William S. Simmons, "Of Large Things Remembered: Southern New England Indian Legends of Colonial Encounters," *The Art and Mystery of Historical Archeology: Essays in Honor of James Deetz* (Boca Raton, Fla.: CRC Press, 1992), pp. 324–325.

with his transformation of the Pacific Coast's last remaining monsters into rocks. Leaving behind a world safe for human occupation, he then enacted a final commentary on the unbridgeable gulf between mythic and contemporary times by turning himself into stone as well.

In a variant from the Winnebago, or Ho-Chunk, from Wisconsin, the Trickster's last fling, coming at the close of the tale cycle analyzed by Paul Radin, climaxes with a mouse tying him to a dead horse's tail; the animal (representative of white society?) awakens to drag him off. But Radin's informant tacks on an epilogue in which Trickster heads on a last ride down the Mississippi, removing waterfalls and other obstacles "that might annoy the people who will later live there." At first, this seems like he's switching to his good-guy side. But as if he cannot resist flipping us latecomers one final bird, before he disappears to become potentate of the underworld, he sinks a permanent imprint of his buttocks into the rock where the Missouri River enters the Mississippi.[29]

In another narrative, which sounds more like *memorate* than folktale, Tsimshian lore also leaves our deathless one with an escape hatch. The story came from a tribal cannery worker, who lost all his money to gambling. Retreating deep into the wild mountains, the man runs into a Big Foot sort of creature who lives in a pit and claims to be the present incarnation of Raven. Much like my macho spirit Indian from Indian Island, Trickster had transformed and gone to ground.[30]

A slightly different clue to Coyote's present refuge was recorded by linguist Anthony Mattina from the Colville storyteller Peter Seymour in Washington State. It concludes a "shamans' duel" plot that turns on a dialogue and a test of strength between Coyote and Jesus Christ. As usual, we first meet Coyote ambling about the countryside. When he runs into a little boy, the kid claims to be his "older brother" and challenges Coyote to move a mountain. That much he can do, but then he can't return it to its original location. Now the child announces that he is actually Jesus Christ, and he claims credit for Coyote's supernatural

[29] Paul Radin, *The Trickster: A Study in American Indian Mythology* (New York: Schocken Books, 1956), pp. 50–53; but I was led to this by *Raven Tales: Traditional Stories of Native Peoples*, selected and edited by Peter Goodchild (Chicago: Chicago Review Press, 1991), p. 125.

[30] Ralph Maud, editor, *The Porcupine Hunter and Other Stories: The Original Tsimshian Texts of Henry Tate* (Vancouver: Talonbooks, 1993), pp. 146–156.

ability to shift mountains from place to place and to slaughter man-eaters to ready the world for human habitation. Because Coyote "threw my words away," Jesus Christ next tosses him into prison, allowing that "on the last day you'll get back with the people on earth." As if still wary of Coyote's cunning and undying commitment to his own people, however, Christ finally exiles him to an island in the middle of the ocean. And storyteller Seymour closes with Coyote retaining his unassimilated mystery:

> And they say, these white people say that if you look with binoculars, you can see him there walking around. But if they go over there in a boat, trying to reach him, they can never reach. When they get close it disappears before their eyes.[31]

---

[31] Anthony Mattina, *The Colville Narrative of Peter J. Seymour and Peter J. Seymour's Man-Eater Stories: A Colville Trilogy* (Nespelem, Wash.: Colville Business Council, 1976), pp. 130–131.

—◀◉▶—

FIVE

Anchoring the Past in Place

Geography and History

These places are very important for us. Those who know about them. They are something that is proof of our past. But it seems that something that is proof of our past is not as sacred as things that are sacred to Europeans.[1]

Sto:lo

In the spring of 2000 I retraced in a friend's Twin Cessna the traditional territory of the Mohave Indians. From Laughlin, Nevada, we soared above the lower Colorado River down to Blythe, California. To the Mohave Indians this is an especially storied stretch of the 1,700-mile-long waterway that is often referred to as America's Nile, as I learned when I researched it for the Native American Rights Fund a dozen years ago. Just northwest of Bullhead Lake we circled above the Mohave's pivot for all beginnings, Avikwame, "Spirit Mountain" (Newberry Mountain). Near this crinkled uplift, baking under the noonday sun, lived their creator, Mastamho. His son Matilveya (sometimes described as his brother) was born and died near its forbidding summit. Through binoculars I tried to locate the eroded pinnacles said to be the remnant pillars of his cremation "cry house."

Before non-Indian farmers commenced their tunneling and damming of the Colorado in 1868, every spring this floodplain spread with acres

---

[1] Quoted in Gordon Moh, "Sto:lo Sacred Ground," in *Sacred Sites, Sacred Places*, edited by David L. Carmichael, Jane Hubert, Brian Reeves, and Audhild Schanche (London and New York: Routledge, 1994), p. 184.

of snowmelt off the high Sierras. It oozed over the desert to create a brown organic soup five to seven miles wide. Once the runoff subsided, all the Mohaves settled along its banks had to do was cast their corn, beans, and squash seeds upon the cake of fertile silt – no rituals were necessary. Instead of that messy annual contraction and expansion, today our plane banked over the river's manicured valley floor with its mechanically irrigated acres, squared like a checkerboard, colored in every hue of green, and diminishing in mathematical perspective toward the hazy southern horizon – with any wayward drops of water captured by a dozen dams.

Rare people, those old riverine Indian dwellers of this region, sequestered since the 1860s on the ever-shrinking Fort Mohave and Colorado River Tribes reservations and now hemmed in by recreation vehicle parks, retirement communities, and powerboat marinas. Tallest of all Native Americans, inveterate dreamers, Rasta-haired warriors, sinewy runners covering a hundred miles a day and long-distance middlemen on trade routes that linked the Pacific Coast to the Pueblo Southwest, the Mohave were also said to stand apart from other southern California Indians in possessing a national identity. Their in-migrating totemic clans only acquired "completeness," it has been argued, once each of them claimed its own permanent riverfront location hundreds of years ago. And when their nation marshaled its warriors to defend this landscape, they were also fighting for their history.

No matter how concrete their inventories of old place names and accounts of migrations and intertribal warfare were, when anthropologist Alfred Kroeber evaluated Mohave narratives around the turn of the twentieth century, he likened them to the sort of "pseudo-history" he found in the Book of Mormon. This verdict was sealed when Kroeber discovered that to the Mohave these stories of ancient beginnings, clan movements, and epic battles received their stamp of historical veracity through the "power dreams" (*sumach ahot*) received by individual tale-tellers.[2] First and foremost, Mohave national identity and homeland

---

[2] See A. L. Kroeber, *A Mohave Historical Epic*, Anthropological Records 11(2) (Berkeley: University of California Press, 1951), and A. L. Kroeber and C. B. Kroeber, *A Mohave War Reminiscence, 1854–1880*, University of California Publications in Anthropology Series, V(10) (republished in abridged form: Mineola, N.Y.: Dover Publications, [1973] 1994).

were dreamed and sung realities. They emerged in the era of supernatural ancestors such as Frog, Serpent, and Buzzard, whose homes and exploits were commemorated in place names. Then human ancestors claimed these places, amalgamated them into a sacred geography, and through more dreaming and singing maintained communication with Frog and Buzzard's parallel plane of existence.

In 1902 Kroeber's key Mohave consultant, Jack Jones, tried to impress upon him the critical links between myth, song, geography, and history. But more detailed information on Mohave songs would not come to light for another century. That rediscovery began in 1972, when the last of the Mohave Creation and Traveling Song singers took twelve hours to record on reel-to-reel tape his corpus of 525 ceremonial songs. Finally translated in 1998 by contemporary Mohave elders, their verses contained dozens of place names and geographic stories about the wanderings of mythical precursors up and down this once wild river.[3]

From the Mohave perspective, the dream narratives and song cycles that stamped their geographic histories as authentic held a deeper mystery. The majority of mature Mohave dreams were replications of what one might call an individual's proto-dreams; for most coveted and credible of those in the "lucky" or "power dream" category were the ones received before one's actual birth or in the years of innocent childhood shortly thereafter. "Before I was born," remembered one Mohave shaman, "I would sometimes steal out of my mother's womb while she was sleeping, but it was dark and I did not go far. Every good doctor begins to understand before he is born. When I was a little boy I took a trip to Avikwame Mountain [in a dream] and slept at its base." Later, this "doctor" climbed that same mountain many times (again, in dreams), not only hearing about the universe's creation from Mastamho's very

---

[3] Attempting to link cultural and environmental protection, geographer Philip M. Klasky has directed the Storyscape Project, which curated and translated the tapes of the deceased Mohave singer Emmett Van Fleet; see Klasky's thesis, *An Extreme and Solemn Relationship, Native American Perspectives: Ward Valley Nuclear Dump* (Master of Arts Thesis in Geography, San Francisco State University, May 1977), which contains a rough map of California locating Van Fleet's place names, and Klasky's "House of Night: The Mohave Creation Songs Return to the Keepers of the River," *News from Native California* 13(10) (Fall 1999), pp. 15–18. A comparable place name recovery effort from the Plains is *The Apsàlooke [Crow] Cultural Landscape Project*, directed by Tim McCleary and accessed on the Internet through *www.lbhc.cc.mt.us/crownames*.

own lips but *actually experiencing* the world's origins in real time during the four days and nights of the dream's telling.[4]
This was some feat. It was just as perilous to dream of scaling this mountain as to attempt it. Whites who tried were said to lose their way and die.[5] Subsequent power dreams were repeat performances of these embryonic dreams. And what a non-Indian scholar might identify as compositional "patterning" in these dream narratives was to Mohaves as factually accurate as anything reported in yesterday's newspaper.[6]

Leaving Avikwame we rode the mellow currents south, skimming the Indian reservation's western border, scanning the gravel river terraces for the large scraped-earth markings, known as "intaglios," that are said to be early Mohave commemorations of Mastamho's creations. Alongside fertilizer drying vats we made out furrowed remains of the once eighteen-acre "Topock maze" scratched from the desert surface. Past the Chemehuevi Mountains, where Mohaves evicted the tribe of the same name in the early nineteenth century, on the eastern skirt of the Big Marias Mountains, we finally made out thirty- to forty-foot images of humans and animals staring up at us, "guardians of the land who assist the Mohave in their spiritual and physical well being."[7] Perhaps a thousand years old, scarred by off-road vehicle tracks but now fenced off and semiprotected on the National Register, these largest pieces of North American landscape art looked vulnerable and irrelevant to the vacationers' metropolis expanding from the shoreline.

From Spirit Mountain to these Blythe figures, we'd coasted over a hidden Mohave world whose interminglings of dream, story, geography and history remains a blank to most of us. From Avikwame (Spirit Mountain) to AviKwahath (South Mountain) in Arizona to AviKoovoTut

---

4 From Alfred L. Kroeber, *Handbook of the Indians of California* (Washington, D.C.: U.S. Government Printing Office, 1925), p. 783. Donald Bahr also discusses how mythic events become "presentized" in "Native American Dream Songs, Myth Memory, and Improvisation," *Journal de la Société des Américanistes* 80 (1994), pp. 73–93.

5 George Devereux, *Mohave Ethnopsychiatry: The Psychic Disturbances of an Indian Tribe*, Bureau of American Ethnology, Bulletin 175 (Washington, D.C.: U.S. Government Printing Office, 1961), pp. 248–249.

6 W. J. Wallace, "The Dream in Mohave Life," *Journal of American Folklore* 60 (237) (July–September, 1947), pp. 252–258.

7 Charles A. Lamb, "A brief description of the cultural significance of Intaglios and the present status of preservation efforts," *Colorado River Indian Tribes Museum* (June 12, 1986), p. 2.

(Monument Peak) just southwest of Parker Dam, this habitat and history sank deep into the Mohave psyche. Their supernatural precursors and human forbears had created it, their songs and narratives continued to claim it; as a one hundred-year old Mohave said of Monument Peak:

> Many Ages ago the Mohave God drove a great wooden stake into the earth. He told the Mohaves this marked their land. Today that stake has turned to stone but the Mohaves are still here. This is our homeland. We never want to leave it.[8]

Studying the ethnic minorities that managed to hold together in Asia and Europe, the Cherokee scholar Robert K. Thomas saw that they usually shared four vital characteristics. Each clung to some form of a *distinct language*, even if it was more revered than functional; to a *unique religion*, even if it was only their regional or syncretized version of a world religion like Christianity or Islam; and to a *sacred history*, which told them who they had been and were and why they must endure.[9] These three expressions of identity were bundled together in mutually reinforcing, culturally specific, and often unexpected ways.

But Thomas also noted that most of their accountings for recent and ancient happenings were rooted in visible, and visitable, corners of their familiar landscape. Even when these physical places were virtually erased by conquest or progress, some reemerged as what French historian Pierre Nora has labeled *loci memoriae* ("memory places"), spots of cultural-historical significance that provided spatial centers and moral touchstones within various oral genres.[10] Thomas's own familiarity with

---

[8] Charles F. Thomas, Jr., "Ah-Ve-Koov-o-Tut, Ancient Home of the Mohave," *The Desert Magazine* 9(1), November, 1945, p. 17.

[9] Robert K. Thomas, "Language and Culture: Persistence, Change and Dissolution of Tribal Society," in *New Directions in Indian Purpose: Reflections on the American Indian Chicago Conference* (Chicago: Native American Educational Services College, 1988), pp. 70–71 (emphasis mine).

[10] Pierre Nora, "Between Memory and History: *Les Lieux de Memoire*," *Représentations* 26 (Spring 1989), p. 25. This overview sidesteps the "fundamental opposition" that Nora draws between Memory, "[which] is life, borne by living societies founded in its name. It remains in permanent evolution, open to the dialectic of remembering and forgetting, unconscious of its successive deformations," and History, "[which,] on the other hand, is the reconstruction, always problematic and incomplete, of what is no longer. Memory is a perpetually active phenomenon, a bond tying us to the eternal present; history is a representation of the past" (p. 8). If the two are imagined as

the intimate bonds between culture and landscape among the Yaqui, Pima–Papago, and Navajo communities he encountered at the University of Arizona-Tucson campus confirmed the primacy of this existential grounding. Whether in physical reality or cultural memory, language, religion, and history always "took place." In deep ties of blood and nostalgia, the face-to-face communities whom Thomas called "persistent peoples" and historian Anthony D. Hopkins termed "ethnie" were usually attached to "*a particular piece of land, a homeland, and a holy land.*"[11] Indeed, to the Yankton Sioux writer Vine Deloria, Jr., a close friend and colleague of Bob Thomas, the preeminence of topography over chronology remains a key diagnostic of Indian historicity in general:

> The contrast between Christianity and its interpretation of history – the temporal dimension – and the American Indian tribal religions – basically spatially located – is clearly illustrated when we understand the nature of sacred mountains, sacred hills, sacred rivers, and other geographical features sacred to Indian tribes. The Navajo, for example, have sacred mountains where they believe they rose from the underworld. Now there is no doubt in any Navajo's mind that these particular mountains are the exact mountains where it all took place. There is no beating around the bush on that. No one can say when the creation story of the Navajo happened, but everyone is fairly certain where the emergence took place.[12]

For Thomas's and Deloria's colleague, the late Pueblo Indian anthropologist Alfonso Ortiz, most tribes' interwoven concepts of history, identity, and destiny rested on this pride of *place*. "Historians need to develop a sensitivity," Ortiz believed, "to certain tribal traditions that

polar opposites on a continuum, most of the episodes or duration-marking modes discussed in this book would fall on many points between them. For exemplary treatment of cultural-historical-environmental ties in a specific North American region, see James S. Griffith, *Beliefs and Holy Places: A Spiritual Geography of the Pimeria Alta* (Tucson: University of Arizona Press, 1992).

11 To Hopkins, the proto-nationalistic identity and character of such groups are "directly influenced by collective perceptions, encoded in myths and symbols, of the ethnic 'meanings' of particular stretches of territory, and the ways in which such stretches (and their main features) are turned into 'homelands' inextricably tied to the fate of 'their' communities" (*The Ethnic Origins of Nations* [Oxford: Blackwell Publishers, 1986], p. 183, emphasis mine).

12 Vine Deloria, Jr., *God Is Red* (New York: Grosset and Dunlap, 1973), p. 138.

have a bearing on a people's past, present, and aspirations for the future, to wit, on their history, *which have no meaning apart from where they occur.*" As a university professor and board chairman of Chicago's D'Arcy McNickle Center for the Study of Indian History, Ortiz knew many non-Indian scholars and was well aware that these place-specific traditions made little literal sense to most of them. But "to keep the debate on that level is to miss the point," he argued; "these kinds of traditions [are not] irrelevant to the historian's task if he or she is to represent a given tribe's view of reality accurately and fully."[13]

The full-bodied role of nonbuilt environments in American Indian history is more than painted canvas backdrops for human events. Mountains, canyons, springs, rivers, and trees often enjoyed the capacity for volition and intentionality. They demanded allegiance to and remembrance of their significance as full players in tribal passages through time. Regardless of when a group historically came to occupy a locale, it commonly felt compelled to construe some "primordial tie" to the topography it thereafter called home.[14] As this umbilical link between historical geography and self-image was articulated by Taos Pueblo authorities in New Mexico in 1968 when they were fighting to recover their sacred Blue Lake watershed:

> Our tribal government is responsible to this land and to the people. We have lived upon this land from days beyond history's records, far past any living memory deep into the time of legend. The story of my people and the story of this place are one single story. No man can think of us without also thinking of this place. We are always joined together.[15]

[13] Alfonso Ortiz, "Some Concerns Central to the Writing of 'Indian' History," *The Indian Historian* (Winter 1977), p. 20 (emphasis mine).

[14] Borrowing a concept from Edward Shils, David Reed Miller sees land as fundamental among the "primordial ties" that, for Assiniboine and Stony Indian peoples, incarnate ultimate, inviolable, sacred values; see Miller, "The Assiniboines and Their Lands: The Frameworks of a Primordial Tie," *Chicago Anthropology Exchange*, Special Issue: *Native American Land* 14(1–2), 1981.

[15] Quoted in Alfonso Ortiz, "Indian/White Relations: A View from the Other Side of the 'Frontier,'" in *Indians in American History*, edited by Frederick E. Hoxie (Arlington Heights, Ill.: Harlan Davidson, 1988), p. 11; directly after this quote, Ortiz comments, "When historians can understand and deal with this view of self in relation to the land, then they will begin to understand the Indian spirit of place."

For the Navajo, Taos Pueblo's neighbors to the west, hundreds of sacred places converted their landscape, in the words of Sam Bingham and Janet Bingham, who studied Navajo subsistence ecology, into something "like a book. A wise person can look at the stones and mountains and read stories older than the first living thing ... and since the first people made homes on the land, many people and many tribes have come and gone. The land still remembers them, however, and keeps ... the things they left behind."[16] To communicate the authoritative presence of his people's penultimate sacred places, one Navajo elder conflated politics and religion much as he might have myth and history: "Sitting somewhere is he who is Washington (the President); he is the boss of all the white people, and they all look to him. In a like way we look to Sierra Blanca Peak, to Mount Taylor, to San Francisco Peak, to La Plata Mountain, to Huerfano and to Gobernador Knob."[17]

Sweeping claims about the hallowed nature of Indian environments demand localized refinement lest defining distinctions between tribal traditions get submerged beneath romantic or eco-pious clichés about Indians and nature. Take the contrast between Cheyenne and Creek notions of territoriality, which anthropologist John Moore points out.[18] The Creeks are a Muskogean-speaking tribe from the Southeast. Throughout their history their spatial traditions have emphasized a civic identity. Since the precontact era of their mound-building ancestors, their sense of sacred space is aligned to each town's "heart" – its annually renewed sacred fire.

---

[16] Sam Bingham and Janet Bingham, *Between Sacred Mountains: Navajo Stories and Lessons from the Land* (Tucson: University of Arizona Press, 1984), p. 1.

[17] Robert W. Young and William Morgan, *Navajo Historical Selections: Selected, Edited and Translated from the Navajo*, Bureau of Indian Affairs (Phoenix, Ariz.: Phoenix Indian School Print Shop, 1954), p. 17. Another Navajo analogy likens their land to the Good Book, as Douglas Preston was told by two separate men: "So when we look out here, at the land, what we see is our history. This land, it's our bible. Like you have your Bible, all black and white, written down, fresh and new. And we have our bible, old, worn, which is the land and the songs about the land." *Talking to the Ground: One Family's Journey on Horseback Across the Sacred Land of the Navajo* (New York: Simon & Schuster, 1995), p. 97.

[18] John H. Moore, "Truth and Tolerance in Native American Epistemology," in *Studying Native America: Problems and Prospects*, edited by Russell Thornton (Madison: University of Wisconsin Press, 1998).

Today's self-identified "traditional" Creeks in Oklahoma still acknowledge this covenant and their sacred history not by paying homage to outlying sacred sites but through symbolic reconstitutions of this sacred, four-log "town" fire during their late summer Green Corn Ceremonials. The fire is kindled before dawn with flint and steel. The hearth is surrounded by clan "beds," leafy arbors for housing the old Creek social units that get reconstituted during the gathering's four days of all-night dancing, feasting, oratory, prayer, and imbibing of natural "medicines." For Creek people, it is this ceremonial "square" or "stomp" ground in which is encoded the symbols of their cosmology and sociology, and where their dances give thanks for a history that produced a domesticated world.

Among the Cheyenne and other Plains peoples, on the other hand, the geographical fount of spiritual sustenance often lies on lonely promontories or mountainous overlooks, beyond the safety of the camp circle and often outside today's reservation confines. To renew their communities, Cheyenne from both Oklahoma (southern Cheyenne) and Montana (northern Cheyenne) reservations wend their way, in solitude or close-knit groups, to the northeastern rim of the western Black Hills of South Dakota. Their destination is an isolated, mounded *lacolith*, a volcanic surge that never quite reached eruption, known to the Cheyenne as *Nowah'wus*, or Bear Butte, and now protected as a state park. In the cavernous hollow of this promontory their long-ago hero, Sweet Medicine, received their Sacred Arrows medicine bundle together with instructions on how the Cheyenne should make it in the future.

As Father Peter J. Powell, scholar of the Cheyenne, remarks of this butte: "For those who climb Nowah'wus, glimpses of the Cheyenne past still lie all around." Partly because it requires a healthy walk to the fasting beds, followed by private suffering from thirst, hunger, wind, and elements on its slopes – replicating the actions of their culture hero – the comfort and power that Cheyenne draw from the spot may be intended for everyone, but they are relayed only through the self-sacrificing few who bear its blessings and stories back home.[19]

---

[19] Peter J. Powell, "Power for New Days," in *The Plains Indians of the Twentieth Century*, edited by Peter Iverson (Norman: University of Oklahoma Press, 1985), p. 249.

A crude way of distinguishing Indian sites of historical-religious significance is by their roles in either creation or migration tribal origin scenarios. In the folklore of the Eastern Shoshone, as among other northwestern Plains Indian peoples, it is the Trickster Coyote, in his garb as culture hero, who initiates historical time by establishing (or "transforming" a former world into) the known landscape. In a narrative told to Ake Hultkrantz about how the first animals were distributed, his storyteller validated the account through geographical specificity: "This is a really true story, told to me by my grandfather, and the place it tells about is in Nevada. There is a well there, and Coyote, still petrified, southwest of Reno."[20] Even when locations associated with the historical figure of a creator Trickster have been obliterated, as in south-central British Columbia's Nicola Valley, geographically precise memories of the local Interior Salish people can, for the time being, preserve them as *loci memoriae*:

> Right at the King Garden Manor there was a low-lying mountain – a little hill. I've seen it. It's called Senk'iyapaplhxw – Coyote's House. That house was pure gravel, and they used it to pave the road to Merritt, up the Nicola, to Sulus, and up towards Princeton Road – as far as they could while the gravel lasted. It was pea gravel. The hill was beautiful. . . . That was his house. The town of Merritt, or the government, or the highways, or whatever leveled it. That was where he lived.[21]

Among the southwestern Pueblos it is the lengthier, more formalized creation epic that stipulates sites associated with an origin-by-ascent

---

[20] Ake Hultkrantz, "Religion in Shoshoni Folk Literature," in *Culture in History: Essays in Honor of Paul Radin*, edited by Stanley Diamond (New York: Columbia University Press, 1960), p. 559. North of Shoshone country, the Columbia Plateau is particularly interesting for studying the formation of today's topography through the adventures of Coyote-as-World-Maker; see Jarold Ramsey's *Coyote Was Going There: Indian Literature of the Oregon Country* (Seattle: University of Washington Press, 1977), Ella E. Clark's *Indian Legends from the Northern Rockies* (Norman: University of Oklahoma Press, 1966), and Donald M. Hines's *Tales of the Nez Perce* (Fairfield, Wash.: Ye Galleon Press, 1984).

[21] *Our Tellings: Interior Salish Stories of the Nilha7kapmx People*, compiled and edited by Darwin Hanna and Mamie Henry (Vancouver: University of British Columbia Press, 1995), p. xvi.

scenario. For the Hopis of Arizona, paramount among such (often multiple) emergence locations is the travertine dome along a tributary of the Little Colorado River where the Hopis claim their distant ancestors first saw daylight after crawling through three subterranean realms of existence before emerging, still moist, upon this fourth, earthly plane. To this day, Hopis plant little feathered sticks as prayer messages to the supernatural beings here; indeed, their reverence is such that when a scholar announced his intention to publish its role in the tribe's traditional pilgrimage for salt, the book was suppressed.[22]

Other American Indian traditions, by contrast, emphasize origin by descent from a sky world, a celestial domain of prototypical existence to which one often returns after death. At the convergence of North Dakota's Turtle Creek and the Missouri River, for instance, Hidatsa Indians identify one old village location as the landing place for a magical, flaming arrow whose shaft was divided into thirteen sections. As it hurtled down to earth, the missile carried each of the tribe's founding thirteen clans. Upon landing, a culture hero named Charred Body fought monsters in the vicinity to clear it for their safe habitation.

Even after nearly two hundred years of epidemic disease, population loss, and sequential dislocations, the importance of this origin account to twentieth-century Hidatsas remained strong enough for archaeologist-ethnographer Alfred W. Bowers to take its geographical implications seriously when he studied them in the 1930s and 1940s. This is a nation, we may recall, that belonged to the same Plains Village world whose oral traditions were questioned in 1832 by the artist-explorer George Catlin, as quoted in Chapter 1. In July 1983 I arranged for Dr. Bowers, then in his eighties, to join me at this Flaming Arrow site while archaeologists from the University of North Dakota finally picked up those hints he had received from Native descendants of Catlin's hosts. As they excavated a flat table about twenty miles below the Knife River, where what Indians called Charred Body Creek (today's Turtle Creek) empties into the Missouri, we watched them tweezer out rotten chunks of buried house posts. Within a few months, these organic remains established the

---

[22] Chris Raymond, "Dispute Between Scholar, Tribe Leaders Over Book on Hopi Ritual Raises Concern About Censorship of Studies of American Indians," *The Chronicle of Higher Education* 37(70) (October 17, 1990), pp. A6, A8–A9.

spot as the oldest radiocarbon-dated Plains Indian Village culture site in the entire middle Missouri region.[23]

More compatible, perhaps, with non-Indian expectations of reputable history than creation myths, migration narratives to predestined homelands also memorialized portions of their landscape. Sometimes they scripted pilgrimages that reenacted a group's formative experiences across it. As with the Mohave, the stories functioned as "topographic mnemonics" for recalling place names and way stations linked, to choose a few examples, to early relocations of Creeks, Arikaras, Kiowas, and the Montana Crows. Among the Ojibwas of the upper Great Lakes, however, their migratory history was resurrected through a major ritual that became a virtual geography lesson. Within the tribe's *mitewiwin* ceremonials, ritual dramaturges planted numerous references to their origin-migration experiences. Especially precise were the prayers and songs that described earlier journeys around Lake Superior.

This sacred body of water was also represented by the oval floor space of the bark-walled ceremonial enclosure, around which celebrants circulated in solemn procession. According to Thomas Vennum, Jr., who studied these *mite* rites in exacting detail, "Portions of the origin tale were reenacted symbolically by the candidate in initiation rituals, and the journey to the west finds its parallel in the new member's 'path of life,' which originates in the sudatory [sweat bath] located to the east of the medicine lodge (*mitewikan*), leads into the lodge, 'passes through' it (Ojibwa terminology for initiation) and emerges from its westerly exit."[24]

Vennum's major discovery was the geographical precision of the *mite* song corpus. Ojibwas anchored their collective past to sequences of specific "resting places" on the epic journey of mythologized forebears to their present "homeland." Like giant footsteps, their verses fixed sites such as "Lake of Eddying Waters" (Lake St. Clair) and "long rapids" (Sault Ste Marie) in their memories, at once legitimizing territorial claims and indoctrinating new members into their territorial legacy. Ritual songs of the Mandan of North Dakota, heard during their major Okipa

---

[23] For this validation of oral tradition, see Stanley A. Ahler, Thomas D. Thiessen, and Michael Trimble, *The Prehistory and Early History of the Hidatsa Indians* (Grand Forks: University of North Dakota Press, 1991), pp. 27–30.

[24] Thomas Vennum, Jr., "Ojibwa Origin-Migration Songs of the *Mitewiwin*," *Journal of American Folklore* 91 (1978), p. 754.

religious festival, likewise memorialized their geographic past. Celebrating village names and locations founded and abandoned over the decades
of gradual Mandan ascendance from the Grand to the Knife rivers, they
were sung in chronological order so as to evoke the tribe's upstream
progress, just as their prophets had forseen.[25]

When Indian peoples gravitated between creation or migration scenarios, depending upon who was reciting an origin narrative or which
version suited their present advantage, their historical geography com-
plied. A suggestion of this topographic flexibility comes from the
Mississippi Choctaw who revered a genesis site in southern Winston
County known as Nanih Waiya, meaning the "slanted" or "bent" hill.[26]
Although scholars postulate that the Choctaw ethnogenesis resulted
from a seventeenth-century synthesis of two or more groups, the prevailing tribal version identifies this flat-topped Woodland Period mound as
the climax of their ancestors' journey from the northwest. They were led
by a chief named Chahta, and it was here that his sacred pole no longer
leaned forward but stuck straight up, the sign that their odyssey was
over. The place did function as a capital of sorts; in 1828 a national
council of all Choctaw convened here. With the mound as their new
burial center, some of these Choctaw successfully resisted the removals
of the 1830s, and their economic success from the mid-twentieth century
on still causes admiration.

Walk about two miles from this temple mound, however, and you
reach a *second* site that is likewise known as Nanih Waiya. Often called
simply the "cave mound" because of a perfectly round opening at the
base of a tree-covered natural hill, it leads to a subterranean cave. Bend
your ear to this manhole-sized aperture and you hear dripping water
echoing deep within. This second site fits with a second body of Choctaw
stories that described the first human beings born out of the ground,
with different southeastern ethnicities – Cherokees, Creeks, Shawnees,
and Delawares – dispersing elsewhere, but which had the Choctaw settle

[25] Alfrred C. Bowers, "Chronological Sequence of Missouri River Cultures in the
Dakotas," *Logan Museum of Anthropology*, Beloit College, Beloit, Wisconsin, 1935,
typescript, p. 2.
[26] William Brescia, Jr., "Choctaw Oral Tradition Relating to Tribal Origin," in *The
Choctaw Before Removal*, edited by Carolyn Keller Reeves (Jackson: University Press
of Mississippi, 1985), pp. 3–16.

here, as if alongside their primordial earth womb. Were earlier Choctaw enjoying a sort of backup protection offered by the two sites, citing one to support their autochthonous claim to being among the "first humans" but turning to the other when it was instrumentally advantageous to associate with a "chosen people's" migratory scenario"?[27]

Where tribal formations are multistranded, their stories record multiple geographies that are indexed to the travails and arrivals of separate clans, tribal divisions, or family lineages. This seemed a prime rationale for clarifying territoriality by Northwest Coast clan- and lineage-based peoples like the Kitwancool.[28] In lieu of tight plotting, their narratives are preoccupied with formulaic accounts of successive resettlements by aristocratic families between some aboriginal homeland and their present coastal inlet. But personal life stories could show the same pattern. When Julie Cruikshank listened to elderly Yukon women recite these clan stories, she likened them to "travelogues" in which the narrators "seemed to be using locations in physical space to talk about events in chronological time."[29] As each woman placed her clan at a specific location and then tracked a move to a new start in another spot, the precise place names and memories of incidents along the road "become mnemonic devices linking segments of [each woman's] life experience." And Cruikshank concluded that "Although chronology may be ambiguous, the named locations are not."

Ancestral narratives that were the proud property of Northwest Coast lineages revolved around their accumulating prestige over time. Their high points commemorate the acquisitions of the (ancestor) animal "crest" identities, which they can portray on honorific statuary and

[27] Both creation and migration narratives sanctify Hopi sites, but the migratory tales divide into those that commemorate journeys of the Twin War Gods and the legendary Tiyo, originator of the Snake rites, and those marking peregrinations by ancestral clans. For the Tiyo and Twin War Gods narratives see Jesse Walter Fewkes's "The Snake Ceremonials at Walpi," *Journal of American Ethnology and Archaeology* 4 (1894), pp. 1–126, and "Hopi Tales," *Journal of American Folklore* 42 (1929), pp. 1–72.
[28] Wilson Duff, editor, *Histories, Territories and Laws of the Kitwancool* (Victoria: British Columbia Museum, 1959).
[29] Julie Cruikshank, in collaboration with Angela Sidney, Kitty Smith, and Annie Ted, *Life Lived Like a Story: Life Stories of Three Yukon Native Elders* (Lincoln: University of Nebraska Press, 1990), p. 347.

ceremonial attire. Adding economic consequence were clan claims to preferred fishing beaches, river mouths, and berrying, timber, and hunting resources. On the Northwest Coast, public recitations of such narratives still function as Native America's most legalistic hybrid of history and geography, blending approximations of the non-Indian practices of posting a "land deed" and registering a "historical copyright."

Unfolding ties between Indian peoples and places continue to provide grist for emergent Indian ways of history. Evidence for earlier reconceptions of tribally claimed territories suggests that whether territory accrued to groups by social inheritance or by divine revelation, geographic imaginations could also serve expansionist ends. Among the Hopi, the synchronizing of separate clan narratives produced an episodic epic for collective origins that, when circumstances called for clarification of its territorial implications, amounted to a Hopi *locus carta*. Although the thirty or more in-migrating clans that constitute today's Hopi Indian tribe, for example, originated from every conceivable direction and showed up in their Arizona mesa lands at different times, through the process of selective adaptation that Hopi tribal member and scholar Hartman H. Lomawaima calls "Hopification," they congealed into a hierarchy of clan groups dispersed into separate villages, each retaining, however, its own migration stories and hallowed sites of arrival.[30]

Taken in the aggregate, the land delimited by and periodically renewed at these clan shrines became known under the cover term *Hopitutskwa* ("Hopi Land"), a bounded landscape whose political integrity scholar Peter Whiteley traces at last back to the mid-nineteenth century. By then this geographical affiliation was so entrenched in Hopi thought that their elders attributed these territorial boundaries to their all-powerful

---

[30] Hartman H. Lomawaima, "Hopification, a Strategy for Cultural Preservation," in *Columbia Consequences*, V. 1, *Archaeological and Historical Perspectives on the Spanish Borderlands West*, edited by David Hurst Thomas (Washington, D.C.: Smithsonian Institution Press, 1989). William K. Powers's related concept, "Lakotification," is another "ethnification" process for which the Lakota themselves actually have a term, *yulakota*, meaning "to make (things) Lakota" ("Innovating the Sacred: Creating Tradition in Lakota Religion," *European Review of Native American Studies* 9(2) (1995), p. 24.

Masau'u, the powerful "Earth God" in charge of this terrestrial plain as well as the underworld.[31]

Due to a U.S. government edict, in 1868 the new reservation of their later-arriving neighbors, the Navajo, alarmingly surrounded this Hopi world. And like the agricultural Hopi, these hunting and gathering new-comers also staked their histories of in-migration with place-specific narratives describing their piecemeal entry into the Four Corners region as separate matrilineal clans. Over time the Navajo sacralized their new residence as a traditional homeland, Navajoland, or *Dinetah* or *Dine Bikeyah* ("Land of the People").[32]

In Navajo eyes, this territory is bounded by their four sacred mountains (and embraces thousands of other sacred places, "homes" of sacred entities and locations of mythic and historical actions that remain vital to Navajo identity). Even before Navajo and Hopi territorial disputes were aggravated by the superimposition upon Native land-tenure practices of reservation boundaries decreed by the U.S. government, this *Dinetah* surrounded, overlapped, and competed with *Hopitutskwa*. But when and why the Navajo explicitly advanced this unifying territorial claim, as if positioning their amalgam of dispersed clan settlements alongside that of the Hopi, remains unclear. Their tense relationship today can be viewed as North America's closest equivalent to the more deadly stand-offs between competing mytho-historical geographies that have made headlines in the Middle East and South Asia.[33]

Shadowy suggestions of a similar impulse to consolidate defensible holy lands come from the northern plains, thanks to Alfred W. Bowers's fieldwork in the 1930s with North Dakota's Hidatsa tribe. Among their more recent rituals was an "Earthnaming" ceremony, which was held at

---

[31] Peter Whiteley, *Hopitutskwa: An Historical and Cultural Interpretation of the Hopi Traditional Land Claim,* expert witness report presented to the district court in Arizona for *Masayesva v. Zah v. James* (1989).

[32] For discussions of Dinetah and Navajo sacred places, see Laurance D. Linford, *Navajo Places: History, Legend and Landscape* (Salt Lake City: University of Utah Press, 2000), Klara Bonsack Kelley and Harris Francis, *Navajo Sacred Places* (Bloomington: Indiana University Press, 1994), and Douglas Preston, *Talking to the Ground* (New York: Simon & Schuster, 1995).

[33] For a brilliant comparative case, see Meron Benvenisti, *Sacred Landscape: The Buried History of the Holy Land Since 1948* (Berkeley: University of California Press, 2000).

various promontories in present-day North Dakota.[34] Originally these buttes were ranked by the relative authority of their respective animal spirits, who had provided supernatural aid to legendary vision questers. But when Hidatsa chiefs were required to synthesize their territorial claims prior to attending the Fort Laramie Treaty council of 1851, this hierarchy was set aside. Politically, it was more urgent for the sum total of these Earthnaming sites and their presiding spirits to represent something akin to a national "holy land," with lines connecting the four most outlying sites demarcating its perimeter.[35]

Other tribes commemorated their historical experiences by carving, painting, or otherwise sculpting them onto the land itself. Some rock art has been hypothesized to record, implicitly, precontact historical processes, such as adoption by precontact Pueblo peoples of the new Katsina Cult in the early fourteenth century.[36] More explicitly, perhaps, it can illustrate postcontact encounters, with Navajos depicting priests wearing cross-emblazoned tunics on horseback in Canyon del Muerto or Makah Indians carving a three-masted schooner on the rocks near Ozette village on the Washington State coast.

Among the Chumash of southern California, according to rock art scholars Travis Hudson and Georgia Lee, sandstone surfaces of boulders or caves served to connect the greater – and future – community with its past: "Their specific location within the community served as a 'story display' of their past and present within the total realm of the universe."[37] Working on the aspects of Zuni Indian history in present-day New Mexico that were linked to rock art symbols, archaeologist M. Jane Young termed such graphic designs "metonyms of narrative." Through

---

[34] "Earthnaming," in Alfred C. Bowers, *Hidatsa Social and Ceremonial Organization*, Bureau of American Ethnology, Bulletin 194 (Washington, D.C.: U.S. Government Printing Office, 1965), pp. 433–438, with a map of sacred buttes on p. 12.

[35] This territorializing process, and the maps of Hidatsa lands produced by Poor Wolf, Big Cloud, and Four Bears, are described in Bowers's unpublished manuscript, "Crow's Heart Autobiography," n.d. (manuscript copy provided to me by Dr. Bowers), pp. 90–92.

[36] E. Charles Adams, *The Origin and Development of the Pueblo Katsina Cult* (Tucson: University of Arizona Press, 1991).

[37] Travis Hudson and Georgia Lee, "Function and Symbolism in Chumash Rock Art," paper presented at the annual meetings of the Southwestern Anthropological Association, Santa Barbara, California, March 1981, and the Society for American Archaeology, San Diego, California, April 1981, p. 25.

these depictions, anonymous Zuni ancestors locked their myth-historic narratives to place – often blessing and empowering the very spots where these events were said to transpire.[38]

Cairns, piled-up rocks, were another way that Plains Indians marked their historical landscape for future generations. The heaps of rock in and around Pryor Gap, Montana, denote where Crows still commemorate supernatural and historical occurrences; visitors add offering rocks, coupled with prayers, for the Little People, remembering how they rescued a long-ago abandoned baby, and tribal storytellers take youngsters to cairns where famous warriors fell in battle.[39]

In other cases it is the stories alone, or resurrected place names, that release memories of a once-owned landscape, even when the visible topography has become modernized beyond recognition. That was what linguist Sally McLendon discovered when she drove an Eastern Pomo narrator around northern California. McLendon was shown specific places where the Pomo myths she was hearing had actually taken place, "despite the fact that none of the significant landmarks remained."[40]

Even though most younger Mohaves might be hard put to locate the sites and their place names where their long-ago supernatural beings readied the lower Colorado River Valley for them, hope is not lost. An increasingly appealing technique for Indian peoples to at least conceptually "reinhabit" their age-old tribal territories, together with the histories that transpired on them, is through toponymic research – collecting place names, "remapping" terrain, and, in a virtual sense at least, "reclaiming place."

This was also the goal of language scholars collaborating in recent years with the Tolowa Indians of northwestern California. As part of

---

[38] M. Jane Young, *Signs from the Ancestors: Zuni Cultural Symbolism and Perceptions of Rock Art* (Albuquerque: University of New Mexico Press, 1988).

[39] See Timothy P. McCleary's *Aluutalaho/Where There Are Many Arrows: The Cultural Landscape of the Pryor Mountains Report* (Crow Agency, Mt.: Little Bighorn College, 1999) and "Stone Memorial Cairns on Little Bighorn Battlefield," *The Research Review* 2 (1998), pp. 2–7; also Stephen L. Riggs, "Sioux Memorials," *South Dakota Historical Collections* 2 (1904), pp. 103–111.

[40] Sally McLendon, "Cultural Presuppositions and Discourse Analysis: Pattern of Presupposition and Assertion of Information in Eastern Pomo and Russian Narrative," in *Linguistics and Anthropology*, edited by Muriel Saville-Troike (Washington, D.C.: Georgetown University Press, 1977), p. 163.

the Tolowa Language Program's dictionary project, they moved beyond assembling vocabulary to summarizing traditional history, cosmology, and territory. The maps that they compiled featured forty-three of their old village sites and fifty-seven other culturally sensitive locations; interviews with elders also identified ten villages and nine prominent places that extended their remembered habitat into southern Oregon. As articulated by ethnohistorian James Collins, the project's guiding vision was that "the importance of a 'name for every riffle' is that it is part of a complex historical knowledge, a knowledge that much of the past, 'tradition,' has been disrupted, if not destroyed, and that it lives on as a possibility."[41]

Instead of the "settler vocabulary" found on Triple-A tourist maps, through the Tolowa project's "counter-cartography" of Del Norte County, one could now trace prior occupations of, and possible historical relationships between, long-ago settlements within a recovered cultural landscape.[42] For tribal members, voicing these reasserted place names released pent-up emotions and resurrected scandals of land theft and stolen cultural treasures. Not only did the Tolowa document become an argument "for the ancientness of Tolowa occupation of the region," according to Collins, "it also argues for a link between that archaicness and the present period, through genealogies that connect current Indian families to 'the ancestors' and that connect 'the ancestors' and current families to particular places."[43]

Your personal history might be similarly grounded, as Tom Ration remembers of his fellow Navajos: "Long ago it was traditional custom to return to one's birthplace now and then and roll in the earth there."[44] Or at life's end you might yearn for remembered ground, as was said of the great Crow Indian medicine man Big Ox: "Although he was traveling all over the country, he made the last request that he shall be returned to

---

[41] James Collins, *Understanding Tolowa Histories: Western Hegemonies and Native American Responses* (New York: Routledge, 1998), pp. 149–150.

[42] See "Introduction" and "Appendix: Village and Geographical Locations," in Loren Bommelyn and Berneice Humphrey, *Xuss We-Yo': Tolowa Language*, 2nd ed. (Crescent City, Calif.: Tolowa Language Committee, 1989).

[43] Collins, *Understanding the Tolowa*, p. 150.

[44] Quoted in Peggy V. Beck and Anna L. Waters, *The Sacred: Ways of Knowledge, Sources of Life* (Tsaile, Ariz.: Navajo Community College Press, 1977), p. 334.

the place that [sic] he was born.... And this is again the custom among
the Crows...in the old days when people deceased they were buried
close to where they were born."[45]

One can never predict where an investigation into a society's language,
geography, and history will lead, as linguist Keith Basso found out in
the 1970s when he innocently began collecting place names among the
Western Apache, whose homesteads are dispersed throughout the scrub
hills near Cibique, Arizona. During this chapter's overview of Indian
links between landscape and history, I have generally begun with group
perspectives, in which place becomes the consecrated setting through
mythic events, and here I wind up reflecting on their importance to
individuals. Lest one read my own cultural bias into this rhetorical move,
I turn to Basso's astonishing discovery of an American Indian connection
between history and geography that also inventively binds personality
to particular place and to an underlying moral code.

Initially, Basso was studying Western Apache linguistic codes when
he stumbled upon a type of historical narrative utterly new to him, the
agodzaahi, or "historical tale." Its time frame was usually only two or
three generations removed from today, it underscored the importance
of hundreds of specific place names, the stories were almost anecdotal
in their brevity, and they usually described someone violating Apache
norms of behavior and dramatized the social costs of doing so.

Basso's turn to "ethno-geography" took him into a decade of close-
grained fieldwork. Analyzing the role of place names, for instance, he
became aware of the way that they coerced tribal members into perceiving the past through the eyes and orientations of ancestors. These Native
names directed their listeners to "look 'forward' into space" and also
positioned them to "look 'backward' into time." Hearing such names,
Apaches imagined themselves standing directly before the physical site,
stepping into their ancestors' "tracks" and collapsing their two time
frames, and *turning* their minds around so that they identified emotionally with their struggles and travels. Like Bommelyn, Humphrey, and

---

[45] Quoted in Peter Nabokov and Larry Loendorf, *Every Morning of the World: Ethnographic Resources Study of the Bighorn Canyon National Recreation Area*, unpublished report (Denver: National Park Service, Rocky Mountain Regional Office, 1994),
p. 105.

Slagle, who used "remapping" strategies among northern California's Tolowa, Basso also worked closely with the Apache to remap their geography – almost as insurance against future threats.

Next, Basso pursued those "historical stories" that promised to reveal deeper levels to the landscape Apaches could see and name. He learned to identify this genre, in part, by its formulaic sign post: an opening line that was repeated at the end – "This happened at . . . [such and such a specifically named place]." These place names tied the Cibique Apache to spots with which anyone from the immediate area would, or should, be familiar. Sometimes the toponyms referenced the deed described in the story; more often they were abbreviated, pictorially accurate, offhandedly poetic descriptions of the location. Like a parable, however, this brand of narrative "shot," as the Apache phrased it, its moral lesson into any of its human targets who had spoken too loudly, worn their hair like a whiteman, were disloyal to tribal customs, or otherwise violated the code that makes Apaches Apaches.

These historical stories struck their listeners' consciences like barbed arrows that could not be pulled out. Instead, people were summoned to ponder their transgressions, to work on "replacing" themselves, as the Apache put it to Basso. Even when the aunt or grandmother who originally aimed the story at the listener died, the place name itself kept people reminded of its moral lesson, "stalking" them until they changed their ways. These stories of place preserved the underlying "why" of historical action rather than its particular "what." And they brought the "where" into the moral equation to create a landscape replete with ethical references for their closed circle of Apache listeners.[46]

Place remains a bone of historical contention in the fraught discourse of Indian–white relations. Accusations that Indians are "inventing their tradition" often focus on claims regarding religious-historical places. No less in the New World than in the Old, sacred landscapes "emerge as both culturally constructed and historically sensitive. . . . Far from being immune to developments in other aspects of human life, [sacred

---

[46] This material is from Keith H. Basso, "Stalking with Stories," Chapter 2 of his prize-winning *Wisdom Sits in Places: Landscape and Language among the Western Apache* (Albuquerque: University of New Mexico Press, 1996).

landscapes] can reflect a very wide cultural and political milieu."[47] But quarreling over ethnographic minutiae to support or refute claims that Point Conception on California's Santa Barbara Coast was regarded by Chumash Indians as the sacred "western gate" to the Land of the Dead,[48] or that a proposed uranium mine site south of Arizona's Grand Canyon was regarded as the "Abdomen of the Mother" by Havasupai Indians,[49] is often beside the point.

Those arguments overlook the reality that most Indian history is culturally strategized and situationally contingent and has always been interpreted by Indian peoples through references to mythic thought. They forget that the indisputable nature of whatever is prefaced by that loaded word "sacred" always makes conversation a lost cause. They also ignore the fact that even if some religious traditions are self-conscious re-creations by contemporary mixed-bloods yearning to repair and repatriate their tattered pasts, how could any self-respecting American Indian not begin with the ground beneath his feet?

When Indian claimants do lose the argument and their lands, our shared cultural folklore grants their history one last ace up its sleeve. It slips into the earth to haunt our dreams. Both white and Indian literatures remind us how memories of the Native American's recriminating shadows and uncompensated losses still inhabit America's dark forests, bottomless lakes, mountain mists, and midnight crossroads.[50] And in

[47] S. Alcock, *Graecia Capta: The Landscapes of Roman Greece* (Cambridge: Cambridge University Press, 1993), p. 172.
[48] See Brian D. Haley and Larry R. Wilcoxon, "Anthropology and the Making of Chumash Tradition," *Current Anthropology* 38(5) (December 1997), pp. 761–794.
[49] Carma Lee Smithson and Robert C. Euler, *Havasupai Legends: Religion and Mythology of the Havasupai Indians of the Grand Canyon* (Salt Lake City: University of Utah Press, 1994), p. x.
[50] "To be haunted," writes sociologist Avery Gordon in *Ghostly Matters: Haunting and the Sociological Imagination* "is to be tied to historical and social effects... [and imbues place with] rememories that you can bump into, even if they did not happen to you personally, that are waiting for you, even if you think they are finished and gone" (Minneapolis: University of Minnesota Press, 1997, p. 190, 197). It produces a situation in which, as Walter Benjamin writes in *The Origins of German Drama*, "history has merged into the setting" (London: New Left Books, 1977). Priscilla Homola unearths one of many literary examples of Indian history haunting the New World's environment and conscience in "The Indian Hill in Rolvaag's *Giants in the Earth*," *South Dakota Review* 27 (1) (Spring, 1989), pp. 55–61. On the Indian side, the New England oral traditions collected and analyzed by William S. Simmons (*Spirit of the*

more tangible ways, Indian history continues to hinder and haunt the doctrine of progress by placing human remains in its path.

The power of ancestral bones to mobilize emotions was observed by Thomas Jefferson in 1750 when he noticed some Indians in his Virginia backyard. They assembled by the same "barrow" mound that Jefferson would excavate thirty years later. He was struck by the fact that the Indians "went through the woods directly to it, without any instructions or enquiry, and having staid about it some time, with expressions which were construed to be those of sorrow, they returned to the high road, which they had left about half a dozen miles to pay this visit, and pursued their journey."[51] Over the following centuries, former village locations and their cemeteries exerted a sentimental pull on Indian groups, without the new landowners having an inkling of what was going on when Indians quietly paid their respects and were gone the next morning. As Alfred Bowers recalls being told by the Hidatsa, "It was the custom of many families to return to living sites and to point out to the younger people the depressions of lodges where certain relatives had lived, their graves, or earth rings on the prairies where various ceremonies such as the *Naxpike* or Wolf ceremonies were held."[52]

Whenever Indian bones are denied due respect and peaceful rest, modernization offers today's Indians a rare opportunity to turn their histories around. Due to strict legal penalties, stumbling upon human remains has become a particular nightmare for American developers and archaeologists. The universally charged subject of care and feeding of the dead creates tremendous potential for activating historical memory, community regeneration, and moral outcry. It also refocuses attention on the

---

New England Tribes: Indian History and Folklore, 1620–1984 [Hanover, N.H.: University Press of New England, 1986]) provide ample evidence of the ghostly persistence of Indian spirits; see also Simmons's "Of Large Things Remembered: Southern New England Indian Legends of Colonial Encounters," in *The Art and Mystery of Historical Archaeology: Essays in Honor of James Deetz*, edited by Anne Elizabeth Yentsch and Mary C. Beaudry (Boca Raton, Fla.: CRC Press, 1992), pp. 317–329, and Constance C. Crosby's "From Myth to History, or Why King Phillip's Ghost Walks Abroad," in *The Recovery of Meaning: Historical Archaeology in the Eastern United States*, edited by Mark P. Leone and Parker B. Potter (Washington, D.D.: Smithsonian Press, 1988), pp. 183–209.

[51] Thomas Jefferson, *Notes on the State of Virginia* (Chapel Hill: University of North Carolina Press, [1787] 1955), p. 100.

[52] Bowers, *Hidatsa Social and Ceremonial Organization*, p. 2.

power of place, refreshing the relevance of what Mark Nuttall, working with the Inuit of northwestern Greenland, has called "memoryscape," by which he means peoples' sensual and mental apprehension of their environment, "with particular emphasis on places as *remembered* places."[53]

Graves are among memory's key symbols, and secondary burials only intensify their importance. Although a small community of Interior Salish Indians from British Columbia was declared extinct by Canadian authorities, in the late 1980s disturbance of graves belonging to ancestors of "Arrow Lakes" survivors inspired them to revivify their memoryscape. As dispersed community members organized around the issue of reburial, involving geographic research and what one might call the "imaginative rehabitation" of their ancestral village and graveyard locations, a reemergent community began to reforge its primordial ties.

Furthermore, argues Paula Pryce, the anthropologist who chronicled the Lakes' reburial campaign, this "recreation of their moral world" could be interpreted as a current manifestation of the community's documented implication, over a century before, in the Interior Plateau Prophet or Ghost Dance movement: "I found that ideas of prophecy, the destruction of present reality, and resurrection exist side by side with discussions about the importance of protecting the graves of the ancestors." And Pryce adds, "For the Lakes' protecting the ancestors is a way of protecting their world from collapse."[54]

In this chapter we have looked at the interconnected fortunes of history and the nonbuilt environment. Next, we turn to the world of Indian material culture and review the ways that histories can circulate around and through objects – from grand earth lodges to tiny shell beads.

---

[53] Mark Nuttal, *Arctic Homeland: Kinship, Community, and Development in Northwest Greenland* (London: Belhaven Press and Scott Polar Research Institute, University of Cambridge, 1992), p. 54 (emphasis mine).
[54] Paula Pryce, *'Keeping the Lakes' Way': Reburial and the Re-creation of a Moral World among an Invisible People* (Toronto: University of Toronto Press, 1999), p. 9.

SIX

——◄◦►——

Memories in Things

Material Culture and Indian Histories

Totem poles were our history books. Unfortunately, the missionaries who came early on in the 1800s and the public officials thought that totem poles were our idols. They weren't. They all told a story, usually of achievement or the overcoming of some obstacles.[1]

Judson Brown, Tlingit

On my table are some old tools I picked up at pawnshops on a road trip through the high plains – an awl shaved from a deer bone, a hoe made from a buffalo shoulder blade, a hide scraper cut from an elk antler. Seemingly inert and mute, given the right sorts of contextualization, in situ as well as in isolation, these examples of what anthropologists lump together as "material culture" can stand up and speak. Their stories are all about history of many kinds. For want of data, one of their shared attributes has been underplayed in the chapters so far – the role of female activities and perspectives in the Indian past and historical consciousness. Each of these tools belonged to some Plains Indian woman's work kit.

Imagine an idealized Upper Missouri archaeological site, perhaps a cutbank sheared by a flash flood, with all three items visible at different strata. Jutting out of a lower layer might be such an awl, a woman's primary tool from an early plains or prairie hunting-gathering

---

[1] Nora Marks Dauenhauer and Richard Dauenhauer, editors, *Haa Kusteeyi, Our Culture* (Seattle: University of Washington Press, 1994), p. 146.

campsite.[2] Like my example – a five-inch piece of deer metapodial bone tapering to a point from its joint knob, which was left as a pushing grip – this awl may not have been created for punching holes in hides, that is, for processing materials procured by men. Conceivably it could have helped to interweave porcupine quills for decorative work or to split and ply plant fibers that women gathered, dried, and fashioned into burden baskets whose forms came out of a woman's craft tradition, even possibly being passed on as women's heirlooms and intrakin gifts. Depending on her cultural beliefs, this woman's constant companion might also turn up within or atop her gravesite, the way an old Alabama-Coushatta tribal cemetery I visited in East Texas years ago displayed women's thimbles and beads on their rain-beaten mounds of earth, shaving mugs on the mens', and, most touchingly, chipped cast-metal toys on the tiny graves. Like the bone-handled, iron-tipped awl from a Minnesota site on which archaeologist Janet D. Spector builds her case for a feminist archaeology, some of these tools might also record more personal moments, as we shall soon see.[3]

In the bank's somewhat higher lens you might extract my chipped-edge hoe blade, formed from a thin, flat, triangular buffalo scapula or shoulder blade bone, with its glossy patina resulting from considerable chopping into floodplain soil. Probably originating from a Middle Missouri hunting/agricultural village, this was also a woman's tool. Lashed with rawhide to a relatively short ash-wood handle, there is no telling how long such a blade would have held up for breaking soil and weeding the rich silt before it was discarded. With women's farming duties at least as economically vital to their cultural survival as men's hunting, it is no wonder that these particular tools sometimes became proud emblems of the female role in Plains village societies. When Hidatsa women dressed up for early photographers, they sometimes

---

[2] The Clackamas Chinook of Oregon saw this instrument as so synonymous with womanhood that one story, "Awl and Her Son's Son," has a solitary man's longing for a mate transforming the item itself into Awl Woman, "who can function like a valued tool for domestic chores and can employ an awl herself." Melville Jacobs, *The Content and Style of an Oral Literature* (Chicago: University of Chicago Press, 1959), p. 98.

[3] Janet D. Spector, *What This Awl Means: Feminist Archaeology at a Wahpeton Dakota Village* (St. Paul: Minnesota Historical Society Press, 1993).

gripped such buffalo shoulder blade hoes, much as men proudly posed with their pipes; bone hoes also played a conspicuous part in the altar-piece and ritual enactment of the "Mother Corn Ceremony" practiced by the Arikara long after the Indians had replaced them with metal hoes.[4]

Nearer grass level you might spy my third item, the L-shaped hide scraper handle, part of a tool used to scrape off hair and meaty lumps so that finished buffalo hides would have uniform thickness. This one caught the blade of a local Indian mowing his front yard. Cut from the thick beam of an elk rack with its bent, right-angle branch shaved from a side tine, it is about a foot long and lacks the chipped stone or metal chisel-like edge that would have been tightly bound to the tine with hide-and-sinew wrapping.

Once horses allowed these newly rich tribes to splinter into smaller hunting bands, hunting at will and easily acquiring sufficient meat, this scraper became a ubiquitous woman's tool. Yet this equestrian revolution wrought a demotion in women's status. Their former prestigious work as gardeners gave way to toiling over buffalo carcasses, processing meat, bones, and internal organs, and producing tipi covers, clothing, footgear, and furry robes for trade from buffalo hides. Meanwhile, their menfolk developed their fondness for intertribal feuding, which took center stage and brought them both glory and death, with women as booty or mourners.

On the underside of my horn handle is faintly incised a series of little cuts. Did they record the number of buffalo the owner had tanned, I wondered?[5] Then I read the life of Iron Teeth, the personal testimony of a ninety-two-year-old Northern Cheyenne woman whose own

---

[4] George F. Will, "Arikara Ceremonials," *North Dakota Historical Quarterly* 4(4) (July 1930), pp. 247–265. In "Shelling Corn in the Prairie-Plains: Archeological Evidence and Ethnographic Parallels Beyond the Pun," David Mayer Gradwohl proposes a similar ritualized perpetuation of antiquated tools – clam shells used for shelling corn – in use among contemporary Prairie Indians (*Plains Indian Studies: A Collection of Essays in Honor of John C. Ewers and Waldo R. Wedel*, edited by Douglas H. Ubelaker and Herman J. Viola [Washington, D.C.: Smithsonian Institution Press, 1982], pp. 135–156).

[5] According to Royal B. Hassrick, this was the practice among Lakota women, who recorded achievements on their elkhorn handles: black dots for each tanned robe, red dots for every ten robes (one tipi), and an incised circle for a hundred robes (or ten tipis' worth). Hassrick, *The Sioux: Life and Customs of a Warrior Society* (Norman: University of Oklahoma Press, 1964), pp. xiii, 42.

grandmother remembered raising corn in South Dakota's Black Hills in the late 1700s. Over her mother's and her own lifetimes, their economic base became exclusively dependant on horses and the buffalo-hunting, intertribal raiding way of life. As escapees from forced containment in Oklahoma Territory, her particular band, under the leadership of Morning Star (Dull Knife), also became hunted outlaws. With remarkable ease, Iron Teeth's story telescoped the full drama of nineteenth-century Northern Cheyenne history, blending sharp details with a marvelous command of a century's major events. Her husband was killed during Col. Ronald S. Mackenzie's raid on Nov. 25, 1876; three years later, she lost her son in her band's tragic breakout from the Fort Robinson brig in Nebraska. Closing her story, she held up her hide scraper and said:

> Besides using them in tanning, the women made marks on them to keep track of the ages of their children. The five rows of notches on this one are the age-records of my five children. Each year I have added a notch to each row, for the living ones. Any time, I can count up the notches and know the age of any of my children. Throughout my 92 years it has always been part of my most precious pack. There were times when I had not much else. I was carrying it in my hands when my husband was killed on upper Powder River. It was tied to my saddle while we were in flight from Oklahoma. It was in my little pack when we broke out from the Fort Robinson prison. It never has been lost. Different white people have offered me money for it. I am very poor, but such money does not tempt me. When I die, this gift from my husband will be buried with me.[6]

Examined separately or scrutinized in the aggregate, these three tools carry any number of historical messages: cultural change within one gendered segment of society, the impact of introduced items (horses) on a society's technological inventory, the history of human–animal relations (domesticated and otherwise), shifting methods of land use and their social consequences, the rise of new prestige categories (family horse ownership and men's war honor acquisition), and the more intimate record keeping of particular individuals. All are plausible avenues

---

[6] Thomas B. Marquis, "Iron Teeth, a Cheyenne Old Woman," in *The Cheyennes of Montana* (Algonac, Michigan: Reference Publications, 1978), p. 80.

for further study extracted from our hypothetical dig. Let me explore other ways in which the things that Indians made provide windows into various kinds of American Indian history.

Recovering History

To generate new explanations for changes in Indian pasts, archaeologists compare Indian-crafted tools, weapons, and ornaments, and their contexts, in order to discern social alterations over time[7] and to trace diffusion of cultural ideas over space. Usually the layer cake of items at a site, its stratigraphic sequence, records the superimpositions of ordinary life, tools discarded when they become dull or broken, clay vessels thrown away when they are improperly fired or crash to the floor, charcoal from ancient fires, and bones that are tossed away once their marrow has been sucked out. They fall into our hands un-self-consciously as the detritus of ordinary domestic life.

Some of these chronological layerings were intentional, however, as if Indians were building up a material archive. Within burial and temple mounds of the Southeast, for instance, were superimpositions of interred corpses, together with sacrificed subordinates and grave goods whose selection bore symbolic, social, and utilitarian meanings. We cannot know how the compacted history, upon which sat a mound's latest thatch-roofed building, might have been expected to inspire or sanctify its current priests or dignitaries who walked, talked, and performed rituals atop all this potent material, or how its mounded structure, which would eventually add another level upon their deaths, might have been considered "alive" because of this growth process.

Another candidate for such "indigenous curatorship" may be the care that Taos Pueblo still accords its four hemispherical "ash piles," where for generations residents have dumped their household leavings during

---

[7] A now classic example of artifacts revealing historical shifts in social practice is James Deetz's comparative analysis of how changing Arikara women's pottery styles reflected postcontact ecological changes that, in turn, caused women to change residence rules, finally affecting the styles of their ceramics (*The Dynamics of Stylistic Change in Arikara Ceramics* [Urbana: University of Illinois Press, 1965]).

the late summer cleanups prior to their annual San Geronimo fiesta. Their preservation offers a working hypothesis for how earlier Pueblo peoples might have regarded similarly designated zones. Explained archaeologist Florence H. Ellis during a visit to the thirty-foot refuse heap at Chaco Canyon's "great house" ruin of Chetro Ketl:

> Some people have the impression that the Indians had garbage dumps. They were ash dumps, really, and they referred to them as ash piles. They put with the ashes the broken shards, the broken implements and everything that comes sweeping out from their houses. Now, when this stuff is deposited, it all goes back to nature and this is the Pueblo idea of what is good in the world – things should go back to nature. The point is then, you do not have messy stuff that was thrown all around in here, and it's a rather sacred spot, totally, and in the modern Pueblos they don't let white people walk over their dumps, and they put prayer offerings on top of the dumps, periodically, on ceremonial occasions.[8]

Hypothesizing about ancient Pueblo Indian behavior by examining contemporary Indian practice is the method of making informed conjectures within the same cultural flow over time that Iroquois scholar William Fenton once dubbed "upstreaming." On rare occasions the archaeological recovery of material culture can almost allow one to "downstream" as well and derive even more definitive conclusions about the Indian past. In the early 1970s, for example, the Makah Indians of the Olympic Peninsula found themselves in court defending their right to use gill nets, which Washington State insisted were not part of the tribe's traditional fishing methods to which they were restricted by their treaty of 1855. Although their oral histories talk of men netting halibut, ling cod, and salmon, along with harpooning whales from their dugout canoes, word alone was not enough. Then excavations at the archaeological site of Ozette revealed a four-house Makah village that had been suffocated by a sudden mudslide a little over two hundred years before.

---

[8] Florence Hawley Ellis, quoted in *The Chaco Legacy*, transcript of a documentary film (Boston: Public Broadcasting Associates, 1980), p. 3. Pueblo Indian respect for these "ash piles" offered author Oliver La Forge the contested ground for his short story about archaeological versus Native priorities, "The Ancient Strength," in his collection *The Door in the Wall* (Boston: Houghton Mifflin, 1965), pp. 105–131.

Among the 55,000 salvaged artifacts from the Ozette site, including perishable items that were sealed from the air, was their missing evidence. Once a fragment of old gill net, whose fragile fiber webbing was the right size for snagging such fish, was sealed in plexiglass and presented to a judge, as one Makah fisherman said with satisfaction, "end of story."[9]

Registering History

Whether accumulated by design, neglect, or some in-between custodianship, refuse can also yield "exotic" materials, to adopt archaeological parlance, which, implicitly, register all manner of historical interactions. To strike it rich in an excavation by turning up Wyoming grizzly bear claws, North Dakota flint, Pacific Coast dentalium shells, Great Lakes copper, Gulf of Mexico tortoise carapaces, Minnesota Catlinite, North Carolina mica, California abalone shells, or Mexican red argelite far from their points of origin is to suggest long-distance trade routes, cross-cultural pillaging, or ceremonial exchanges for social or diplomatic reasons. Where such items circulate, so might ideas clustering around their uses and meanings, even though their new cultural homes will generally become quite proprietary, and acculturate them much as they might want to create fictive kinship relationships, through adoption, with any equally "exotic" visitors who intend to stay.

Material culture whose contextual circumstances refine our hypotheses about historical interactions, and which, under lucky conditions, can identify the ethnic groups involved, relate to those intense periods of cross-cultural interaction that the French historian Fernand Braudel referred to as the "conjuncture," usually spanning only ten to a hundred years. From the earliest trade transactions between American Indians and Euro-Americans, what people wore, the tools they used, and how they adorned themselves registered all of these historical changes and altered value systems. The pace and intensity with which their material, social, and political lives were transformed by horses, glass beads,

---

[9] From the documentary film *A Gift from The Past* (Washington, D.C.: Media Resource Associates, 1994, Sixty Minutes).

trade cloth, metal wares, firearms, and the like can yield rich "implicit documentation" of many kinds of history.[10]

Old relics that were sanctified through their association with earlier times often acquired numinous or sentimental significance, and still do – as described later. These include ancestral bones carried in portable ossuaries, such as the traveling tabernacles that Choctaw oral traditions say were borne by their leaders during tribal migrations. Then there are the communal medicine bundles, such as star- or planet-connected talismans that were treasured by the Skidi Pawnee. As additional evidence of Indian intentionality in these living historical souvenirs, one might also cite outmoded styles of domestic architecture that metamorphosed into religious spaces because of their close association with earlier cosmological and sociological ideas. Examples range from old pithouses of the Southwest that were remodeled into ceremonial *kivas* after their occupants came to reside in multistoried domestic room clusters, to rectangular Mandan earth lodges of the Missouri Plains, one of which was retained in each village as its *Okipa* ceremonial lodge – and as a historical reminder of former days – once most Mandans moved into circular earth lodges arranged around a common plaza, to the construction and ritual protocols associated with the Delaware Big House ceremony, which deliberately conjured up their multiethnic past.[11]

Recording History

Indians crafted other devices to mark occurrences or facilitate their oral recountings, which were usually referenced to those remarkable events or experiences characterized by Braudel as "surface oscillations." Many are mnemonic aids, memory helpers that kept recitations on track during oral presentations of a political, social, religious, or historical nature. Some were for initiates only, to be revealed and used during religious occasions. Only trained specialists decoded the symbols

---

[10] For an example of how to interpret such materials, see Cynthia R. Jaspers "Change in Ojibwa (Chippewa) Dress, 1820–1980," *American Indian Culture and Research Journal* 12(4) (1988), pp. 17–37.

[11] Frank G. Speck, *The Celestial Bear Comes Down to Earth* (Reading, Pa.: Reading Public Museum and Art Gallery, 1945), pp. 20–25.

scratched on Great Lakes birchbark scrolls associated with the *mitewiwin* or Grand Medicine Society. According to Thomas Vennum, Jr., these pictorial "migration charts" were cross-indexed to "song scrolls" and allowed an Ojibwa priest to "retain knowledge of the Ojibwa past . . . a reference text for the geohistory of his people."[12] What sounds like an old mnemonic device enabled the earth lodge–dwelling Arikaras of the Missouri River to recollect their genesis narrative. This sheaf of thirty-four thin sticks was preserved by an old Arikara priest named Four Rings. Arranging them in six piles around a firepit, Four Rings moved from pile to pile, each stick enabling him to conjure up separate scenes in the creation of his people's complex cosmology, their value system, their early history, and their cultural destiny.[13]

Jogging the memory with such aids was not limited to the Plains Indians. Among the Pimas of Arizona are found two- to five-foot-long incised "calendar sticks," which Frank Russell prefers to characterize as "annals," since their "Chronologic sequence is subordinated to narrative."[14] Oratorical crib sheets among the Iroquois peoples achieved greater complexity. Like the Pimas, the Iroquois possessed ceremonial canes, carved with pictographs and fitted with tiny birchwood pegs, which during installation rituals for new leaders reminded speakers of the roll call of chiefs who had founded the Confederacy of the Five Nations. Actually, they combined two different mnemonic systems: the pictographs, which depict such items as a claw hammer or a log house, were, according to William Fenton, "not the clues to titles but rather reflect the interpretations current among nineteenth-century Iroquois ritual leaders"; the arrangement of pegs, however, was an older device, probably dating back to the origin of their Confederacy.[15]

---

[12] Vennum, 1978, p. 760.

[13] Melvin R. Gilmore, "The Arikara Book of Genesis," *Papers of the Michigan Academy of Science, Arts and Letters* 12 (1929), pp. 95–120.

[14] Frank Russell, "Pima Annals," *American Anthropologist* 5(1903), p. 76. See also "A Chronology of Papago and Pima History Taken from Calendar Sticks" (Papago Indian Reservation: Papago Tribe of Arizona, Bureau of Indian Affairs, U.S. Public Health Service, 1975).

[15] William N. Fenton, "Field Work, Museum Studies, and Ethnohistorical Research," *Ethnohistory* 13(1–2) (1966), p. 81; see also Fenton's *The Roll Call of the Iroquois Chiefs: A Study of a Mnemonic Cane from the Six Nations Reserve*, Smithsonian Miscellaneous Collections, 3(15) (Washington, D.C.: Smithsonian Institution Press, 1950).

More widespread was the mnemonic and record-keeping use of shell beads, which we know generically by the Algonquian term *wampum*. Formed into strands or woven belts, throughout the entire eastern woodlands these were vital backup for the reliable transmission of historical data. In the late eighteenth century, for instance, a visitor noted that among the Creeks

> the old chiefs had often spoken to me of their ancestors, and they had shown me the belts, or species of chaplets, which contained their histories. These chaplets were their archives; they are of little seeds like those which are called Cayenne pearls; they are of different colors and strung in rows; and it is on their arrangement and their pattern that their meaning depends. As only the principal events are preserved on these belts and without any details, it sometimes happens that a single chaplet contains the history of twenty to twenty-five years.[16]

In Iroquois diplomatic discourse, shell-bead belts did more than join with condolence canes in abetting collective memory. "The interpretation of these several belts and strings brought out in the address of the wise-man," wrote Lewis Henry Morgan, "a connected account of the occurrences at the formation of the confederacy."[17] But the belts also became material embodiments of "pledges or records of matters of national or international importance," in the words of Iroquois scholar Arthur C. Parker. According to linguist Michael Foster, they functioned both "retrospectively," for calling up past events, and "prospectively," as a means of organizing present, and even future, events. In contrast to (or complementary to) the pictographs on their "condolence canes," their colored bands and linked stick figures served as conceptual code that enabled users to evaluate the current status and desired direction of alliances between Indians and Indians or between Indians and Euro-Americans.[18]

---

[16] In John R. Swanton, *Social Organization and Social Usages of the Indians of the Creek Confederacy*, Bureau of American Ethnology, Annual Report 42 (Washington, D.C.: U.S. Government Printing Office, 1928), p. 455.

[17] Sir William Johnson in 1753, quoted in Lewis Henry Morgan, *League of the Ho-de-no-sau-nee, or Iroquois* (Rochester, N.Y.: Sage & Brother, 1851), p. 121.

[18] Michael K. Foster, "Another Look at the Function of Wampum in Iroquois–White Councils," in *The History and Culture of Iroquois Diplomacy*, edited by Francis

Other Indian mnemonic records were more autobiographical, such as the "string balls" that Yakima girls began winding in childhood from stands of dogbane bark, attaching dentalium shells, glass beads, and colored cloth, and tying hundreds of knots in them as life experiences accumulated, each an exclamation point for some personal experience. At death the balls would hang near their graves or be buried with them.[19] A similar purpose was served by the "history baskets" woven by Yup'ik people from Alaska's Nelson Island. Their colors represented women's work – black and brown for the drying and storing of meat, green, blue, and red hues for the grasses they picked, brighter colors for berries, and pink for fish. While their covers rattled with seashells and pebbles – making warning noises if thieves poked around – they held umbilical cords, hair and nail cuttings, and bird feathers to recall multiple generations of women.[20]

With horses and intensified intergroup feuding, it became customary for Plains Indian warriors to portray battle exploits with pictographic figures on shirts, robes, and even tipi covers. An early example of these self-promotional "partisan histories" came to light after Lewis and Clark collected a Mandan painted buffalo robe depicting a fight between horsemen believed to have taken place about 1797. It is not clear if these early individual "brag robes" of Plains warriors preceded the community records painted by Plains Indian chroniclers that were collected by travelers and ethnographers afterward. Known as *waniyetu yawapi*, or "winter counts," to the Dakotas and as *sinaksin*, or "picture-writing," to the Blackfeet, their images were used as chronological "shorthand," highlighting the notable event of a given year.

Although a collective diary, they were generally the work of self-appointed historian-artists. Starting at the center, their symbols might spiral outward, with each standing, as a Sioux named Good Wood

Jennings (Syracuse, N.Y.: Syracuse University Press, 1985). See also Lynn Ceci, "The Value of Wampum among the New York Iroquois: A Case Study in Artifact Analysis," *Journal of Anthropological Research* 38(1) (1982), pp. 97–107.

[19] J. D. Leechman and M. R. Harrington, "String Records of the Northwest," *Indian Notes and Monographs*, series 216 (New York: Museum of the American Indian, Heye Foundation, 1921).

[20] Pat Hickman, *Innerskins/Outerskins: Gut and Fishskin* (San Francisco: San Francisco Craft and Folk Art Museum, 1987), p. 27.

put it, for "something put down for every year about their nation."[21] Among the oldest winter counts on record was one by a Lakota named Baptise Good, which its mixed-blood "author" began with the year 1779. Rather than producing complete historical records, these visualizations linked what Raymond D. Fogelson might call each year's "epitomizing event" in order to bring to the surface what Vine Deloria, Jr., has described as "the psychic life of a community."[22] They located key happenings from this collective life in time, as Raymond J. DeMallie points out, but he also stresses that they enabled good storytellers to enliven the "message" of each event with humor, drama, and relevant anecdotes; through the mediation of a master "keeper," winter counts instructed *and* entertained.[23]

While Deloria may be correct that they ignore a people's "continuous subject matter," they can document personal chronologies, as Marion Smith learned by extracting census data from a Mandan pictographic robe. "History to the Mandan," she concluded, "seems to be composed in large part of a set of interlocking life histories remembered in terms of a relatively few criteria such as birth, initiations, war deeds, supernatural displays, place in council, chieftanship and death."[24]

---

[21] Helen H. Blish, "Dakota Histories and Historical Art," in *A Pictographic History of the Oglala Sioux* (paintings by Amos Bad Heart Bull)(Lincoln: University of Nebraska Press, 1967), p. 23.

[22] Vine Deloria, Jr., *God Is Red* (New York: Grosset and Dunlap, 1973), p. 112. See Linea Sundstrom, "Smallpox Used Them Up: References to Epidemic Disease in Northern Plains Winter Counts, 1714–1920," *Ethnohistory* 44(2) (Spring 1997), pp. 305–343; for a old Kiowa example that marks annual events from the great meteor shower of November 13, 1833, to the measles epidemic that killed about 15 percent of the Kiowa people in the summer of 1882, see *A Chronicle of the Kiowa Indians (1832–1892)* (Berkeley: R. H. Lowie Museum of Anthropology, University of California, 1968); Joyce M. Szabo's ideas about how the genre evolved during the reservation era are presented in "Shields and Lodges, Warriors and Chiefs: Kiowa Drawings as Historical Records," *Ethnohistory* 41(1) (Winter 1994), pp. 1–24.

[23] DeMallie's useful explanation of Lakota concepts of history, time, and winter counts is in James R. Walker, *Lakota Society*, edited by Raymond J. DeMallie (Lincoln: University of Nebraska Press, 1982), pp. 111–122. He also distinguishes between their counts based on the "year," *omaka*, or "winter," *waniyetu*, and on the rarer form of pictographic reckoning based on a "generation," *wicoicage*, or seventy years, roughly equivalent to the life of an old man.

[24] Marion Smith, "Mandan History as Reflected in Butterfly's Winter Count," *Ethnohistory* 7 (1960), p. 202.

Resisting History

Ceremonial regalia, magical wearing apparel, and even architectural forms aided and abetted a slew of Indian revitalization movements. Erupting shortly after first contact and continuing into the twenty-first century, Native spiritual crusades and charismatic leaders sought to turn back the clock, to counter Euro-American diseases, overwhelming numbers, technological superiority, introduced symbols of time keeping, Christianity, and imposed lifeways. Some encouraged almost suicidal, apocalyptic confrontations; others favored less drastic forms of resistence or separate-but-equal coexistence. All provided succor and hope for tribespeople overcome by physical and psychological distress. Best known are the muslin and hide shorts and dresses of the Plains Indian Ghost Dance. On their fronts and backs were emblazoned the supernatural power of crows, stars, dragonflies, and cedar trees that were intended to restore the old Indian cosmos that seemed irretrievable.[25]

Many revitalization movements featured distinctive flags or banners, storytelling aids, and even wearing apparel, as if their followers were unified and protected within magical zones and spiritual body armor.[26] Uniform-cut frock coats of the Faw-Faw movement among the Otos of Oklahoma blended the military potency of white soldiery with visionary insignia, applied in beadwork, of stars, moons, and trees.[27] In northern California, the "dream" religion revival of the 1950s known as Bole Maru saw the prophet Essie Parrish inspiring the production of "holy" handkerchiefs, flags, skirts, and headdresses. While their imagery derived from the revelations of individual women, their aim at the time was to protect Pomo men in the armed forces then engaged in the Korean conflict.[28]

---

[25] Catalog for *I Wear the Morning Star: An Exhibition of American Indian Ghost Dance Objects* (Minneapolis: Minneapolis Institute of Arts, July 29–September 26, 1976).

[26] For a discussion of material culture in an early revitalization movement, see James H. Howard, "Kenakuk Religion: An Early 19th Century Revitalization Movement 140 Years Later," *Museum News* 26(11–12) (Vermillion: University of South Dakota Press, 1965), pp. 1–48.

[27] David Wooley and William Walters, "Waw-No-She's Dance," *American Indian Art Magazine* 14(1) (Winter 1988), pp. 36–45.

[28] Clement W. Meighan and Francis A. Riddell, *The Maru Cult of the Pomo Indians: A California Ghost Dance Survival*, Southwest Museum Papers N. 23 (Highland Park, Calif.: Southwest Museum, 1972).

A number of these movements spawned unique architecture. It may be disputed whether the Delaware Big House and the Ojibwa Grand Medicine Lodge were revitalization movements or not, but there is no doubt that these buildings were created to function as special chambers for summarizing their ideologies. The California Ghost Dance spawned an altered architectural form, the oversized earth lodges dreamed up by north-central California prophets in 1870. The revelations of these prophets, which attracted followers for a short spell, called everyone to cluster inside newly built earth-covered buildings while the world outside was destroyed by fire or flood. Inside, the "saved" would have visions of a greater earth lodge, home of their Earth spirit, which was carpeted with spring poppies and lupine. Although this "Earth Lodge Cult" lost its appeal, California Ghost Dance–inspired rituals continued to be held inside roundhouses, although they were then built of the milled lumber and split shingles that Indians scavenged from nearby lumber yards.[29]

Roles in History

Like the myths of which they are material proof, certain American Indian items lift the possibility of tribal persistence out of history's grasp altogether. Enshrouded with the sort of fetishistic status accorded a European royal scepter, the original Declaration of Independence, or a splinter of the True Cross, these revered key symbols emerge out of well-established typologies. These belts, bundles, pipes, or buildings are displayed or used on formal occasions. Around them swirl the heroic biographies and personal charisma that we associate with prominent individuals who gained divinity upon their demise.

The origins of the sacred compacts, which such tactile symbols often seal between groups of people and their supernatural protectors, are rooted in supernatural milieu. In creation narratives we discover the chartering accounts behind the stone sun image in old Natchez

---

[29] Peter Nabokov, "Hidden Blueprints [Roundhouses of the Reservation Era]," *North Dakota Quarterly*, American Indian Issue, 67(2&3) (Summer–Fall 2001), pp. 256–315.

city-states,[30] the Lone Man shrine of the Mandan,[31] the flat pipe of the Arapaho,[32] the copper and brass plates still preserved by the Upper Creek community of Tuckabatchee,[33] or the sacred pole complex of the Omaha.[34] Yet we find no clear division between these myths and icons and those that sanctioned the reconsolidations of ethnic groups who seem to have fused, frequently under adverse conditions, either shortly before or after white contact. The Sacred Pipe associated with the White Buffalo Maiden story, the Sacred Arrows of the Cheyenne, and the Tai-Me effigy of the Kiowa might be classified among more recent collective symbols, except for the fact that their emic interpretation and urgent mandate exempt them from chronological comparison. Often there are prescribed opportunities for the privileged or supplicants to glimpse, touch, and pray to these charmed items so that they will protect one's people, clan, or family throughout all conceivable periods of time.

Even when revered items of material culture emerge from unquestionably historical conditions, such as the wampum belts that cemented diplomatic encounters in the Northeast, a personalized identity envelops them. I have witnessed their presence at semipublic gatherings, as when the Western Cherokee Keetowah Society wampum belts, which were safeguarded over the infamous "Trail of Tears," are displayed to fellow Cherokees during the Redbird Smith birthday commemorations in eastern Oklahoma.[35] I have also seen their more private care and feeding, as

---

[30] John R. Swanton, *Indian Tribes of the Lower Mississippi Valley*, Bureau of American Ethnology, Bulletin 43 (Washington, D.C.: U.S. Government Printing Office, 1911), p. 175.

[31] Alfred W. Bowers, *Mandan Social and Ceremonial Organization* (Moscow: University of Idaho Press, 1991 [1950]), pp. 115–117.

[32] Loretta Fowler, *Arapahoe Politics, 1851–1978* (Lincoln: University of Nebraska Press, 1982), pp. 107–109, 118.

[33] Angie Debo, *The Road to Disappearance: A History of the Creek Indians* (Norman: University of Oklahoma Press, 1941), pp. 160, 293.

[34] Robin Ridington and Dennis Hastings, *Blessing for a Long Time: The Sacred Pole of the Omaha Tribe* (Lincoln: University of Nebraska Press, 1997).

[35] For a description of these belts' role in recovering Cherokee history see Robert K. Thomas, "The Redbird Smith Movement," Paper. N. 16 in *Symposium on Cherokee and Iroquois Culture*, Smithsonian Institution, Bureau of American Ethnology, Bulletin 180 (Washington, D.C.: U.S. Government Printing Office, Smithsonian Institution, 1961), p. 164.

at the thousand-year-old Acoma Pueblo in western New Mexico, where a tribal official led me up to his hereditary adobe house's upstairs room. In his hands were a bowl of water and a pouch of cornmeal for nourishing the silver-headed ebony Lincoln Canes, emblems of tribal sovereignty that President Abraham Lincoln distributed in 1863 among these autonomous villages (following practices of early-seventeenth-century Spanish governors), for which he was responsible during his term of office. Considered numinous elders and guides in their own right, the staffs are also tangible emblems of the Acoma Pueblo's autonomy.

When enshrined objects are desecrated, destroyed, or disappear, feelings of confusion, panic, or fury weaken a community's self-confidence. Well before passage of the Native American Graves Protection and Repatriation Act of 1978, (known as NAGPRA), Indians sought cultural treasures that wound up in eastern repositories, as expressed in the Cayuga leader Deskadeh's 1925 final speech begging the Canadian government to return his people's beaded "records of our history"[36] and Hidatsa Indians' efforts to recover their Waterbuster Bundle in 1938 from New York's American Museum of Natural History.[37] Repatriation efforts gained legal backing and public visibility in the 1980s as Native groups repossessed Iroquois masks, Northwest Coast potlatch goods – confiscated by the Canadian government when the ceremony was outlawed – and other prized possessions.[38] A noteworthy case was the gradual disappearance from the Zuni Pueblo since the late nineteenth century of wooden effigies representing their Twin War Gods, or *Ayahu:da*. Recarved each year, with older examples expected to weather away in peace in their sacred cave, over the years nearly a hundred of these enigmatic cylindrical effigies were stolen and stashed in private collections or flagrantly displayed in public museums. Over a decade eighty-five of the carvings, considered the entire

---

[36] Speech quoted in *Native Literature in Canada: From the Oral Tradition to the Present,* edited by Penny Petrone (Toronto: Oxford University Press, 1990), pp. 102–104.

[37] Carolyn Gilman and Mary Jane Schneider, "Wolf Chief Sells the Shrine," in *The Way to Independence: Memories of a Hidatsa Indian Family, 1840–1920* (St. Paul: Minnesota Historical Society Press, 1987), pp. 296–301, 314–315.

[38] See Rayna Green, compiler, *American Indian Sacred Objects, Skeletal Remains, Repatriation and Reburial: A Resource Guide* (Washington, D.C.: American Indian Program, National Museum of American History, 1994).

tribe's property or sacred trust, were eventually repatriated from twenty-six different sources.[39]

Less successful were efforts by Tlingits from the old village of Klukwan, in southeastern Alaska, to retrieve their world-renowned Whale House carvings, which were sold surreptitiously by members of the owner's family in the 1880s. Although complicated legal proceedings resulted in a court decision ordering a private collector to return the posts and screens, appeals kept some of the artifacts, which recorded the history and legends of one of villages' leading aristocratic families, sealed in a Seattle warehouse.[40]

As each year brings new artifact collections to light, Indians groups are given fresh cause for rallying fellow members and new hopes for recovering their past. Lamented one tribesman upon learning of a 150-year-old collection of eighteen items sent east by the Presbyterian missionary Henry Spalding, "The Nez Perce need it for our culture and younger generations. Our culture is disappearing so fast."[41]

Representing History

How contemporary Indians self-consciously reflect upon and depict the connective tissue between material culture and history has undergone considerable change in the last quarter-century. Twentieth-century

---

[39] Roger Anyon, "Zuni Repatriation of War Gods," *Cultural Survival Quarterly*, (Winter 1996), p. 47. Another case study with a less auspicious outcome is Catherine Banett's "Of masks and marauders" (*Arts and Antiques 7(7)* [October 1990], pp. 99–109, 140, 142, 147–148), which retraces the journey of an improperly sold 150-year-old "Long Beak" Kachina mark from the Hopi Pueblo of Old Ovaibi.

[40] Proprietary opinions diverge: non-Indian connoisseurs consider the Whale House's material ensemble world-class art and "belonging" to all humankind; the courts deemed it the property of the entire village; but to its extended-family owners its art pieces remain what Tlingit author Nora M. Dauenhauer calls an unalienable part of a "copyright system," by which particular clans and families customarily asserted their history of social status and property rights ("Context and Display in Northwest Coast Art," review essay in *New Scholar* 10(1&2) [1986], p. 425). The Whale House controversy is well covered in Marilee Enge's five-part series "Treasure of the Tlingit," *Anchorage Daily News*, April 4, 1993, pp. A1, A6, A7, A9; April 5, 1993, pp. A1, A4, A5, A7; April 6, 1993, pp. A1, A4, A5, A6; April 7, 1993, pp. A1, A4, A5, A6; April 8, 1993, pp. A1, A4, A5, A6.

[41] *Billings Gazette*, August 29, 1995, p. 7B.

Indian Painters have depicted historical events that transpired before the advent of photography – new imagings of the Pueblo Indians' 1680 all-Pueblo Revolt, the Cherokee Trail of Tears of the 1830s, the Navajo Long Walk of 1864, and even the Gallup Intertribal Ceremonial, itself a distilled self-representation of Indian cultural history that began in the 1920s.

As showcases for Indian material culture that must continuously revise their explanatory contexts, the "truth factories" that we call museums find themselves in the line of fire during heated debates over historical and cultural representation. And as their cross-cultural exhibitions inevitably interrogate history, the oppositional agendas of non-Indian and Native museum facilities should come as no surprise. While Robert Cantwell claims that the Smithsonian Institution's mandate, for example, is "to be the repository of the enchanted objects around which the narrative of our history has been formed," he candidly notes that Smithsonian exhibitions tend to support a progressivist time perspective and technologically-advanced subject matter.[42] In the face of this uncongenial master narrative, over the past decade Indians have mounted their replies.

At a tribal museum like the Ned Hatathli Cultural Center Museum at Navajo Community College in Tsaile, Arizona, the Native emphasis on emergence out of underworlds by mythic supernatural figures is given equal play alongside the non-Navajo archaeological story, thereby "exhibiting the debate." In Connecticut, the Institute of American Indian Studies premised its summer 1990 exhibition, "As We Tell Our Stories: Living Traditions and the Algonkian Peoples of Indian New England," on the theme of cultural continuity. Its message that "we are still here" refutes the older museum habit of exhibiting artifacts from Indians "who *were* here."

Revisionist approaches to Indian history have reached the uppermost echelons of American popular culture. The prevailing mandate of the Smithsonian Institution's new National Museum of the American Indian, according to Director W. Richard West, Jr., is "to describe a

---

[42] Robert Cantwell, *Ethnomimesis: Folklife and the Representation of Culture* (Chapel Hill: University of North Carolina Press, 1998), p. 114.

non-European view of the world" by employing "the first person voice of the Indian peoples to communicate it."[43] Its flagship exhibit, the "Pathways of Tradition" show at New York City's U.S. Custom House, conspicuously omitted dates in its labels. "When you start pegging dates to items in the collection," explained Director West, "it connects to a linear time-line. We want to get away from that perspective."[44] The show's curator, Rick Hill, added, "What we are looking at in this show is not art as an evolutionary process but how ideas and beliefs remain strong through time."[45]

A beautiful example of an "epitomizing object" that continues to reference traditional ideas about time, narrative, space, tribal identity, and Native history is the circular Tohono O'odham basket. It features a sticklike representation of their mythological Elder Brother, I'itoi, standing at the mouth of a circular maze at whose center is a dark circle that represents the tribe's sacred world-center mountain, Baboquivari Peak, in southern Arizona. Regardless of the dramatic particulars of a given narrative, the way the basket's coils are woven around the cardinal-directional crosspieces reflects how the characters in legends, old and new, move through their conflicts and dangers in a counterclockwise direction, from a state of harmony to one of increasing trial and conflict. A narrative may open with the phrase *sh hab wa chu'i na'ana,* meaning "They say it happened long ago." With the eventual resolution

[43] Quoted in the *Washington Post,* November 23, 1992, "*Style,*" pp. B1, B8. "In N.Y., Indian 'Traditions,' with a Twist; An Exhibit That Promises a New Look at Native Americans."

[44] Quoted in the *Wall Street Journal,* "Indian Museum Takes Shelter in Beaux-Arts Wickirp," November 17, 1992, p. A6. See Director West's further thoughts and other essays in *The Changing Presentation of the American Indian: Museums and Native Cultures* (Washington, D.C.: National Museum of the American Indian/Smithsonian Institution Press and Seattle: University of Washington Press, 2000). The most ambitious recent efforts to achieve such "representational repatriation" by Indian museums are the $135 million Mashantucket Pequot Museum and Research Center in southeastern Connecticut, which opened in August 1998, and Washington, D.C.'s $110 million National Museum of the American Indian, slated to open in 2002. And a recent museum exhibition focused on one American Indian idea that has prevailed over time is "Gifts of Pride: Kiowa and Comanche Cradles," which demonstrates how southern Plains women used a key symbol of genealogical continuity to defy the history impinging on them (catalog with the same name edited by curator Barbara A. Hall, Bristol, Rhode Island: Haffenreffer Museum of Anthropology, Brown University, 2000).

[45] Quoted in the *New York Times,* "Museum Displays Indian Artifacts," Section 1, November 15, 1992, p. 43.

of its troubles, however, the storyteller will close by declaring *am o wa'i at hoabdag*, meaning "that's the center of the basket," evoking Elder Brother returning to the security of his house on the sacred mountain. Harmony is restored, and all is well again.[46]

Renewing (Despite History)

This overview of the interplay between Indian history and material culture would be incomplete without a reminder of how certain objects provide Native societies with counterweights to rapid change. A gentler, more inward-looking, private category of symbol-rich commodities, with historical shading if not direct import, helps to bind Indians together through their traffic back and forth among kin, friends, and ceremonial associates.

At the end of their traditional four-day summer dances, for instance, the Osage held a massive giveaway at which virtually no participant, either relative or guests from afar, left empty-handed. Today's intertribal powwows carry on this custom of handing out specially designated goods, typically blankets for men and shawls for women. For over a century an especially esteemed gift has been the uniquely Indian "Star Quilt," whose central radiating-star motif has been traced to either the Morning Star symbol that Plains Indians painted, quilled, and beaded on hide robes or the Anglo-American Star of Bethlehem design that was used by eighteenth-century American and British quiltmakers. Whether cloaking shamans in Lakota *yuwipi* rituals, draped over caskets, given to newlyweds, or newborn babies, and whether originating in the Plains or the Great Lakes, the Star Quilt has become a key symbol of identity for Indians everywhere.[47]

The outlays of gifts in Indian giveaways commonly link hosts and guests beyond the immediate event through subtle but tenacious ties

---

[46] From Dean Saxton and Lucille Saxton, *O'othham Hoho'ok A'agitha: Legends and Lore of the Papago and Pima Indians* (Tucson: University of Arizona Press, 1973), pp. 371–373.

[47] Marsha MacDowell and Margaret Wood, "Sewing It Together: Native American and Hawaiian Quilting Traditions," in *Native American Expressive Culture* (Ithaca, N.Y.: Akwe:kon Press, 1994), pp. 108–113.

of reciprocity. Either they are continuations of long-recognized alliances through fictitious kinship, such as the annually maintained link between age-old "cousins" like the Kiowas and Crows and other historically "paired" tribes for centuries, or they are initiations of such ties for mutual aid, with the intention that they will oscillate back and forth through similar exchanges in the future. Participants might keep mental accounts of who gave what to whom, with the mechanism called "delayed reciprocity" requiring recipients to play host and return the favor some day, only to incur new obligations for the future.

American Indian gift-giving practices between kin and visitors are part of a venerable etiquette, and the primary category for acceptable presentations – essentially "containers of culture," since they mostly turn out to be wrappings or enclosures for people, goods, and food – also displays remarkable continuity. On the Northwest Coast, plank boxes and woven blankets were passed around this way, while wooden bowls and buffalo robes circulated to the east. Upon the appearance of white traders and their standardized wares, however, Pacific Coast peoples like the Kwakiutl considered piles of Hudson Bay blankets and stacks of enameled metal dishes replacement tokens in grand-scale give-away ceremonies known as "potlatches," while an appetite for metal kettles and trade woolens took over formal feasts among Great Lakes peoples.[48]

One might view this adaptation, however, as the material counterpart to "reverse assimilation," whereby in the colonial period whites abandoned their former identities after absorption into Indian social worlds. This is what happened, as ethnohistorian Calvin Martin demonstrates, when the Micmacs of Nova Scotia "Indianized" a simple copper pot

---

[48] For a brief analysis of how potlatch interchanges of Hudson's Bay blankets came to "transcend the boundaries between [Kwakiutl] groups" and "make it possible to compare on a scale of greatness chiefly names and lineage privileges (*tlogwe*) that are otherwise incommensurable," see Marshall Sahlins, "Cosmologies of Capitalism: The Trans-Pacific Sector of 'The World System'," in *Culture/Power/History: A Reader in Contemporary Social Theory*, edited by Nicholas B. Dirks, Geoff Eley, and Sherry B. Ortner (Princeton, N.J.: Princeton University Press, 1995), pp. 435–438. Further comparison of the commodity concept in Native and European trade and diplomatic contexts is found in Bruce M. White's "Encounters with Spirits: Ojibwa and Dakota Theories about the French and their Merchandise," *Ethnohistory* 41(3) (Summer 1994), pp. 369–405.

they obtained in trade. Apart from its utilitarian function, its historically bounded cultural "lives" included its highly valued role in the colonial exchange economy, its key place in ceremonial life as a burial vessel, its animated life as a member of the overarching belief system, and its circumstantial impact in altering older settlement patterns, which had been constrained by the inability to find proper woods for carving into feast bowls. Martin also might have mentioned the new historical life accorded those old-fashioned wooden bowls. While they might have dropped from everyday usage, they acquired heightened prestige as traditional feast dishes, brought out on only special occasions.[49]

Rather than dooming the old-time socializing protocols, as often as not these modern substitutes – easier and cheaper to secure in bulk than hand-crafted items – enabled elaborations of ceremonies and likely reinforced preexisting world views and social customs. And while the institutionalized trade exchanges such as otter pelts for Hudson Bay blankets or beaver skins for copper pots made Indians dependent upon the "world systems" of the Pacific Rim and the colonial Northeast, Native conservatism still moderated the adaptation, into these formal exchange systems at least, of enticing new wares. Foods, metal pots, tools, and cloths were the objects back then, and updated materials like dried noodles, plastics, and rayons can fulfill the same function today. Back and forth they circulate as Indians strengthen their ties with one another, with dollar bills sometimes tossed into open Star Quilts carried around the edge of powwow arenas to defray expenses or thrown with abandon into a visitors' section during potlatchs. When Indians come together at these cooperative and self-celebrating moments, something far more valuable than money, or even history, is apparently at stake.

[49] Calvin Martin, "The Four Lives of a Micmac Copper Pot," *Ethnohistory* 32 (1975), pp. 111–113. See also Laurier Turgeon, "The Tale of the Kettle: Odyssey of an Intercultural Object," *Ethnohistory* 44(1) (Winter 1997), pp. 1–29. Bill Cronon and Richard White add that Indians also cut up their trade kettles to make arrowheads and high-status jewelry, and that, from the Native perspective, their role as grave goods to serve the dead in the afterlife was equally "utilitarian" (see "Indians in the Land: A Conversation Between William Cronon and Richard White," *American Heritage* 37(5) [August–September 1986], pp. 18–25).

SEVEN

—◄◦►—

Renewing, Remembering, and Resisting

Rituals and History

The white people had their own religion and churches; all kinds of churches to go by. Now we want to protect our redskins from the white people. We'll let them have dreams through fasting. We'll give them a religion to go by too – the *Midewiwin* (Medicine Dance), the Drum Dance, and the War Dance. That's what *Manido* [Spirit] arranged for all the nations. That's part of Indian history.[1]

John Thunderbird, Chippewa

The first time I saw an American Indian piece of ritualized history, I had no clue what was going on. It was in early summer 1962. During a Saturday stroll along the banks of the Little Bighorn River on the outskirts of Crow Agency, Montana, I broke into a clearing to find a procession of about twenty women wearing what today constitutes "traditional" attire – long-sleeved calico dresses, leather-tooled heavy belts and pouches, and high-top moccasins. Bringing up their rear walked a line of men beating thin, single-sided, hand-held drums, some of them sporting the old-style reservation black hats with high, round crowns and wide, flat brims. All of them were heading for an oversized tipi composed of two regular-sized tipi covers flung over a frame of ten poles, their canvas sides rolled up at around shoulder height with a fringe of leafy willow boughs tucked into the furl. The solemnity and concentration of

---

[1] Quoted in Victor Barnouw, *Acculturation and Personality Among the Wisconsin Chippewa*, Memoirs of the American Anthropologist, N. 72 (1950), p. 108.

the moment were obvious. Noticing my presence, one drummer walked directly towards me without a smile on his face. It was an adoption ceremony of the Tobacco Society of the Crow Indians, but I didn't know that. All I learned was that I had no business there.

For any people to make genesis accounts, turning points, and even key figures in their collective past convincingly part of their present, they usually do more than talk together. To imprint their preferred versions of deep or shallow history so thoroughly that they feel their very survival depends upon them, they script opportunities for stepping through the veils of time and into the vestments of these narratives. Inverting that proposition, if moments of symbolic manipulation intended to renew the world, sanctify rites of passage, restore distressed individuals, usurp a former political or religious order, or steer community behavior in new directions require "recentering" their fellowship into a credible cosmology, people often feel the need to move together.

They commit bodies, gestures, voices, and stagecraft to dramatized and/or danced enactments or tableaus of the sacred histories that either originally chartered or, more commonly, reconsolidated their ancestral communities. "Whatever the ontological status of culture as such," writes Robert Cantwell, "it must be embodied, enacted, performed, represented, and reproduced in order to have any social reality."[2] These ritualized representations are not especially self-reflective: without apology, they portray idealized stories of collective struggle, coherent sociology, partisan politics, unified geography, shared symbols, and common destiny.

These participatory occasions also dissolve the performer–audience division implied in the term "historical reenactment," where picnickers or tourists watch businessmen and truck drivers costumed as Yankees and rebels fire long-barreled rifles and pretend to die. They ask everyone to temporarily evacuate their current personalities and submerge in the stream of time – becoming the past for the sake of the future.[3] They

---

[2] Robert Cantwell, *Ethnomimesis: Folklife and the Representation of Culture* (Chapel Hill: University of North Carolina Press, 1997), p. 30.
[3] As critic Margo Jefferson described the thrall of enacted pasts: "When history and theater meet on equal terms something extraordinary happens. History becomes

generally reverse the old idea of "command performances," in which the compulsion to participate is ordered from on high. Here that responsibility falls upon everyone, through the gossip and peer pressure that have always made community members shape up.

These collective representations breach the divide between creative illusion and magical transformation, which the scholarly term "cultural performance" misguidedly still perpetuates. Here we are not geared to "suspend disbelief" or induce introspection from uninvolved spectators. Nor are these cultural dramas sympathetic with sociological definitions that see performance as the manipulative "impression management" of self-interested individuals during their face-to-face interactions.[4] Here everyone must capitulate and join in, implicating themselves almost as coconspirators. At the very least, one should walk away a sort of witness, who can testify that one social world has kept itself on track – for the restabilization of everyone else too, believe the Pueblo people: "We help him [the sun] daily to rise and to cross over the sky," explained Mountain Lake of Taos Pueblo to the psychologist Carl Jung. "We do this not only for ourselves, but for the Americans also. Therefore they should not interfere with our religion. But if they continue to do so and hinder us, then they will see that in ten years the sun will rise no more."[5]

Two decades after I first glimpsed that adoption ritual, I devoted four years to putting it under a magnifying glass. My study took issue with accounts written by the renowned Crow Indian scholar, the late anthropologist Robert Lowie. After his impeccable ethnographic descriptions of them, Lowie concluded that the Tobacco Society planting and adoption rituals resembled "not a unified plot, but rather a chain of casually coupled episodes from the tribal repertory."[6] Now Lowie knew full well that the Montana Crow were a Plains Indian hunting people,

three-dimensional, and an audience of strangers become united in its willingness – its need – to live it all again" ("Familiar History Meets Theater and Turns into Epiphany," *New York Times*, March 27, 1997, p. C 9).

[4] See Edward L. Schieffelin, "Problematizing Performance," in *Ritual, Performance, Media* edited by Felicia Hughes-Freeland (London: Routledge, 1998).

[5] Quoted in Michael Serrano, *C. G. Jung and Hermann Hesse: A Record of Two Friendships* (New York: Schocken Books, 1966), pp. 87–88.

[6] Robert H. Lowie, *The Crow Indians* (New York: Holt, Rinehart and Winston, 1935), p. 296.

who readily admitted to him that their forefathers split off from the Hidatsa, the farming culture based in the Middle Missouri River region of central North Dakota. His best guess was that this happened sometime shortly after 1500 A.D. Yet he also chose to devalue statements by his key Crow consultants that their very existence depended upon the regular observance of these Tobacco Society rituals, and he never asked what their "parent tribe," the Hidatsas who still lived on North Dakota's Fort Berthold reservation, might have to say on the split. Crows insisted that their original migration west from North Dakota was inspired by a legendary leader's sacred vision quest, and clearly preferred this story over that Lowie emphasized, which attributed the fission to a women's squabble over the fair distribution of the succulent vegetal contents of a buffalo's stomach following a collective hunt.

My investigation took me two summers and one winter (when Lowie never visited the reservation) in Crow country and archival research in Chicago, Bloomington, New York, Beloit, Washington, Wyoming, and Montana. It yielded over a dozen variants of the tribe's preferred storyline that had been told among themselves for over a century. Soon a finer-grained understanding of Crow historicity began to emerge. In the Crow collective memory – sanctioned in 1983, when a revised standard text was published by the Crow Bilingual Program for dissemination throughout reservation classrooms – the tribe's separate identity was born when two brothers set out for a resting place on a high overlook to fast and seek their life-guiding visions.

In his out-of-body experience, one brother was granted corn as his "medicine," after which he fathered the agricultural Hidatsa people. But the other brother's vision won him the power of sacred tobacco seeds (actually a rare subspecies of *Nicotiana* known by botanists as *multivalvis*). He was also instructed to shepherd his small band of followers on an epic circulatory tour of the Plains. On this search for their predestined resting place, they encountered the cold winds of the north (Canada), the damp climate of the west (Colorado), and the dry grasslands of the south (Oklahoma) before looping back into the heart of the plains – the game-rich, well-watered Bighorn heartland. Here they coalesced as the Absaroke ("Children of the Large-Beaked Bird') or "Crow" tribe – a "chosen" people in their "promised land" at last, as the foremost Crow historian, Joseph Medicine Crow, once put it. The storyline provided a sacred narrative that validated the Crow's presence as a new ethnic entity on the plains and substantiated their claim to the coveted valley between the Absaroka and Bighorn mountain ranges.

The symbolic manipulations of that Tobacco Society adoption procession I had interrupted years before, I would argue, only brought this story to life. Its three "stops" along the way, for song and prayer, and the fourth, climactic entry around the oversized tipi's cedar-lain altar (which symbolized the Bighorn Valley), dramatized what the Crow cared to remember and/or reconstruct about their past. Rather than origins forged out of anger or disagreement, this narrative grew out of a cultural logic that "naturalized" their migratory history and rendered it harmonious and inevitable. As one of Lowie's Crow consultants put it, in a comment that Lowie recorded in his notebook but that never made it into the 2,000-odd pages he published on the tribe: "This is how we became people."

At the close of my field studies, I had a chance to witness the adoption ceremony again and this time was invited to stick around. From the sidelines I saw two young initiates halt four times during their solemn procession, duck under the hem of the initiation lodge – whose two overlapping canvas covers, I knew by now, symbolized the amicable consent of their "giving" and "receiving" parents – and acquire songs and other insignia of membership. At the climax, I saw the truckloads of fruit being distributed, symbolizing the earth's natural bounties by which the Sacred Tobacco – a female entity – got her adopted tribe through hard times.

Suddenly everyone broke into clan clusters for ritual consumption of watermelon and oranges. A Whistling Water clan member frantically motioned to me, yelling out in Crow, "*Issaatxalvash*" (Two Leggings) – the name of a 19th-century Crow warrior whose life story I had edited. No one should observe "outside" this symbolically created world or fail to ratify its power; bystanding was not an option. Momentarily conscripted into the social persona of my old book's protagonist, I stepped into his grinning circle of clan descendants. With pulp and seeds running down our chins, we internalized the only historical truth that mattered: the power of the Crow's "national totem" to nourish her people.[7]

---

[7] Peter Nabokov, "Cultivating Themselves: The Interplay of Crow Indian Religion and History," Ph.D. dissertation in anthropology, University of California, Berkeley, 1988.

Not all Indian rituals call upon their practitioners to embody this degree of historiographic purpose. Seasonal rites of thanksgiving, sometimes called "First Fruits" rituals, do not seem informed by Native theories of change or memories of older actions, even though they may be coupled with enactments that do, as American society does with its own annual Thanksgiving ritual, which melds a fictionalized master narrative of Indian–white harmony with a harvest celebration.[8] Drawing upon timeless cosmogenic powers, shamanic performances likewise rarely hint at enacted histories, although to take effect they must transport their practitioners to some "time before time," and may acknowledge some critical divide in Native thought, bendable or bridgeable as it may be, between cosmology and chronology. But without half trying, many Indian religious pageants or ritual cycles of central sacramental significance to their tribe's identity *do* seem to fit the Native requirements for "doing history" – honoring and preserving their self-conceived pasts by representing them through symbolic regalia and routinized, if rudimentary, expressive behaviors.

Interested in how traditional peoples represent and reconnect with their heritages, Paul Connerton has alerted us that "if there is such a thing as social memory, we are likely to find it in commemorative ceremonies."[9] In some Indian religious schemes, historical references are usually so enmeshed within a mythologizing narrative that one need not digress into the chicken–egg debate of which came first, rituals or myths,[10] to appreciate the necessity for the two to unite in some participatory ceremonial, such as the Busk of the southeastern Creeks and others, the Okipa of the Plains Mandan, or Powamu of the southwestern Hopi. Collective as they may be, these representations usually differentiate between religious choreographers, role impersonators, and community observers,

---

[8] See Peter Nabokov, "Red Herring or Real Turkey: The Race for an American Founding Rite," in *Folklore Interpreted: Essays in Honor of Alan Dundes*, edited by Regina Bendix and Rosemary Levy Zumwalt (New York: Garland Publishing, 1995).

[9] Paul Connerton, *How Societies Remember* (New York: Cambridge University Press, 1989), p. 71.

[10] While "rituals consist of 'doing,' myths are 'talk about doing,'" writes Karl W. Luckert; in Navajo tradition, "these are two sides of the same coin." "An Approach to Navajo Mythology" in *Native Religious Traditions* (Waterloo, Ontario: Wilfrid Laurier University Press, 1979), p. 117.

but in ways that nonetheless draw all of them into a moral community with common concerns and the binding force of a shared past.

The historical content found in American Indian rituals is often delivered through accompanying oratory, with a trained speaker using stylized cadences and perhaps sprinkling his address with archaic terminology – the unfamiliar words acquiring occult prestige through their aural evocations of a sacralized past. Official Cherokee orators chose their national Green Corn ceremony for the annual recitation of how the tribe "came from the upper part of the Ohio, where they erected mounds on Grave Creek, and that they removed hither [to east Tennessee] from the country where Monticello is situated."[11] Among the Mescalero Apache of south central New Mexico, the ritual opportunity for their self-history lesson, according to Claire R. Farrer, is the annual girls' puberty ceremony, also known as *Na in es*, or the "Sunrise Dance." Presiding male "holy men," or singers, "memorize long stories of the people, their travels, and accounts of tribal interactions from the beginning to the present." These narratives are recited during the ritual so that, in Farrer's words, "The Ceremony is thus a reenactment of events from the beginning of cosmological time and a recitation of ethnohistory."[12] For the Osage of northern Oklahoma, however, installations chiefly became a major opportunity for remembering the past. Through their allegorical references and symbolic actions, the entire arc of tribal history, from cosmic origins to clan chronologies, focused upon the present task of adding a new chapter, a new officeholder, to this sequential heritage.[13]

But it would be hard to find a grander blend of worship, multimedia, mythology, sacred history, and compulsory participation – what

[11] J. Haywood, *Natural and Aboriginal History of Tennessee* (Nashville: Printed by George Wilson, 1823), pp. 224–237.

[12] Claire R. Farrer, "Singing for Life: The Mescalero Apache Girls' Puberty Ceremony," in *Southwestern Indian Ritual Drama*, edited by Charlotte J. Frisbie (Prospect Heights, Ill.: Waveland Press, 1989), p. 126.

[13] Described in Carter Revard's "History, Myth, and Identity Among Osages and Other Peoples," in his *Family Matters, Tribal Affairs* (Tucson: University of Arizona Press, 1998), pp. 126–141, but based upon Francis La Flesche, *The Osage Tribe: Rite of the Chiefs; Sayings of the Ancient Men*, Smithsonian Institution, Bureau of American Ethnology, Annual Report N. 36 (Washington, D.C.: U.S.Government Printing Office, 1921).

performance scholar Richard Shechner classifies as "Performances of Great Magnitude" – than the fourteen-day Shalako Ceremony of the Zuni Indians of New Mexico, which officially ends the Zuni year every late November or early December. In venues that tie together unseen sacred springs, lakes, mountains, and a distant haven for spirits of the dead with these historical, snow-swept village streets, plazas, back alleys, a sacred race course, and seven house interiors colorfully appointed to house all-night performances – an orchestration of public enactments, lengthy prayers, colorful dances, and myth recitations contributes to the tribe's continuing health and prosperity and the well-being of their architecture, livestock, and cornfields.

In this reunion between Zunis and their personified symbols during this "coming of the gods" festival, key personages from the tribe's sacred past come to life. The festival culminates with the twilight arrival of six ten-foot-tall "messenger spirits" who escort a "council" of deities for their all-night sojourn in the village. Roaming through the decorated houses are other teams of other characters from Zuni mythic history, "mudhead" clowns, animal dancers, and impersonated (and lampooned) members of neighboring tribes such as Comanches and Navajos. Yet Shalako is only the pinnacle of the Zuni year's ritual round, as critic Edmund Wilson wrote after witnessing the ceremony in 1947 and realizing how it drew participants into a fairly nonstop renewal of their religious, social, and historical identity:

> The ceremonies are partly in the nature of the enactment of a national myth, and they present a sort of sacred drama whose cycle runs through the entire year. The legends show a good deal of art, and the cast is so enormous that a very considerable portion of the little town of twenty-six hundred has, at one time or another, a chance to play some role.[14]

Although categorizing religious expressions is an inexact exercise, in contrast to the primordial re-creations of Shalako, the backdrop for a second category of ritual dramas to which the Crow Tobacco Society belongs is a world already created, human beings already socialized, but perhaps trying to set down roots in unfamiliar terrain and/or threatened

---

[14] Edmund Wilson, *Red, Black, Blond and Olive* (London: W. H. Allen & Co., 1956), p. 3.

with catastrophe or major transformations. Often dubbed a "culture hero," the supernatural protagonist of these mytho-historical dramas sometimes appears alone, sometimes as twins, and occasionally as a married pair. These more common "commemorative ceremonies" frequently *recharter* a geographically removed or politically reformulated constituency, often welding together multiple ethnic factions through dramatic recapitulations of what anthropologist Sherry Ortner would term their "key scenario" of self-re-creation.

Throughout the Great Plains, where Native in-migrants settled over hundreds of years, the historical and ideological dimensions of these "rebirth" dramas were summarized in "earth-claiming" rituals. Not long before whites penetrated the plains, as mentioned in chapter 5 the agricultural Hidatsa, the Crows' parent tribe (in the non-Indian version) or fraternal stock (in the Crow version), appear to have been in the midst of consolidating a number of site-specific vision-quest accounts into one "earth-claiming" ceremony whose topographical referents provided a connect-the-dots perimeter for an emergent holy land.[15]

A similar narrative of divine territory-claiming scripts a major ceremony of the archenemies of both Hidatsas and Crows, the peripatetic Algonquian-speaking Tsistsistas (Cheyenne). When they first showed up in the tall grasses of the Dakotas, these proto-Cheyennes "were confused, and they were starving because animals were withheld from them." Their helplessness caused Thunder Spirit and Old Woman, "keepers of the animal spirits," to favor a shaman-prophet, his sidekick, and a female buffalo spirit turned into a woman. The three were guided inside a sacred mountain named *Nowah'wus*, today's Bear Butte on the northeastern rim of South Dakota's Black Hills. Inside this mountain they sealed what might be called a "covenant of kinship" between the Cheyenne and the animals they hunted, which would be regularly dramatized in their oldest religious pageant, the Massaum. For the emergent Cheyenne, this sacramental experience provided them with a new "world center" (Bear Butte, to which they still return for pilgrimages and vision questing), their four sacred directions, a set of interrelated, (re)chartering narratives, and

---

[15] Alfred W. Bowers, *Hidatsa Social and Ceremonial Organization*, Smithsonian Institution, Bureau of American Ethnology, Bulletin 194 (Washington, D.C.: U.S. Government Printing Office, 1963), pp. 433–438.

a ceremonial mechanism for (re)claiming any contested territories under their guardianship.[16]

A clearer fusion of ahistorical and commemorative features may be found in the old Tohono O'odham (formerly Papago) tribal ceremony known as the Vikita, which was held in their western Arizona homeland every four years. Some say that the individual who fused older and recent elements into this ritual was a foreigner, possibly a Pueblo Indian, who appeared after the ancestors of the Tohono O'odham, those "who came from the east," had already driven out former occupants and founded their premier village of Gu-Achi.[17] The dance he instituted reenacted not only this original community's establishment, but also that of the four successive villages, as well as ensuring that the outlander's role would not be forgotten by making sure he was represented by a hereditary descendant who wore his forefather's distinctive turkey feather headdress. To ensure full community participation, and to mesh its linear-historical and cyclical-calendric references, like the American Thanksgiving the rite became equally important as a group supplication for rain and good harvests.[18]

One searches in vain for much historical reflection in the ritual practices of our third category: the new religious movements, whose visionary leaders and creeds of community transformation we have already heard about in earlier chapters. No wonder; the impatient agendas of these movements is to eclipse the historical crises out of which they erupt. Except for preached recitations of the conversion or transformative experiences of their pivotal prophet, which often function as modal narratives to be replicated by followers, these syncretic belief systems rarely look back. Scrutinizing these revitalizing eruptions from the perspective of a cultural anthropologist, Victor Turner detected how their

---

[16] Karl H. Schleiser, *The Wolves of Heaven: Cheyenne Shamanism, Ceremonies, and Prehistoric Origins* (Norman: University of Oklahoma Press, 1987), pp. 76–80.

[17] This theme of foreigners who revitalize old traditions or establish new ones is reminiscent of the Inka founding scenario explicated by anthropologist Gary Urton in his marvelous study *The History of a Myth: Pacariqtambo and the Origin of the Inkas* (Austin: University of Texas Press, 1990).

[18] Julian D. Hayden, "The Vikita Ceremony of the Papago," *Journal of the Southwest*, Special Issue: The Vikita Ceremony of the Papago, edited By Joseph C. Wilder, 29(3) (Autumn 1987).

processual profile resembled the one he had observed during African initiation rituals.

Building upon the work of earlier scholars, Turner clarified a three-stage process to these rituals, whereby the young underwent a *separation* from the general population with its social structure; then they experienced a betwixt-and-between or *liminal* state, a time of antistructure, when they were freed from the burdens of status, property, and community identity; and lastly a process of *reincorporation*, when they rejoined their community, but with new roles as full-fledged adults. In the emergence of world or historical religions, especially those characterized as "founder faiths" because of their establishment by named prophets, Turner saw a reflection of this trajectory. But after their break from the steady state, these religious innovations did not return to the fold of their preexisting religious system. Instead, their creative *liminal* phase became institutionalized as a "permanent condition." In his review of millenarian religious movements among oppressed peoples like the American Indians, Turner then noticed how "such movements occur during phases of history that are in many respects 'homologous' to the liminal periods of important rituals in stable and repetitive societies, when major groups or social categories are passing from one cultural state to another."[19] This is why, Turner went on, "in so many of these movements much of their mythology and symbolism is borrowed from those traditional *rites de passage*, either in the cultures in which they originate or in the cultures with which they are in dramatic contact."

Whether Indian rituals are historical productions or incorporate history are questions that often strike sparks. Some religious traditions freely acknowledge the semilegendary circumstances of their origins, as with the Vatika ceremony of the Tohono O'odham of Arizona. More commonly, however, Native adherents and some empathetic scholars resent any suggestion that these religious practices are anything but primordial, or maintain that they are too old or spritually profound to be keyed into the mundane, contigent events of their times. But their opponents point out that given the ravages of Euro-American conquest, Native land loss, and depopulation, together with the consequent withering

---

[19] Victor Turner, *The Ritual Process: Structure and Anti-Structure* (Ithaca, N.Y.: Cornell University Press, 1969), p. 112.

of older rites associated with outmoded subsistence bases, rituals like the Midewiwin of the Great Lakes,[20] the Big House Ceremony of the Delaware,[21] the Beautyway of the Navajo,[22] or even the Busk of the Southeast[23] were more likely – like the Iroquois Longhouse Religion, the Plains Ghost Dance, or the pan-Indian Native American Church – syncretic or nativistic religious movements that evolved or were refurbished, in part, as defensive mechanisms to resist absorption by foreign ethnic or cultural forces. In these debates, the histories that swirl around these rites have themselves become volatile symbols in deeper arguments over whether any Indian group's identity is rooted in its culture's deeply psychological, almost genetic predisposition (the "primordialist" argument) or is the result of consolidated communities attempting to maximize and protect their self-intersets against those of adjoining groups (the "instrumentalist" approach).[24]

A fourth category of Indian symbolic performances that comment upon history, the masquerade, either retells it to suit ideological purposes or makes fun of its detrimental consequences. In the music, portrayals, costumes, and choreography of the southwestern Matachines Dance, which is a featured Christmas offering among a number of Rio Grande Pueblo Indian villages as well as well as in neighboring Hispanic hamlets, the performance's Old World origins are inescapable. Lines of mitre-wearing

[20] Harold Hickerson, "Notes on the Post-Contact Origin of the Midewiwin," *Ethnohistory* (9), pp. 404–423. Some Indian spokesmen counter Hickerson's argument by pointing to Midewiwin-associated artifacts which turned up in a precontact burial site in Ontario; see Minnie Two Shoes, "Oral History Confirmed by 'Modern Science,' " *News From Indian Country*, Hayward, WI, 9(24) (December 1995), pp. 1, 5.
[21] Anthony F. C. Wallace, "New Religions among the Delaware Indians, 1600–1900," *Southwestern Journal of Anthropology* 12 (1956), pp. 1–21; and see the vigorous rejoinder by Jay Miller, "Old Religion among the Delawares: The Gamwing (Big House Rite)," *Ethnohistory* 44(1) (Winter 1997), pp. 113–133.
[22] David M. Brugge, *Navajo Pottery and Ethnohistory*, (Window Rock, Ariz.: Navajo Tribal Museum, 1963), pp. 22–27.
[23] Joel W. Martin, *Sacred Revolt: The Muskogees' Struggle for a New World* (Boston: Beacon Press, 1991).
[24] For a fuller discussion of the primordialist, instrumentalist, and constructivist streams of analysis of ethnic identity, see M. Crawford Young, "The Dialectics of Cultural Pluralism: Concept and Reality," in *The Rising Tide of Cultural Pluralism: The Nation-State at Bay*, edited by M. Crawford Young (Madison: University of Wisconsin Press, 1993), pp. 3–35.

male dancers skip to the polka-like melodies of scratchy violins and strummed guitars, and weave around a "monarch" and a little girl wearing her all-white communion attire. Franciscan missionaries may have taught the dance as a way to provide a folk dramatization for the battle between Christians and nonbelievers (Moors). Unlike its adaptation in Hispanic mountain hamlets of New Mexico, among the Pueblos it is better known as "Montezuma's dance," and scholar Sylvia Rodriguez argues that the Matachines provided Pueblo Indians with theatrical release for their sense of historical injustice, emphasizing "an oppositional contrast or juxtaposition between symbols of Indian religion and symbols of Christianity."[25] The Indians' version is also open-ended enough so that local references, casting choices, and moments of burlesque and mockery, allow each village to portray "the particulars of its history, ecology and modern character." Introducing such characters as the "Malinche," the Indian mistress of Cortez, allows the Pueblos a rare opportunity to reflect on the "illicit, bittersweet miscegenation" that remains one of the touchier aspects of the Hispanic–Pueblo heritage.

An often biting historical awareness peers out of masking performances among numerous tribes. When the Hopi kachina named *Yo-we* appears on Third Mesa during the midwinter Powamu ritual cycle, older Indians readily identify him as the killer of the priest at old Oraibi during the 1680 all-Pueblo Revolt, and their children internalize the sobering lesson behind the fact that the earring in his hand was torn from the ear of the priest's Indian mistress.[26] Among the Yup'ik people of Alaska, a dancer with a carved two-masted schooner on his mask recites the tale of a shaman who predicted the arrival – and disappearance – of the first white traders.[27]

Ethnic caricatures played a part in a masquerade that the North Carolina Cherokee staged after the first frost – so as not to harm the harvest. Known as the Booger Dance, it was particularly strong among the Big Cove band, who had evaded capture during the wholesale roundups

[25] Sylvia Rodriguez, *The Matachines Dance: Ritual Symbolism and Interethnic Relations in the Upper Rio Grande Valley* (Albuquerque: University of New Mexico Press, 1998), p. 145.

[26] Barton Wright, *Kachinas: A Hopi Artist's Documentary* (Flagstaff: Northland Press, 1973), p. 50.

[27] Ann Fienup-Riordan, editor, *Our Way of Making Prayer: Yup'ik Masks and the Stories They Tell* (Seattle: University of Washington Press, 1996), p. 111.

of tribal members prior to the government-enforced removals to Indian Territory of the 1830s. Teams of four to ten Boogers forced their way into private houses wearing carved masks, each bearing obscene names and representing "people away or across the water" with bald heads, facial hair, and phallic-like noses speaking ugly languages. Clumsily barging around the building, the intruders demanded "girls," then wanted to "fight," and finally danced boorishly around the room. Their hosts first tried to purify the unwelcome visitors, who were considered bearers of disease and other polluting powers, then to cajole them into departing. Grafted onto an old, complex masking tradition that exposed internal tensions between old and young generations, this added cultural critique reminded Cherokee youth (playing the parts of these Germans, French, Spanish, and other aliens – including other tribes) how these foreigners' bad manners, distasteful looks, and grating voices threatened their isolated mountain enclaves.[28]

In their clowning traditions the Pueblos "neutralize history," according to the late Alfonso Ortiz, drawing contrasts between themselves and the rest of the world and "anchoring the historical events onto symbolic vehicles of expression that are traditional and that, thereby, lock those events comfortably onto their own cultural landscape." As he summarizes Pueblo clowning events:

> They burlesque not only the government agents, Protestant missionaries, and anthropologists who have bedeviled them in modern times, but the Spaniards and their priests who beset upon them in earlier times as well. In the *Sandaro* of the Rio Grande Keresans and other ceremonies, the Pueblos depict the original coming of the Spaniards in extremely humorous, but also extremely instructive, ways. For example, in Jemez Pueblo each year on November 12, the appearance of a clown in black face wearing a long coat representing Esteban, the

---

[28] While Frank G. Speck and Leonard Bloom (in collaboration with Will West Long), in *Cherokee Dance and Drama* (Berkeley: University of California Press, 1951), stressed the performance as a response to European impact, the richer contextual treatment by Raymond D. Fogelson and Amelia R. Bell, "Cherokee Booger Mask Tradition," in *The Power of Symbols: Masks and Masquerade in the Americas*, edited by N. Ross Crumrine and Marjorie Halpin (Vancouver: University of British Columbia Press, 1983), pp. 48–69, added its older roles in eastern masking traditions and mediating internal Cherokee social tensions.

first black to enter Pueblo country in 1537, electrifies those onlookers who know what is going on.[29]

Like comedians everywhere, these satirists exploit the topical. During the heyday of America's Apollo space program, for example, Hopi clowns had a field day. At Hotevilla village on Third Mesa, onlookers watched them stuff a mouse into a toy rocket and fire it over the adobe rooftops. Later in the day, with the skit almost forgotten, the rocket plummeted back from the sky into the plaza. Poking inside, the amazed clowns recovered the mouse alive plus a lump of green cheese – evoking a Hopi narrative of a gourd used as a vehicle to go to the moon. On another feast day, visitors heard a strange sirenlike sound. They ducked as metallic discs sailed over their heads and a group of green (painted) men armored in silver (aluminum foil) entered the plaza. But the aliens seemed confused, babbling in disagreement about who their leader was. Apparently a tribal politico had been making a public fuss about flying saucers, a slavish endorsement of white fads that deserved this classic reproach.[30]

To offset the cultural and historical commitments that were internalized throughout all these rituals, whether somber or satiric, extremist bureaucrats fought fire with fire. In 1916, when U.S. Interior Secretary Franklin K. Lane traveled to Yankton Sioux country, he instituted a script for a counterritual that substituted a ludicrously literal subtext, based upon evolutionary history, for the Indians' sacred, or even diffusionist, history. Lane's ceremony had the Yankton who "wanted" to become a citizen publicly shoot one "last arrow" into the sky. Then, addressed by his new "white" name, the applicant dropped his bow and grabbed a plow by the handle. Men were handed new money wallets (sewing kits and purses for the Yankton women), a small American flag, and a citizen's badge so that "the Indian must give his hands, head, and heart to the doing of all that will make him a true American citizen."[31]

[29] Alfonso Ortiz, "The Dynamics of Pueblo Cultural Survival," in *North American Indian Anthropology: Essays on Society and Culture*, edited by Raymond J. Demallie and Alfonso Ortiz (Norman: University of Oklahoma Press, 1994), p. 303.
[30] Barton Wright, *Clowns of the Hopi: Tradition Keepers and Delight Makers* (Flagstaff: Northland Publishing, 1994), pp. 29–30, 47.
[31] "A Ritual of Citizenship," *The Outlook*, May 24, 1916, pp. 161–162.

My fifth and final category of ritual-as-history concerns self-conscious rejoinders by contemporary Indians to such campaigns to transform themselves, or to "let the past be the past," to "get over it," to abandon their "passive resistance," and to capitulate to assimilation and the sway of non-Indians.[32] To anyone familiar with national statistics related to Indian life expectancy, poverty, youth suicide, alcoholism, and family problems, the differences between these modern Indian symbolic enactments and the earlier revitalization movements already touched upon only appears to be the comparable intensity of physical threat, social desperation, and psychological disorientation that propelled both into being.

Categorized by anthropologist Victor Turner as "public rituals," these modern representations have been revised, inspired by, or patched together out of earlier rituals – often their explicit historical content – and partly modeled after non-Native commemmorative practices.[33] Other external influences include public relations consciousness and popular healing therapies. Some have been inspired by institutional responses to the disorienting social and psychological aftereffects of racism, oppression, and genocide suffered by other minorities, and enfold a range of such themes as reconciliation, repatriation, recuperation and the reversal of historical injustices. Inspired by Jewish Holocaust and African-American slavery discourses, over the last twenty years the concept of "historical trauma" has gained particular currency in American Indian mental health literature.[34] Characterized as "incomplete mourning" for

---

[32] The symbiotic relationship between rituals and history is by no means limited to Indians, as revealed by Douglas C. Comer's *Ritual Ground: Bent's Old Fort, World Formation, and the Annexation of the Southwest* (Berkeley: University of California Press, 1996), in which a U.S. Park Service archaeologist interprets an old trading fort in eastern Colorado as a site for continuous history-creating rituals, from intercultural trade and alliance-making endeavors to today's recastings of the past by history buffs.

[33] As Ronald L. Grimes says of the bipolar (conservative–innovative, exclusive–inclusive) nature of such collective representations, "Public ritual is distinguished by its interstitial position on the threshold between open and closed groups – by its aim to tend the gate which swings in towards those who are ritual initiators and outward towards ritual strangers" ("The Lifeblood of Public Ritual: Fiestas and Public Exploration Projects" in *Celebrations: Studies in Festivity and Ritual*, edited by Victor Turner (Washington, D.C.: Smithsonian Institution Press, 1982), p. 272).

[34] Bonnie Duran, Eduardo Duran, and Maria Yellow Horse Brave Heart, "Native Americans and the Trauma of History," in *Studying Native America: Problems and*

past persecutions, population loss, and survivor guilt, an increasing number of Indian therapists working within what the scholar Robert K. Thomas calls their own "internal colonies" believe that without community healing rituals this syndrome of "acculturation stress" and intergenerational dysfunctionalism will continue.

In their own symbolic ways, Indians have also been turning back the clock in order to restore and recover from their histories. Among the many Indian "dramatized shrines" are Navajo reenactments of their "long walk" of 1864, Crow portrayals of their version of Custer's fight at Little Bighorn in June 1876,[35] and Sisseton Dakota's Gathering of Kinship to honor their ancestral kinfolk who participated in the Birch Coulee fight of August 1862 that triggered the Dakota War of 1862. According to Lakota Indian people, for instance, it was their traditional death wake, known as *washigila*, which the Indians reglossed as "wiping the tears," that provided a prototype for their Bigfoot Memorial Ride (*Si Tanka Wokiksuye*) that was synchronized to climax on the centennial anniversary of the infamous killings at Wounded Knee Creek.

Prospects, edited by Russell Thornton (Madison: University of Wisconsin Press, 1998), pp. 60–76.

[35] Debra Ann Bucholtz provides a rich account of Custer Battle commemorations in her dissertation, "The Battle of the Little Bighorn: A Study in Culture, History and the Construction of Identity" (Department of Anthropology, University of Minnesota, 2000). The celebrated encounter produced three recent dramatizations: one, staged and advertised by Hardin, Montana, since 1987, is a Chamber of Commerce version honoring primarily the doomed bravery of Custer's command. Second is a more diplomatic tableau begun in spring 1993, a multiday observance on the U.S. national park battlefield site, with Indian representatives and Seventh Cavalry reenactors sharing equal space and time. Indians from different tribes give speeches about their historical roles and share meals and songs, all under the rhetorical aegis of "peace through unity." Third is the hell-bent-for-leather version enacted since 1991 at Medicine Tail Coulee by mounted Crows on their own land, where Custer's troops approached the Little Bighorn, a folksy, partisan version that stresses Native retaliation for the loss of buffalo and the massacre of Black Kettle's village on the Washita in 1868 (see "Crow Agency's Real Birds Give Alternate View of History," *Bighorn County News*, June 23, 1993, p. 1). A fourth homage was proposed by an Indian entrant in the open competition for an Indian memorial at Little Bighorn: voluntary destruction of the "monstrous symbol of white domination that is Mount Rushmore" in South Dakota, with its rubble turned into building material for the new Custer battle memorial (*For background see* Douglas C. McChristian, "Burying the Hatchet: Semi-Centennial of the Battle of the Little Bighorn," *Montana: The magazine of Western History* 46(2) [1996], pp. 50–65).

For four years prior to December 15, 1990, the Big Foot Riders undertook the 322-mile trek from Cheyenne River to Pine Ridge, South Dakota. Named for *Si Tanka*, or Big Foot, the leader of the contingent of Ghost Dancers who were mercilessly killed in midwinter 1891, the horsemen were accompanied by runners as well. The rhetoric that emerged from this ritual-in-the-making honored the riders' sacrifices (much as relatives commiserate with the suffering pledgers in modern Sun Dances), their completion of proper mourning that had never occurred, and everyone's recommitment to today's rendition of traditional Lakota values. On this fifth and final year, a group of medicine men, joined by Curtis Kills Ree, whose vision was said to inspire the event, rode for two weeks at freezing temperatures to reach the old Wounded Knee battle site almost a hundred years after the original slaughter. But in the words of Lakota attorney Mario Gonzales, the ride became "a story in itself, a reminder that indigenous people all over the world, in protecting themselves and their histories, are protecting something that is precious to all human kind, the right to possess memory and imagination."[36]

For the most part, these representations were for Indian country consumption, to salve their historical wounds and ponder their futures. But in a society at large whose death cult has recently flowered with street-corner shrines for celebrity deaths and victims of neighborhood violence and automobile accidents, it is no surprise that American Indians should also switch from confrontation to memorial as a way to remind the surrounding society of historical sufferings and outstanding debts that they incurred for the rest of us.

My most memorable encounter with a similarly homegrown, hybrid production came in New Mexico in 1979, after I learned that the Eastern and Western Pueblo leaders were pondering the upcoming tricentennial anniversary of their all-Pueblo Revolt of 1680. Led by a charismatic

---

[36] Mario Gonzales and Elizabeth Cook-Lynn, *The Politics of Hallowed Ground: Wounded Knee and the Struggle for Indian Sovereignty* (Urbana: University of Illinois Press, 1999), p. 110, and see Charmaine White Carver "Wounded Knee: Mending The Sacred Hoop'" (*Native Peoples* [Spring 1990], pp. 9–16), as well as the documentary *Wiping the Tears of Seven Generations*, directed by Gary Rhine and Fidel Moreno (San Francisco: Gary Rhine/Kifaru Productions, 1992).

organizer from San Juan Pueblo named Popé, that year their coordinated might drove Spanish colonizers out of the Southwest. To celebrate this most successful multitribal war for independence in Native American history, the Indian organizers were probably inspired, in part, by the nation's recent bicentennial.

Their plan could also be interpreted as a belated rejoinder to persistent expressions of Hispanic triumphalism. For rural Spanish-speaking villagers, the Matachines Dance performance drew parallels between the Spanish conquests of both old and New Mexico; for urban Hispanics, however, the summertime Santa Fe Fiesta recalled the authority of Hispanic civic, ethnic, and religious symbols. And while the folk script of the Matachines lent its Indian performers opportunities for hidden messages of rebellion and critique, no such undermining subtleties were permitted in the enactments trotted out during the Fiesta. Since 1835, the Fiesta annually reasserted Hispanic reconquest of the region after the 1680 rebellion; despite Santa Fe's obvious demographic and economic takeover by Anglo-Americans, the Fiesta conveyed to residents and tourists alike that the town's original charter as a colonial Catholic capital remained its soul. Where Indians were portrayed during the Fiesta, it was as either bloodthirsty rebels or docile converts, and until Native complaints about these stereotypes grew too loud to be ignored, they were impersonated by non-Indians wearing school pagaent caricatures of old Indian attire.[37]

But now the Pueblo Indian communities of New Mexico and Arizona came up with an ingenious way to resurrect their three-hundred year-old victory and retrieve, if only inferentially and temporarily, their old landscape. They staged a 375-mile run that roughly replicated the routes taken by foot couriers who, back in 1680, synchronized simultaneous uprisings in dozens of far-flung pueblos. These messengers secretly deposited knotted yucca fiber strings in pueblos up and down the Rio Grande, and over to the Painted Desert, with instructions that elders untie a knot each day until the strings were clear. On that Native D-day, separated from each other by hundreds of miles, Pueblo Indians rose up to kill and evict priests and settlers, and demolish chapels.

[37] Ronald L. Grimes, *Symbol and Conquest: Public Ritual and Drama in Santa Fe* (Albuquerque: University of New Mexico Press, 1976).

In the pre-dawn hours of August 5, 1980, the reenacting runners left Taos Pueblo in northern New Mexico, ending up six days later on the Hopi's Second Mesa in Arizona. To leaders in nearly twenty villages up and down the Rio Grande and farther west, these couriers, wearing gym shorts and track shoes, handed leather pouches containing symbolic knotted thongs. Each pouch also held a printed swatch of buckskin that praised, in English, their long-ago military success. No sooner were they a little south of Taos, however, than the Hopi boys were handed an additional assignment: to carry the paramount Pueblo religious icon – an ear of blue corn – in tandem with the political symbol of the pouch. As nightly prayer sessions with priests intensified over the days, it was clear that what had begun as marking a moment in time was verging toward a ritual-in-motion.

Furthermore, the reenactment brought an old Hopi story to light. Right after the original revolt, claimed one revived narrative from Shipaulovi Village, a pregnant woman from the Bear Clan was taken away to distance herself and her unborn child from polluting violence and bloodletting. Just as the birth of this baby symbolized the rebirth of the Bear Clan and the Hopi as a people, this tricentennial would function as a renewal ceremony for Hopi self-determination. When the runners finally ascended to the Hopi Cultural Center perched on the summit of Second Mesa, tribal elders were waiting. First, the pouch's message was translated into the Hopi tongue. Then the ear of blue corn was turned over to the oldest clan mother, to be distributed, in turn, among the tribe's Soyal or New Year Society membership, for crumbling into separate kernels and planting in their cornfields.

Over the entire run, an ill-fitting *modus celebrendi* had been half-transformed into a symbolic manipulation more compatible with older ways by which Hopis, and other Indian peoples, have often tended to turn the noble subject and noun of "history" into a more down-to-earth, active verb.[38]

---

[38] The Tricentennial Run of 1980 is the subject of my book *Indian Running* (Santa Fe: Ancient City Press, 1995).

————◄○►————

EIGHT

Old Stories, New Ways

Writing, Power, and Indian Histories

God made it [the writing], but it came down to our earth. I liken this to what has happened in the religions we have now. In the center of the earth, when it first began, when the earth was first made, there was absolutely nothing on this world. There was no written language. So it was in 1904 that I became aware of the writing; it was then that I heard about it from God.[1]

Silas John, Western Apache

For over a decade, I've been interviewing an elderly man from Acoma Pueblo in western New Mexico whose father recited his people's traditional origin myth to Smithsonian Institution scholars in Washington, D.C., in 1928.[2] Not long ago, my friend showed me two of his father's most precious possessions – a grandfather clock and a Bible embossed with his name: Edward Proctor Hunt. The clock represented Mr. Hunt's shift of allegiance from a social milieu that timed its ceremonies by the sun to one governed by shorter increments of seconds, minutes, and hours. Hunt first learned to wake up and work by the clock as a boy at the Menaul Indian School, a boarding school in Albuquerque, New Mexico. One day school officials gave him a donated coat in whose

[1] Keith H. Basso, "Western Apache Writing Systems," in *Western Apache Language and Culture: Essays in Linguistic Anthropology* (Tucson: University of Arizona Press, 1990), p. 29.
[2] Matthew W. Stirling. *Origin Myth of Acoma and Other Records*, Bureau of American Ethnology, Bulletin 135 (Washington, D.C.: U.S. Government Printing Office, 1942).

pocket was a Bible with a written note from a Cleveland physician that said that whoever received this garment could take the name in the book – Edward Proctor Hunt.

That Bible represented Hunt's conversion to Christianity. As a former initiate in the Kachina medicine men's and sacred clown societies, Hunt knew Acoma society from the inside and remained proud of his origins. When he first returned from boarding school to his mesa-top village, Hunt hid his Bible and kept secret his Protestant allegiance while participating in tribal rituals. A requirement of his induction as a sacred clown, in fact, was memorization of the origin myth that he gave the Smithsonian. Deep in Hunt's heart, however, he had become a Christian for life, a follower of the Book, and, thanks to his apprenticeship at the Cubero trading post run by the famous Jewish trader Solomon Bibo, a capitalist as well.

Even though Hunt's progressive and entrepreneurial disposition eventually forced his rupture with Acoma, all his life he retained deep respect for his tribal roots, offering his children and grandchildren to the sun upon their birth, conferring Keresan names on them, telling tribal stories (with his sons translating) to Boy Scouts and audiences around the world, and, somewhat surreptitiously, sharing his culture with South-western Indian investigators like Elsie Clews Parsons, Charles Lummis, John Peabody Harrington, Edward S. Curtis, and Leslie White. After the U.S. Bureau of Ethnology finally published Hunt's mythic history of Acoma, few Indian myths were as thoroughly mined by scholars, anthologizers, and historians seeking an authentic presentation of the conservative Pueblo Indian world view.

At the outset of Hunt's version, two sisters are born underground and ascend to the earth's surface. A spirit gives them baskets containing items with which they will animate and benefit the world. In the basket of Iatiku, who will become the "mother of all Indians" and whose name means "Bringing to Life," are wild seeds and fetishes of wild animals.

But her sister is named Nautsiti, or "more of everything in the basket"; in other Keresan origin stories, she is known as "the father of white people." Compared with her sister, Hunt characterized Nautsiti as lighter-skinned, quicker-minded, selfish, a hoarder, ambitious, solitary, and susceptible to temptation by a serpent. Into her basket go domes-ticated animals, and the wheat and vegetable seeds that Iatiku feels are wrong for her children. Nor does Iatiku care for the "many metals" also found in her sister's basket. When Nautsiti digs deeper into her magical basket, she also turns up "something written (*ti'thyatra'ni*)," and shortly afterward she departs toward the east.

Until his death in 1948, as Hunt maintained the complex relationship toward his origins that is reflected in what we might presume to be his embellishments of his people's myth, that Bible and clock rarely left his side. When Hunt told the anthropologist Leslie White of his conversion to Christianity, he described a dream in which God was dressed like a "successful American Indian businessman." The deity explained to Hunt that while the traditional Pueblo "prayer stick" remained the Indians' "key to paradise," the Bible guaranteed Euro-Americans their entry into heaven.

The personal story behind Hunt's mythic history explains one way that the present and the past become intwined and mythologized so as to acculturate new phenomena by "naturalizing" them into usable symbols.[3] Despite his own conversion to Nautsiti's alien spirits of capitalism and the Protestant work ethic, Hunt kept his narrative's authority firmly in the hands of its nativist heroine, the sister named Iatiku. In a larger sense, the story Hunt recited in Washington and his own biography also reiterate the significance of literate discourse as a marker of non-Indian affiliation.[4]

Over the centuries, Indians have plumbed the contrasts between orality and literacy as a way of meditating upon and mediating between their separate worlds.[5] For many of them, it became their defining difference.

---

[3] Carobeth Laird, *Mirror and Pattern: George Laird's World of Chemehuevi Mythology* (Banning, Calif.: Malki Museum Press, 1984), p. 17.

[4] See Peter Nabokov, "A Life Behind a Myth: The Passages of Edward Proctor Hunt," in *American Indians as Anthropologists*, edited by Douglas R. Parks and Raymond J. DeMallie (Lincoln: University of Nebraska Press, forthcoming), and for more on "culture brokers" like Hunt, see *Between Indian and White Worlds: The Cultural Broker*, edited by Margaret Connell Szasz (Norman: University of Oklahoma Press, 1994).

[5] In this overview, my thoughts about this oral–literate divide are necessarily skin deep. Would that more American Indian cultural historians comparatively tested Jack Goody's long-term archaeology of the intermediate forms – such as admistrative lists,

Through the sorts of retrospective formulations to be discussed in the final chapter, the generative symbols of writing and the Book became such diagnostics for the invasive society, and of its ominous, depersonalized efficiency, as to insinuate themselves into their most ahistorical genres.[6]

First and foremost, "the Book" frequently meant the Good Book. And perhaps the greater individuality enjoyed within other American Indian communities beyond Acoma Pueblo allowed their storytellers to feel freer than Hunt about interlarding their traditions with biblical references and influences.[7] Among the Okanagan of the northern Plateau, for instance, the narrator Harry Robinson perceived the discourse about print, books, and memorization as the distinguishing factor between the two cultures, but simultaneously he constructed his mythic premises around the white man's foundational mytho-historical text. One of his

---

genealogies, classificatory systems, calendric and event-focused chronicles, and religious formulae – between orality and literacy (most recently explored in *The Power of the Written Tradition* [Washington, D.C.: Smithsonian Institution Press, 2000]) and those of Goody's challengers, such as R. W. Niezen ("Hot Literacy in Cold Societies: A Comparative Study of the Sacred Value of Writing," *Comparative Studies in Society and History*, V. 33(2), [1991], pp. 225–254). Rodney Frey's comments, in his *Stories that Make The World: Oral Literature of the Indian peoples of the Inland Northwest* (Norman: University of Oklahoma Press, 1995, pp. 141–158), which contrast the transitory, event-centered, involuntary, and unifying aspects of orality with the permanent, objectifying, voluntary, and isolating properties of literacy, are a start. Only Frey omits one casualty of transferring the spoken to the written: culturally specific deployments of *silence*, as Keith H. Basso illuminates in " 'To Give Up On Words': Silence in Western Apache Culture," *Western Apache Language and Culture: Essays in Linguistic Anthropology* (Tucson: University of Arizona Press, 1990), Chapter 5.

6 Perhaps because they encountered literacy so early, Southeastern tribes seem especially sensitive to its cultural ramifications, as evidenced by origin stories where it functions as a key marker in prophecies of the future, from the Creek (Adam Hodgson, *Remarks During a Journey Through North America* [New York: Samuel Whiting, 1823], p. 278), the Yuchi (David I. Bushnell, "Myths of the Louisiana Choctaw," *American Anthropologist* 12 [1910], pp. 526–535), and the Cherokee (Clemens de Baillou, "A Contribution to the Mythology and Conceptual World of the Cherokee Indians," *Ethnohistory* 8 [1961], p. 101), among others.

7 On the other hand, in tense times, when one's cultural affiliations were closely monitored from all sides, an Indian's public adoption of literacy and the Bible could put him in harm's way, as Jill Lepore describes in "Dead Men Tell No Tales: John Sassamon and the Fatal Consequences of Literacy," *American Quarterly* 46(4) (December 1994), pp. 479–512.

tales has God, a "long long time ago before Christ," instilling "power" in Indian brains and hearts, while keeping it external on paper for whites. His God, or "Big Chief," not Coyote, is the world's arranger; whatever He "thinks" suddenly happens. And what He bestows upon the first people is a paper telling them how to live. For Robinson, who was as intimately familiar as Edward Hunt with the Old Testament, the prior Indian occupation of the New World was also attributed to decisions by the two peoples' common ancestors, Adam, Eve, and Noah.[8]

Indians were not above questioning the appropriateness of these texts as supernatural authorities or selling points for the white man's communicative medium. For the early Great Lakes visitor J. G. Kohl, one Ojibwa man drew a fundamentalist's uncompromising comparison between his people's birchbark scrolls, in which their Supreme Being bestowed upon his Indian people pictographic histories of their migrations and their *midewiwin* ritual's secret teachings, as well as the dubious gift to them of the Bible, which, he declared, came straight from the Devil.[9] Somewhat more diplomatically, the Seneca leader Red Jacket initiated a logical interrogation concerning this particular text's claim of universal primacy: "We understand that your religion is written in a book," he told a missionary in 1805. "If it was intended for us as well as you, why has not the Great Spirit given to us, and not only to us, but why did he not give to our forefathers, the knowledge of that book, with the means of understanding it rightly?" Perhaps in a dig at print's weakness from the perspective of a society that put so much energy into reaching consensus through oral argument, Red Jacket also asked: if this text was so

---

[8] Harry Robinson, *Nature Power: In the Spirit of an Okanagan Storyteller* (Seattle: University of Washington Press, 1992), pp. 13–15. Ojibwas also "amalgamated Biblical and traditional characters of myth, for example, Noah and Nanabozho," according to Christopher Vecsey and John F. Fisher in "The Ojibwa Creation Myth: An Analysis of Its Structure and Content," *Temenos* 20 (1984), p. 88. For more on how Native Bible stories reveal practical circumstances of evangelical work among the Indians, theological dispositions of tribes before and during Euro-American contact, governing principles and relative adaptability of Indian myth systems, and, for our purposes especially, Indian imaginative responses to traumas of conquest, see folklorist Jarold Ramsey's "The Bible in Western Indian Mythology" in *Reading the Fire: The Traditional Indian Literatures of America* (Seattle: University of Washington Press, 1999), pp. 208–221.

[9] J. G. Kohl, *Kitchi-Gami. Wanderings Round Lake Superior*, translated by Lascelels Wraxell (London: Chapman and Hall, 1860), p. 72.

authoritative, "why do you white people differ so much about it? Why not all agree, as you can all read the book?"[10]

Moving from the Book to printed words in general, as Indians weighed the relative merits of spoken and written traditions, some of their verbal comparisons remained, paradoxically enough, rhetorically effective on the page. "I am very glad to demonstrate to you that we also have books," explained Waihusiwa, a Zuni storyteller, to Frank Hamilton Cushing, "only they are not books with marks in them, but words in our hearts, which have been placed there by our ancients long ago, even so long ago as when the world was new and young, like unripe fruit."[11] Then the Zunis wove this comparison into their song for Cushing's initiation into the Bow Society: "Once they made a white man into a Priest of the Bow / he was out there with other Bow Priests / he had black stripes on his body / the others said their prayers from their hearts / but he read his from a piece of paper."[12] When Indians invoked this body–mind opposition to suggest the moral superiority of memorization over archiving, they almost seemed to be savoring the image of pale-faced bookworms squirming through unfamiliar (and unwritten) terrain. "The Indian needs no writing," the Ogalalla Sioux Four Guns stated in 1891. "Words that are true sink deep into his heart where they remain. He never forgets them. On the other hand, if the white man loses his paper, he is helpless."[13]

In the mythic explanation of a Cherokee headman named Elk, books became indexed to Euro-American identity through a notably Old Testament-like domestic drama. An origin narrative he shared with a Moravian missionary in 1815 features a primordial couple with two

---

[10] This citation ("Indian Speeches Delivered by Farmer's Brother and Red Jacket, Two Seneca Chiefs," which was prepared in a pamphlet by James D. Bemis [Canadaigua, N.Y., 1809]) is also in a provocative essay by Sam Gill that addresses a number of themes in this chapter: see "Holy Book in Nonliterate Traditions" in *A Performance Approach to Religion* (Columbia: University of South Carolina Press, 1987), pp. 131–132.

[11] Frank Hamilton Cushing, *Zuni Folk Tales* (New York: Putnam, 1901), p. 92.

[12] Dennis Tedlock, "Verbal Art," in *Handbook of North American Indians*, V.1 (Washington: Smithsonian Institution Press, chap. 50, in press).

[13] Jerry D. Blanche, *Native American Reader: Stories, Speeches and Poems* (Juneau, Alaska: Denali Press, 1990), p. 85.

sons. When the father discovers that they intend to murder their mother – fearing she is a sorceress – he gives them a book "to learn how to act and behave." But one brother snatches the book for himself and goes to the "far side," whereupon the father creates a sea dividing them and their houses, separating forever, in scholar Frank J. Korom's words, "that which is familiar from the unknown other."[14]

Some Indians weighed in with more conciliatory contrasts, as when Luther Standing Bear asserted, "Our stories are our libraries."[15] Even when Native observations about literacy sounded benign, however, some degree of cultural critique often lurked within, some dig about the superiority of the oral, and its irreplaceable rhetorical and even ideological advantages. Here, for instance, a Navajo "singer" and practiced stargazer named Son of the Late Cane subtly conveys to the ethnographer Father Berard Haile his preferred, more kinetically communicated pedagogy:

> Whatever you commit to paper is not lost, and you get and remember your knowledge from that paper. What I know I had to learn with my middle finger. My brother was a singer like myself, and took great pains to teach me. On cloudless, moonless nights we used to spend the time in watching for the appearance of the various stars. He would then explain the constellation, its head, hands, feet, wings, fire, and the like, until sunrise, when we would snatch a few hours sleep. After that we would carry sand into the hogan, level it out and then trace the constellations with my finger. That continued until now I am able to trace them in the dark.[16]

Other Indian judgements were more pointed; as a Stony Indian told an interviewer:

> If you take all your books, lay them out under the sun, and let the snow and rain and insects work on them for a while, there will be

---

[14] Frank J. Korom, "Writing the Cherokee: An Ethnohistorical Inquiry into the Uses and Abuses of Literacy," an unpublished paper that condensed Elk's Cherokee narrative from Clemens de Baillou, "A Contribution to the Mythology and Conceptual World of the Cherokee Indians," *Ethnohistory* 8 (1961), p. 101.

[15] Quoted in Jay Miller, *Oral Literature*, D'Arcy McNickle Center for the History of the American Indian, The Newberry Library Occasional Papers in Curriculum Series, N. 13 (Chicago: The Newberry Library, 1992), p. 4.

[16] Father Berard Haile, *Starlore Among the Navajo* (Santa Fe: William Gannon, 1977), pp. 5–6.

nothing left. But the Great Spirit has provided you and me with an opportunity for study in nature's university, the forests, the rivers, the mountains, and the animals which include us.[17]

For anthropologist Diamond Jenness, a member of the Carrier tribe from western Canada clarified his people's view of this "university's" faculty: "The white man writes everything down in a book so that it might not be forgotten; but our ancestors married the animals, learned their ways, and passed on the knowledge from one generation to another."[18] For an old Inuit woman who talked with Danish ethnologist Knud Rasmussen, the reasons for preferring interactive verbal exchanges over those scribbled on paper were more ethical and pedagogical: "Our forefathers...did not understand how to hide words in strokes, like you do; they only told things by word of mouth, the people who lived before us; they told many things, and that is why we are not ignorant of these things, which we have heard repeated time after time."[19] Momentarily ignoring his own role as an author, Luther Standing Bear took pride in the ways his people's oral histories, "recorded some event of interest or importance, some happening that affected the lives of the people.... The seasons and the years were named for principal events that took place...a people enrich their minds who keep their history on the leaves of memory. Countless leaves in countless books have robbed a people of both history and memory."[20]

For the religious movements that rolled across Native America after first contact, the trinity of literacy, printing, and sacred text posed challenges and aroused ambivalence. Whatever Indian history was promulgated through their doctrines was less a view of any collective past than the chronicle of otherworldly experiences of personal salvation that had to

---

[17] John Walter Grant MacEwan, *Tatanga Mani, Walking Buffalo of the Stonies* (Edmonton, Alberta, M. G. Hurtig, Ltd., 1969), p. 60.
[18] Diamond Jenness, "The Carrier Indians of the Bulkey River," Bureau of American Ethnology, Bulletin 133 (Washington, D.C.: U.S. Government Printing Office, 1943), p. 540.
[19] Knud Rasmussen, *The People of the Polar North: A Record* (London: Kegan Paul, Trench, Trubner & Co., 1908), pp. 99–100.
[20] Luther Standing Bear, *Land of the Spotted Eagle* (New York: Houghton Mifflin 1933), p. 27.

be sufficiently persuasive to substitute for prior discourses and over-whelm written ones. To the degree that these movements envisioned societal rebirth, the testimonies that catalyzed them became replace-ment mythic charters. The turning-point experiences of visionaries like Handsome Lake of the Longhouse Religion, John Slocum of the Shaker Church, Tailfeather Woman of the Dream Drum Religion, and John Wilson of the Native American Church became gravity centers for a new historical discourse that marked the onset of ecstatic New Days.

Since the Bible, with its testimonies of prophets and miracles, most resembled the tribes' own supernatural mechanisms for turning history around, it also represented the stiffest competition: the Europeans' better funded and institutionalized messianic cult, known as Christianity, ver-sus theirs. Indian visionaries felt compelled to promote their alternatives to the communicative powers of writing that strangers could use silently between each other, and to the fetishistic powers of mass-produced Bibles that everyone could carry in their hands. To Smohalla, the influential Wanapum visionary from the Columbia Plateau, the white man's reli-gious texts represented the clearest dividing line between emulators of white society like Edward Proctor Hunt and followers of his Prophet Movement:

> Many Indians are trying to live like white men, but it will do them no good. They cut off their hair and wear white man's clothes, and some of them learn to sing out of a book.... No one has any respect for book Indians. Even the white men like me better and treat me better than they do the book Indians.[21]

For at least one anonymous member of the Native American Church, which spread across western North America in the late nineteenth cen-tury, printed words could never duplicate the educational rewards of submission to his ritual. "I wish to say that the Peyote is not a written history, or a book available as a reading matter for study by learning its principles," he insisted. "A person must actually use Peyote himself and really participate in the ceremony, for no microscope can reveal

[21] E. L. Huggins, "Smohalla, the Prophet of Priest Rapids," *Overland Monthly*, 2nd Ser. 17, no. 98 (January–June 1891), pp. 212–213.

the secret within."[22] This contrast between secondhand Bible teaching about the past and direct, person-to-person preaching and raw firsthand revelation instigated a crisis within the Shaker Religion, a religious movement from the Pacific Northwest associated with a Coast Salish Indian named John Slocum. Begun in 1881 with Slocum's near-death visionary experience, the church was plagued by an abiding debate between "progressives" who read the Bible as a source of inspiration and purists who believed that Slocum's message required those unmediated seizures by the divine that produced the faith's distinctive shaking or twitching motions. Said one traditionally oriented Shaker, "No, we do not believe in the Bible.... We all believe that John Slocum died and went to heaven, and was sent back to preach to the people. We all talk about that and believe it."[23]

Whether they openly admitted it or not, the majority of American Indian prophets who inspired revitalization movements were exposed to the Bible, literacy and Christian proselytizing early on. The Delaware visionary of 1762–1763, Neolin, peddled multiple copies of his buckskin chart of a saved soul's progress through this world, which he called "the Great Book of Writing," even though it communicated his vision through hieroglyphics that only he could decipher.[24] The leader of the syncretic Hudson Bay Cree religious movement of 1842–1843, Abishabis, printed hymns and texts about the Great Spirit using a phonetic writing system developed by a Christian priest and sewed them between hide covers.[25]

At the age of eighteen in Nevada, a northern Paiute named Jack Wilson (soon to gain renown as Wovoka, prophet of the Plains Indian Ghost Dance of 1890) joined daily prayers at a neighbor's Protestant home and attended Baptist temperance and evangelical camp meetings.

---

[22] Quoted in J. S. Slotkin, *The Peyote Religion: A Study in Indian–White Relations* (New York: Octagon Books, 1975), p. 114.

[23] H. G. Barnett, *Indian Shakers: A Messianic Cult of the Pacific Northwest* (Carbondale: Southern Illinois University Press, 1957), p. 145.

[24] Anthony F. C. Wallace, "New Religions among the Delaware Indians, 1600–1900," *Southwestern Journal of Anthropology* 12(1) (1956), pp. 1–21.

[25] Jennifer Brown, "The Track to Heaven: The Hudson Bay Cree Religious Movement of 1842–1843," in *The Native Imprint: The Contributions of First Peoples to Canada's Character*, edited by Olive Patricia Dickason, V. 2 (Athabasca, Alberta.: Athabasca University Educational Enterprises, 1996).

Scholar Michael Hittman believes the man surely noticed the deference paid to the Methodist "saddle-bag riders" who made the rounds of pious homesteads. Contemporaries may never have seen Wovoka kneel down to pray, but he certainly kept his ears and eyes open. Soon he was dunking followers in the Walker River following his own "miracles," claiming the power to save them from "hell fire," and word had him drawing down rain just like the Old Testament's Elijah.[26] Literacy also came to Wovoka's aid in New Testament style through the epistolary testimonies of boarding school–educated Indians, who had experienced his preachings and spread the word through their letters; Wovoka's own correspondence enabled those he never met to receive through the U.S. Postal Service their seer's trademark packets of sacred body paint.

Perceiving the inescapable powers of script, some Indian groups such as the Micmacs of Newfoundland, the Yaquis of the Southwest, and the Aleuts of Alaska also sought to appropriate them by coming up with their own syllabaries. For the most part, however, these indigenous symbol systems did not produce any upsurge in the recording of community histories. Rather than embracing print's promise of opening up communication and making information public and impersonal, it was often the magical, sacred, secretive, symbolic, and iconic aspects of letters that appealed to Indians.

The symbols for recording Cree Indian speech that Protestant missionaries introduced to Rupert House Natives of eastern Canada in the late nineteenth century were intended for religious observances. But local Indians seized upon the syllabary for private correspondence. And although its use has declined among younger Crees today, the distinctive lettering became a logo of tribal identity, proudly displayed on sweatshirts and sports team jackets.[27] The symbol system developed by the early-twentieth-century Western Apache shaman Silas John Edwards was put to more mystical use. Not a true syllabary, his semipictographic

---

[26] Michael Hittman, *Wovoka and the Ghost Dance* (Lincoln: University of Nebraska Press, 1990), pp. 59–61.

[27] Barbara Burnaby and Marguerite MacKenzie, "Reading and Writing in Rupert House," in *Native North American Interaction Patterns*, edited by Regna Darnell and Michael K. Foster (Ottawa: Canadian Museum of Civilization, National Museums of Canada, 1988).

system for recording sixty-two mystical prayers that came to him in a vision – whose content was marked by early exposure to Lutheran missionaries – perpetuated his syncretic version of Creation, his prescription for "the good life," and prayers for physical and psychological well-being.[28]

The most celebrated Indian writing system was devised by the Cherokee George Guess, popularly known as Sequoyah. And while many Cherokee documents were preserved in this national script, and the phonetic alphabet he invented in 1809 is credited with making his people literate enough to launch their own newspaper, the *Cherokee Phoenix and Indian Advocate*, in 1828, over time his characters were also put to more esoteric purposes.[29] Perhaps the preponderance of material preserved in Sequoyah's script, historian Theda Perdue points out, dealt with traditional religion. His syllabary was largely devoted to recording magical healing formulae of individual shamans who then hid their scribbled bits of paper in secret caches. According to Perdue, the folk wisdom that saw the syllabary coming to Sequoyah in a visionary way "enabled them to view literacy in the Cherokee language as a part of native knowledge, not as a repudiation of their own culture and a step towards 'civilization,' " as non-Indians have hailed it.[30]

Over the years, many Indians capitulated to an invasive world view of which print was a key symbol and applied various forms of methodological triage so that their traditions might live another day. Whereas in the 1880s a Navajo singer might tell the early ethnographer Alexander M. Stephen that "I have no book, we have nothing of writing, but in my memory are many things strange to the Americans,"[31] fifty years later,

---

[28] Keith Basso, "A Western Apache Writing System: The Symbols of Silas John," in *Western Apache Language and Culture: Essays in Linguistic Anthropology* (Tucson: University of Arizona Press, 1990).

[29] In "To Hear an Old Voice: Rediscovering Native Americans in American History," George Miles chides academic historians for ignoring the fact that "between 1772 and 1924 some two thousand Native American writers published in English more than sixty-seven hundred pieces of work, ranging from articles in local newspapers to lengthy academic studies" (*Under an Open Sky: Rethinking America's Western Past*, edited by William Cronon, George Miles, and Jay Gitlin [New York: W. W. Norton & Co., 1992], p. 66).

[30] Theda Perdue, "The Sequoyah Syllabary and Cultural Revitalization," in *Perspectives on the Southeast: Linguistics, Archaeology and Ethnohistory*, edited by Patricia B. Kwachka (Athens: University of Georgia Press, 1994), p. 125.

[31] A. M. Stephen, "Navajo Origin Legend," *Journal of American Folklore* 43 (1930), p. 88.

when Aileen O. Brien was collecting Navajo sand painting designs, a chanter named Sandoval told her, "In time to come my people will have forgotten their early way of life unless they learn it from white men's books. So you must write it all down that I will tell you."[32] More recently, this sentiment was echoed by the Navajo educator John Dick, but likewise addressed specifically to his own youngsters: "From now into the future we should remember our prayers, stories, art and cere-monies...that is why we prepare books like this for you to read."[33] A more optimistic perspective on this bicultural compatibility comes from Native writer Felipe S. Molina and coauthor Larry Evers, who elected to publish the sacred Yaqui deer songs and describe their cultural contexts:

> There is a view that print spells the end of oral traditions, that stories and songs are fast-vanishing relics performed only for anthropologists and folklorists, that in order for them to survive they must be captured between the covers of books. Our experience suggests that Yaqui deer songs and the traditions which surround them are very much alive and that more than sixty years of recording and printing versions of them has complemented and reinforced more traditional oral modes of continuance, rather than contributing to their disappearance.[34]

This did not mean that the Book as a ceremonial object lost all of its talismanic potency. Like Torahs or Korans, for individuals like Edward Proctor Hunt who were introduced to literacy through Chris-tianity, the Bible's presence as what historian of religions Sam Gill has termed a "performative object" held firm. In stark contrast to its rejec-tion by the Wanapum prophet Smoholla, for instance, to the followers of John Solcum and his neo-Christian Shaker movement it joined clang-ing hand bells as mandated media for calling forth semi-Christianized spirits.

---

[32] Aileen O'Bryan, *The Dine: Origin Myths of the Navajo Indians* Bureau of American Ethnology, Bulletin 163, (Washington, D.C.: U.S. Government Printing Office, 1956), p. vii.

[33] John Dick, "A Talk with Navaho Students," *Grandfather Stories of the Navahos* (Rough Rock, Ariz.: Curriculum Center Press, 1979), p. 9.

[34] Larry Evers and Felipe S. Molina, *Yaqui Deer Songs Maso Bwikam: A Native American Poetry* (Tucson: Sun Tracks and the University of Arizona Press, 1987), p. 14.

For some Indians, the shift from orality to literacy entailed a sort of bureaucratic conversion. A Kutenai Indian friend of anthropologist Carling Malouf named Baptiste Mathias inherited his father's traditional mnemonic "string," with its recording of Native lunar months, (Christian-influenced) seven-day weeks, births, and deaths, together with historical events of importance to the entire community – all indicated by knots of different colors. Begun when he was a child, the buckskin string had been kept around the old man's waist. Once it was in Baptiste's hands, however, he memorized some of its key events before writing them down, using his own code for the knots, in a lined notebook, penciling in tangent lines and small dots to indicate births and crosses for deaths. Whereas his father was interested in a broader chronicle of his people's history, Baptiste's more stripped-down view highlighted Christian rites of passage, since his new mental model, in Malouf's opinion, was the record keeping of Catholic parish registers.[35]

Much as Indian storytellers like Edward Hunt and Harry Robinson steered their narratives between the constraints of inherited genres, intervening doctrines, and written discourse, two centuries of writing by or accounts "as told by" Indians produced fascinating admixtures of personal testimonies, convert confessions, oral histories, and angry polemics. Mission-educated converts were the first Indian writers, ranging from the "father of modern Native American literature," Samson Occom, a Mohegan from New England who became a well-known Presbyterian missionary, to Pablo Tac, a Luiseno convert to Catholicism from southern California, who penned a rosy memoir of San Luis Rey Mission life. But some of their early writings were shaded with the same sense of irony we have observed in the tales and *memorates* of Chapter 4.

In the early nineteenth century, the Pequot Indian Methodist minister William Apess conducted his own historical research but could not hold back from interjecting bitter humor into his memoir-cum-chronicles. "I could not find [the word "Indian"] in the Bible," Apess wrote, "and therefore concluded that it was a word imported for the special purpose

---

[35] Carling Malouf and Thain White, "Kutenai Calendar Records: A Study of Indian Record Keeping," *Montana Magazine of History* 3(2) (Spring 1953), pp. 34–39.

of degrading us. At other times, I thought it was derived from the term *in-gen-uity*."[36] Yet, when it came to writing an Indian history that might undermine stereotypes and introduce an Indian-centered narrative, Apess reverted to the dominant society's tendency to apotheosize a Founding Father when he positioned his *Eulogy to King Philip* (1836) in conscious opposition to the prominence enjoyed by George Washington.

Indian writers of the nineteenth century employed oral traditions for a range of purposes. Casting his eye over works by such writers as David Cusick, Elias Johnson, William W. Warren, George Copway, William Jones, and Simon Pokagan, among others, literary scholar William M. Clements pointed out how their prose renditions of spoken narratives provided unique data unobtainable from any other sources, legitimized Indian opposition to government proposals or substantiated Native theories of tribal origin, validated particular family or clan claims, defended the "essential humanity" of Indian people, countered the image of Indians as "vanishing" Americans, and provided bedrock themes, and archetypal characters for Indian novelists and poets to build and improvise upon.[37]

Some of these authors never persuasively dovetailed the canons of oral tradition and written history. In 1852 a mixed-blood Chippewa (Ojibwa) legislator from Minnesota named William W. Warren converted his people's narratives into a tribal history. His first language being his mother's Ojibwa, Warrren sat rapt at the feet of elderly storytellers. But his first book in English opened with an apology for the fact that "Through the somewhat uncertain manner in which the Indians count time," the

[36] *On Our Own Ground: The Complete Writings of William Apess, a Pequot*, edited and with an introduction by Barry O'Connell (Amherst: University of Massachusetts Press, 1992), p. li. "Reading Apess's words can induce historical vertigo," writes O'Connell, for here is an obscure nonwhite author in 1836 turning a national icon (Washington) into a cruel villain and a little-known "devil" (Philip) into a patriot hero. One wonders what other interpretive reversals an open invitation to Indian historical perspectives might yield.

[37] William M. Clements, "'This Voluminous Unwritten Book of Ours:' Early Native American Writers and the Oral Tradition," in *Early Native American Writing: New Critical Essays*, edited by Helen Jaskoski (New York: Cambridge University Press, 1996), pp. 123–124.

two people's dates might differ. Warren forced his blend of historical and cultural information into a linear European model of chronological development.

Similar ambivalence over the compatibility of Indian and European historical discourses weakened the writings of Warren's fellow Ojibwa nonfiction authors in Canada, George Copway and Peter Jones, as well as those of the Tuscarora, David Cusick. In his history, Copway broached the idea of a single combined Indian nation, but his entrapment between the Euro-Canadian and Indian worlds, according to fellow Chippewa author Gerald Vizenor, estranged him: "he could only remember in printed words at a distance from the oral tradition. Those who re-mained at the treeline noticed his transformation from totem to titles since his conversion. At the end of all his speeches, letters, and po-litical ideas, his books, he must have been alone."[38] And while Peter Jones castigated Euro-Canadian culture for the evils besetting his people, he skimpily profiled Ojibwa culture and wound up, again in Vizenor's words, "separated from the traditional cultures in his narrative posture" and seldom removing "the black robe of religious conversion from his prose."

One little-known Indian scribe who creatively blended two cultural modes of historical narration was an Oglala Sioux named George Sword from Pine Ridge, South Dakota. His career led him from a horse-riding warrior against enemy tribes in his youth to an elderly Episcopal deacon and tribal judge. While his autobiographical narrative opened with a genealogy and a list of personal war deeds, it was couched in the third person so as to declare its public, more generally historical function, according to scholar Raymond J. DeMallie. Yet the text switched to the first person wherever the responsibility for historical veracity was placed upon quoted eyewitnesses or historical chiefs. Much like a typical Plains Indian winter count, "Clearly, the important category for Sword's his-tory is the event," says DeMallie, whether they were personal war deeds or collective experiences. Moreover, according to DeMallie, "The narra-tive is told as a series of episodes without drawing connections between

---

[38] Gerald Vizenor, "Three Anishinaabeg Writers," in *The People Called Chippewa: Narrative Histories* (Minneapolis: University of Minnesota Press, 1984), p. 63.

them, suggesting the factors that underlay them, or any making moral judgement about them. Causality is generally implied by an indefinite third-person form: 'they decided' [or] 'it will happen.' " For outsiders to make sense of these "insider" histories and what they might tell us of the motivational context for happenings produced by interactions between different cultural systems, DeMallie continues, "we have to explore the mental worlds in which those actions took place, the cultural knowledge on the basis of which choices were made."[39]

Given their demonstrated ingenuity at what one might call "writing around power," not surprisingly the Cherokee were inventive at establishing a range of these literary "middle grounds." At the same time that their quasi-mythic chronologies of long-ago migrations were regularly recited in oratory, they were being committed to print. The written version that appeared in a bilingual Oklahoma newspaper in 1896 strove, as in its face-to-face oratorical rendition, both to "presentize" the mythic and legendary past, by establishing first causes and principles for Cherokee existence and experience, and to "futurize" it by emphasizing the Cherokees' predestined spiritual strength and success as products of history.[40] But the Cherokee doctor and chronicler Emmett Starr skirted the taxing problem of reconciling Native and non-Indian historical approaches by bequeathing to literate Cherokees his rich compilations of genealogies, laws, and property transfers. This "legislative

---

[39] Raymond J. DeMallie, " 'These Have No Ears': Narrative and the Historical Method," typescript of the shortened version of a paper delivered at the annual meeting of the American Society for Ethnohistory, Salt Lake City, Utah, November 10–11, 1992.

[40] Howard L. Meredith and Virginia E. Milam, "A Cherokee Vision of Eloh," *The Indian Historian* 8(4)(1975), pp. 19–23. In their subsequent, bilingual edition of this work, *Cherokee Vision of Elohi* (Oklahoma City: Noksi Press, 1997), Meredith and Milam add, "the Elohi attempts to overcome the cultural distortions brought on by the over-emphasis on the past as found in the modern Western European sense of history. The Cherokee objection to this modern historical process of analysis is that in a complex system, when the parts are broken down the whole is no longer understood. [Non-Indian] [h]istory relies on a very simplistic framework like correlation or cause and effect. History offers hindsight, which makes everything seem obvious. Such hindsight justification means little. Historical explanation looks backward and is of little importance in identifying a process or pattern in the present. The lessons of modern western history in Cherokee studies are inappropriate and even misleading" pp. 16–17.

history" served the Cherokee fight against assimilationists and the " 'two gun' [non-Indian] historians" sympathetic to them.[41]

One of the earliest literary and historical expressions "by" American Indians was the autobiography. After the publications of those personalized renditions of ethnic history by early-nineteenth-century Indian writings, journalists and friends began eliciting and rewriting "autobiographies" from Indians. But even when notables like Black Hawk (1882), Geronimo (1906), Plenty Coups (1962), or even Charles Eastman (1902) described their lives, they followed no "great man" theory of history. Quite to the contrary: their common inclination was to underscore how their own careers epitomized their culture's ideal for the successful male leader. "The 'wild' Indian," writes the Osage Indian scholar Carter Revard of these autobiographies, with tongue in cheek at his choice of the adjective, "was tied to land, to people, to origins and way of life, by every kind of human ordering we can imagine." According to Revard, the concepts of history, myth, and identity were not "three separate matters here, but three aspects of one identity."[42]

As if in resistance to such externally structured self-representations, however, when anthropologists of the culture-and-personality school began to elicit more comprehensive and less censored accounts from representative members of tribal groups, such as the Winnebago Crashing Thunder (1926), the Chiricahua Apache, "Chris" (1969), the Hopi Don Talayesva (1942), and the Navajo Left Handed (1938), these protagonists were encouraged to divulge unmediated transcripts of their everyday lives. Since high-visibility history rarely intervened in their careers, the relative unrepresentativeness of their experiences could be compared with the collective ethnographic profiles of their societies. Discrepancies revealed how their singular identities emerged from negotiations between group norms, personal predilections, and chance events.

In the 1960s emerged a new form of Indian-authored history. Produced by tribes or Indian organizations, some were collections of transcribed oral histories, and others were written by appointed tribal

[41] Rennard Strickland and Jack Gregory, "Emmett Starr, Cherokee, 1870–1930," in *American Indian Intellectuals*, edited by Margot Liberty (St. Paul, Minn: West Publishing Co., 1978), p. 108.

[42] Carter Revard, "History, Myth and Identity among Osages and Other Peoples," in *Family Matters, Tribal Affairs* (Tucson: University of Arizona Press, 1998), p. 141.

representatives. Occasionally criticized for lacking conventional academic accountability, these new tribal histories from the inside were nonetheless a far cry from the antiquated tribal summaries by old-guard Western historians that were acidly critiqued by anthropologist James Clifton. Usually self-published, occasionally bilingual, and unabashedly partisan, they ranged from the personal profiles of Seneca elders in *That's What It Was Like* (1986), to the Plateau narratives collected in *The Way It Was, Inaku Iwacha: Yakima Legends* (1974) and *Noon Nee-Me-Poo (We, the Nez Perces): Culture and History of the Nez Perces* (1973), to the stream of publications by the Navajo Tribe that resurrected forgotten regional events and neglected local heroes and stressed the persistence of tribal institutions.[43]

When Indians began relating their own histories in their own ways, they sometimes benefited from outside support, as when tobacco heiress and philanthropist Doris Duke earmarked five million dollars for gathering American Indian oral history. Between 1967 and 1972, hundreds of taped conversations with Indian elders were cataloged in seven regional centers across the United States. Not unlike the WPA oral histories amassed during the 1930s under federal government auspices, the sessions followed loose checklists, and once a tribal elder talked, there was meager follow-up questioning. The Duke project yielded only two anthologies, one from the Great Lakes–Plains, *To Be an Indian: An Oral History* (1971) and another from the Pueblo of Zuni, *The Zuni: Self Portrayals* (1972), which provided an interesting glimpse at how one Indian people's history still oriented itself between cosmological mythology and chronological history.

Meanwhile, individual Indian historians weighed in with nonfiction chronicles that ranged from the highly secular and impersonal to the intensely spiritual, compensatory, and polemical. Sometimes the Native authors seemed under tight scrutiny by their ethnic constituency, as with Byron Nelson's account of Hupa political and economic interactions

[43] A regional treatment of this tribal history phenomenon is John R. Alley, Jr.'s "Tribal Historical Projects," in *Handbook of North American Indians* V. 11, *Great Basin*, edited by Warren d'Azevedo (Washington, D.C.: Smithsonian Institution Press, 1986), pp. 601–607. See also Duane Kendall Hale, *Researching and Writing Tribal Histories* (Grand Rapids: Michigan Indian Press, 1991).

with the Euro-American invaders of northwestern California. Nelson's conspicuous avoidance of such sensitive topics as world view and ceremonial life left some readers perplexed about what beat at the heart of the Hupa cultural continuity he extolled.[44] At the other end of the spectrum were Basil Johnston's oral retellings of Ojibwa traditional histories, which almost flaunted their absence of genre distinctions or chronological benchmarks. Readers had to take at face value well told renditions whose subject matter ranged from the exploits of Nanabo'zho, the ahistorical Trickster, to reminiscences of living members from Johnston's southern Ontario reserve.[45]

Directly confronting the dissonance between Indian and European-style historical approaches, a bold Canadian Indian scholar, the Huron (Wendat) Georges E. Sioui, espoused an "autohistory" to tackle "the study of correspondences between Amerindian and non-Amerindian sources." As a polemic, his Indianized history traced the influence of Native American values on the culture at large and argued for replacing the evolutionary bias, which the Sioui perceived as the flawed foundation of Western historiography, with the Indians' devotion to the "sacred circle of life" and its stress on the mutual interdependence of living things. As exemplar, his study rehabilitated the writings of Baron de Lahontan, a neglected seventeenth-century European eyewitness to the positive philosophical and religious values of Huron life, and surveyed the ecological and territorial history of his own Huron people so as to "safeguard the right of an Amerindian group to territories denied it by traditional non-Amerindian history."[46]

The literalist claims often underlying the free-form assemblage of legends, reminiscences, myths, and editorializing found in many collectively and singly authored histories of Native groups were defended by Jemez Pueblo historian Joe Sando. If Western history couldn't bring mythic narrative and Indian ideas of primordial creation in situ into its paradigms,

[44] Byron Nelson, Jr., *Our Home Forever: A Hupa Tribal History* (Hoopa, Calif.: The Hupa Tribe, 1978).

[45] Basil Johnston, *Ojibway Heritage* (New York: Columbia University Press, 1976), and *Moose Meat Wild Rice* (Toronto: McClelland and Stewart, Ltd., 1978).

[46] Georges E. Sioui, *For an Amerindian Autohistory: An Essay on the Foundations of a Social Ethic* (Montreal: McGill-Queen's University Press, 1992), p. 82.

Sando suggested that it might at least grant them equal time or parallel plausibility:

> If we accept Native North American oral history... then we can start with the ancient people who have been in North America for many thousands of years and still allow for European and Mediterranean colonists to strengthen or boost the developing culture. This appears to be what the indigenous people have been saying in their oral history. But later Europeans with their "proof positive" and "show me" attitudes have prevailed, and remain largely unwilling to consider, much less to confirm, native creation accounts.[47]

This position was not without its critics, such as Wilcomb Washburn, who was dissatisfied with the Nez Perce tribal history's vague use of the editorial "we" instead of clear authorship, its disregard for footnotes and other canons of scholarly accountability, its thin-skinned aversion to received terms such as "skirmish," and its reluctance to discuss religious factionalism.[48] From the Indian perspective, however, the challenge of these new publications was not to play by old rules, but to forge new literary genres altogether. Contrary to Washburn, Lévi-Strauss became quite enthused by these written "continuation[s] of mythology." After reading some Northwest Coast examples, he suspected "that the opposition... between mythology and history... is not at all a clear-cut one, and that there is an intermediary level." By close study of these Indian-authored hybrids, Lévi-Strauss concluded, "the gap which exists in our mind to some extent between mythology and history can probably be breached by studying histories which are conceived as not at all separated from but as a continuation of mythology."[49]

As fiction by American Indians gained wide attention in the 1970s, incorporating Native historicities appeared high on their list of artistic goals. The part-Flathead author D'Arcy McNickle was among the first

---

[47] Joe S. Sando, *Nee Hemish: A History of Jemez Pueblo* (Albuquerque: University of New Mexico Press, 1982), p. 2.
[48] Wilcomb E. Washburn, review of *Noon Ne-Me-Poo (We, the Nez Perce): Culture and History of the Nez Perces* (1973), in *Idaho Yesterdays: The Quarterly Journal of the Idaho Historical Society* 18(2) (Summer 1974), pp. 30–31.
[49] Claude Lévi-Strauss, *Myth and Meaning* (New York: Schocken Books, 1979), p. 40.

to dramatize the weight of the past upon the Indian future. In *Wind from an Enemy Sky* (1978), he summed up a lifetime's experience in government service, university teaching, and popular writing on Indian affairs. His tale of a dam threatening a northwestern river brought mythological sensibility – embodied in a sacred medicine bundle appropriated by a New York museum – into direct conflict with the Euro-Americans' determination that nothing must stave off the rush of progress. McNickle saw only cultural conquest and defeat ahead for the values that underlie the traditional Indian sense of history.

On the other hand, Leslie Silko's *Ceremony* (1977), while a gritty depiction of dysfunctional life in Navajoland's border towns, underscored the adaptive ability of Indian cosmological beliefs. Her protagonist, a deeply disturbed World War II veteran, finds psychological recovery through the updated myths and revitalized "ceremonies" of a medicine man whose fixed ethnic identity is less important than his skill at responding to breaking events. Other fiction by Silko engages the different dilemma of communicating histories that are so localized as to require special contextualization for nontribal readers. While this geographic anchoring of community narratives remains a great strength, it also presents problems of a creative and ethical nature. Writes Silko of her personal family memoir that is appropriately entitled *Storyteller*:

> One of my frustrations is that unless you're involved in this, in these stories, in this place, you as a reader may not get it. I have to constantly fight against putting in detail and things that would be too tedious for the "outsider." At the same time I have to have some sort of internal integrity in the piece.... In describing places and directions, there are stories that identify the place. These kinds of things make condensing a problem. It all depends on how much you want to make your stories acceptable to communities outside this one.[50]

---

[50] Leslie Marmon Silko, "A Conversation with Leslie Marmon Silko," *Sun Tracks* 3(1) (1976), p. 31. This chapter does not delve into the possible benefits of insulating Native historical thought through the experimentation, by authors like Silko, with the colloquial "Red English" heard in reservation communities, which Indian stand-up comics parody and which, like the "Indian time" concept, informally but inventively may safeguard ethnic pride and separatism. For more on these dialects, see *Essays in Native American English*, edited by Guillermo Bartelt, Susan Renfield Jasper, and Bates Hoffer (San Antonio, TX: Trinity University, 1982).

Other prominent Indian writers have produced historical fiction, with James Welch, in *Fools Crow* (1986), successfully dramatizing late-nine-teenth-century Blackfoot history through a conventional plot structure but methodically piling up details and motivations no outsider could intuit. Out of her northeastern plains roots, Louise Erdrich has pro-duced, so far, a four-novel epic of North Dakota Indian history that fleshes out a multigenerational kinship chart whose blended racial iden-tities yielded in the nineteenth century a brand new tribe, the Turtle Mountain Chippewas, a new language, Michif, and, one might argue, new cultural structures and psychological patterns that called for Erdrich's more daring literary risks with narrative and dialect in order to bring them to life.

But Indian writers can get into hot water for playing too innovatively with their peoples' traditions. The experimental novel *Seven Arrows* by a self-identified Cheyenne author drew criticism for desecrating Cheyenne tradition. At the same time, Vine Deloria, Jr., championed the book "because an Indian dared to break out of the genre in which people had put Indian literature, and just say, 'I'm going to write a story that destroys chronological time, that intersperses humans and animals, that violates the standards of white society for writing about Indians'."[51] If anyone picked up Deloria's gauntlet, it would seem to be the prolific Chippewa writer Gerald Vizenor. As far as historical writing is concerned, his career has run the gamut from an Emmet Starr–like responsibility for compiling tribal documents[52] to his particular brand of Indian journalism,[53] which blends "instant history" with ironic short fiction that satirically targets all who might appropriate Indian narrative genres.

The special burdens placed upon the creative Indian historian to com-mand cross-cultural genres and multiple voices would seem to have made them proto-postmodernists before the term was ever coined, as Cherokee

[51] Sam Crum, "A Conversation with Vine Deloria," in *Suntracks: An American Indian Literary Magazine* N. 4 (Tucson: American Indian Studies, University of Arizona, 1978), p. 87.
[52] Gerald Vizenor, *Escorts to White Earth: 1868 to 1968, 100 Year Reservation* (Minnea-polis: The Four Winds, 1968).
[53] Gerald Vizenor, *The People Named the Chippewa, Narrative Histories* (Minneapolis: University of Minnesota Press, 1984).

historian and teacher Rachel Caroline Eaton quaintly demonstrates in a 1930 preface to her multilayered account of the Battle of Claremore Mound of 1818, when the resident Osages and removed Cherokee fought a bloody battle in western Arkansas:

> This story is a composite of many sources. The warp is authentic history based on the written records and on the hill which stands as the immutable background of this tragic encounter; the woof is fashioned of legends, traditions and fireside tales passed by word of mouth from generation to generations of each of the tribes that took part in the engagement; but the fabric woven of these elements is shot through with the memory [and] was embroidered with the imagery of one whose childhood was spent under the shadow of the historic hill....[54]

As Eaton describes, Native historians must somehow combine and contextualize raw materials from an alien archival tradition, honor the authority of a specific geography, and interweave their own oral tradition's multiple genres. In addition, they would be fools not to utilize the tactile knowledge that comes from a childhood of finding glass beads, arrowheads, and chipped stone axes on the Claremore battlefield or picking wildflowers and fruits that ripened during the same "Strawberry Moon" when her people's blood soaked into that very ground.

Eaton's comments foreshadow the literary challenge faced by another Indian author thirty-five years later. Like her, N. Scott Momaday retained intimate ties to the Oklahoma landscapes and traditions of his Kiowa childhood; he, too, faced the unique obligations of weaving a multivocal canvas from the same range of personal, white, and tribal elements that she describes. His result, *The Way to Rainy Mountain* (1969), represents an imaginative harmonizing of the contrasting discourses of Indian and Euro-American history. In this disarmingly minimalist prose collage, Momaday successfully orchestrated the seemingly incompatible genres of personal autobiography, objective history, and ethnic tradition. When

---

[54] Rachel Caroline Eaton, "The Legend of the Battle of Claremore Mound," in *Native American Writing in the Southeast: An Anthology, 1875–1935*, edited by Daniel F. Littlefield, Jr., and James W. Parins (Jackson: University Press of Mississippi, 1995), p. 236.

Momaday won the Pulitizer Prize for fiction with his *House Made of Dawn* (1968) in 1969, he had already written an earlier manuscript entitled *The Journey of Tai-Me*, which experimented with his multivocal approach to the story of Kiowa ethnogenesis. Blending different typographies, line drawings (by the author's father, Al Momaday), and rapid cutting between multiple verbal styles that differentiated his mythic, historical, tribal, and personal voices, Momaday swung freely back and forth in time to make his separated paragraphs read like an epic. Published with the title *The Way to Rainy Mountain*, the work managed to depict Kiowa culture history as both contingent and predestined; it blazed a trail for one kind of modern Indian history that could realize the past-in-the-present on paper while retaining an indigenous, even oral, sensibility.

It is hard to imagine even enlightened historians making time to do justice to the intercultural and mixed-genre spectrum of written traditions that have been limned in this chapter and the other historical modalities covered earlier. That challenge only becomes more difficult, and emotionally trying, when it is an American Indian who is struggling to maintain reputations in tribal and university environments. As the Caddo historian Carol Hampton has observed, her fellow Indians academics must dodge stereotypes about the level of "civilization" reached by this or that tribe, retain composure when more established scholars lift, distort, or dismiss privileged information their Indian colleagues have shared, swallow jibes at historical Indian leaders by scholars who never visited their geographic environs or interviewed tribal members, tighten their lips when theories cooked up on faraway campuses wrap up their people's many different pasts, withstand criticism about writing in the "passive voice" about reservation times when the experiences of many Indians was less doing than being "done to," and steer a lonely course between the loyalist "subjectivity" expected from their people and the "objective" standards of academic scholarship that their non-Indian mentors are often secretly dubious they have the sophistication or independence to meet.

Their predicament epitomizes many moments described in earlier chapters when white and Indian ways of making meaning of the past stood at loggerheads. Hampton's optimism about their potential is a beacon for the survival of America's many different Indian histories as well:

> Native American historians have a unique opportunity to contribute and offer new perspectives in comprehending American history in general and American Indian history in particular. Indeed, the trials experienced by American Indian scholars might well serve as a model for a better understanding of all historical experiences.[55]

[55] Carol Hampton, "Tribal Esteem and the American Indian Historian," in *American Indian Identity: Today's Changing Perspectives* (Sacramento, Calif.: Sierra Oaks Publishing Co., 1989), p. 91. For more on the special challenges faced by Indian academics, see Devon A. Mihesuah's excellent "Voices, Interpretations, and the 'New Indian History': Comment on the *American Indian Quarterly's* Special Issue on Writing About American Indians," *American Indian Quarterly* 20(1) (Winter 1996), pp. 91–105.

————◄◦►————

NINE

Futures of Indian Pasts

Prophecy and History

In our society we have many thinkers and philosophers who tell us these things. And this is not something they are making up. This is something they have known before we came to this planet, this world. This is something they knew in the other worlds. This is the pattern of life. This is history.[1]

Alvin Dashee, Hopi

One starry night in the spring of 1967, I had a rendezvous in a sheep-herder's cabin with a man to whom it had been revealed that the Pueblo Indian and European Spanish pasts had produced a "cosmic race" that one day would dominate U.S. history. His name was Reies Lopez Tije-rina, and that evening he was the target of the most extensive manhunt in New Mexico state history. The charismatic leader of a grass-roots movement to recover lands that poor rural Hispanic villagers claimed had been stolen from them in the nineteenth century, two days earlier Tijerina and his armed followers had descended upon Tierra Amarilla, the seat of Rio Arriba County in the northern part of the state. They shot up the courthouse, wounded lawmen, took and released hostages, and hightailed it into the hills.

Like many American Indian prophets whose personalities and mes-sages still engender pride and devotion, along with doubt and division,

---

[1] Quoted in Stan Steiner, *The Vanishing White Man* (New York: Harper & Row, 1976), p. 4.

within today's Indian communities, the self-appointed Tijerina seemed born, or perhaps *reborn*, for this moment. And like the foreign visitors who traipsed to the Priest Rapids stronghold along the Columbia River to interview the Plateau Indian prophet Smohalla in the 1880s, my presence offered this prophet one way to get his word out. Tijerina was not interested in helping a cub reporter get his facts straight. The images and analogies he fired at me kept meandering into some larger vision in which those facts made predestined sense to him. The prophecies he had kept to an inner circle were ready for the world.

Over the following year of covering Tijerina's past and the raid's aftermath, I came to realize how his career fit the classic profile of a revitalization prophet. You could never separate the folklore, history, scripture, and fantasy in his stories, but their themes and references rang old bells. There were the prior golden ages when things were different – the glory days of reputed aristocratic ancestors in the Spanish motherland before they fell down on their luck, the idealized days of pioneering Hispanic settlements in the New World before the gringos crushed them after the Treaty of Guadalupe Hidalgo in 1848, and the family legend of a peasant grandfather who claimed heirship to the Laredo land grant and stood his ground against brutal Texas Rangers, finally eluding their pursuit three times into old Mexico.

There were the more immediate sufferings of deprivation and discrimination. Tijerina's part-Indian, Mexican-born father had supposedly been hamstrung by Rangers, not an unlikely misfortune for Hispanics from South Texas around the turn of the twentieth century. There were early signs of mystical gifts. At age four he fell into a twenty-four-hour trance and experienced Jesus pulling him along in a red wagon. And in what seems today like a forerunner of the seismic religious shifts about to shake all of Latin America, there was the break with mother church and fatherland. Tijerina's conversion to Protestant evangelism in 1942 bestowed legitimacy on the modalities of ecstatic prophecy and its Old Testament themes and metaphors, plus the vision of a mestizo America for which his whole personality seemed prepared.

Too outspoken for church elders in Isleta, Texas's Assembly of God Bible School, Tijerina struck out on his own; the "law of God" propelled him into a series of archetypal experiences. The young man named for the King of Kings had his sojourn in the wilderness (meditating in a cave outside El Monte, California), his political awakening (through a mysterious white stranger who educated him to the darker underside of Hispanic–Anglo relations in the Southwest), and his own utopian compound (the Valle de Paz commune just north of Arizona's Papago Indian Reservation – a "gypsy camp," according to the Pinal County lawmen who rousted Tijerina's "heralds of peace" in what sounds like a rehearsal for the Waco fiasco of April 1993). And he also received the most fateful of his many out-of-body visions.

As a fugitive hiding out in California in 1957, Tijerina dreamed one night of a tumbled-down kingdom in which frozen horses started to melt and three angels offered their assistance. Upon waking up, he felt that the horses represented those old Hispanic land grants he had heard about; the dream confirmed an invitation from a New Mexican to fight for this stolen inheritance, and for the New World's "cosmic race" to whom it rightfully belonged. Nine years before the Courthouse Raid, a band of men in flowing white robes who were soon nicknamed *los barbudos* for their heavy black beards showed up in the town of Lumberton, not far from Tierra Amarilla. This was Tijerina's first appearance in the southwestern landscape where he would carve out his strange place in history.

Three days after our interview in the mountains, Tijerina was nabbed at a highway checkpoint. Over the following years of court appearances, public rallies, and national huddles with other ethnic activists from the 1960s' militant landscape, the more outsiders learned of his uncompromising vision, the less romantic and more anachronistic and egomaniacal he began to seem. His message and chosen media were decidedly not ecumenical. For trusted cadres of like-minded devotees only, this was less reformation campaign than messianic crusade; Tijerina remained impatient with political strategizing, radical networking, and calculated public relations protests. Only when he linked up with the Hopi Indian traditionalist and uncommonly public spokesperson Tomas Banyacya did I sense some deep complicity. Both spoke the language of prophecy.[2]

---

[2] This sketch of Tijerina and his movement is based upon my book *Tijerina and the Courthouse Raid*, 2nd ed. (Albuquerque: University of New Mexico Press, 1970) and on *Grito! Reies Tijerina and the New Mexico Land Grant War of 1967* by Richard Gardner (Indianapolis: Bobbs-Merrill Company, 1970).

To a major sector of Spanish-speaking America, Tijerina shortly become an irrelevant, almost embarrassing throwback. But I shall always be grateful for what that exposure taught me about the probable likes of prophets who led American Indian and other revitalization movements in the past. I had witnessed how their words and deeds were the consequences of communications between their inner selves and unseen forces, a privileged wavelength into which outsiders could never tap. Encountering such a figure in the flesh, or someone claiming to channel unquestioned truths about the past and future, was an unnerving experience, especially for any journalist or academic historian who strove for the detachment and objectivity you can enjoy when you don't have to meet your characters in person or cohabit their terrain or watch their dramas unfold.

They practically begged you to turn cynical. You could never verify their claims. With these sorts, there was no dialogue; one simply received. They seized history by the throat and defied all of its supposed inevitabilities. Their presence argued that a single individual in privileged touch with deeper powers could make all the difference in the world. They seemed to breathe the same air, but then you looked into their unblinking eyes. They spoke with a seductive self-assurance; their words possessed a coiled physical force. Their world views brooked no contradiction or nuance; they were chosen conduits for unarguable forces. Facing the outpouring of their absolutist explications and forecasts, you just buckled your seat belt, fought against the pull of their rhetoric and personality, and noted every eye tick or spittle spray for clues to whether they were gifted charlatans, sincere humanitarians, utterly barking, or possibly could be the One.

Historians may doubt their honesty or sanity, but the central, continuous role of this diverse pool of prophetic individuals throughout Indian history is undeniable. Whether they initiated quiet reformations that persevered beneath the dominant society's radar or inspired violent rebellions to throw off its yoke, they represent some of the greatest change agents in American Indian history.[3] As much as the heroic

---

[3] Sometimes they did both: see Kenneth M. Morrison's plea for a history of the American Revolution "from the bottom up," which positions Indians *in* it, and his main example of Neolin, the Delaware prophet who combined Native and Christian teachings,

military strategists with whom they are often paired, their careers demonstrate the impact of extraordinary personalities on historical processes. This impact was even more creative, it might be argued, when a prophet's sense of political realities limited him or her to conducting a sort of triage on cultural patterns, syncretically mixing and matching with introduced Christian motifs, and, instead of making a clean break with the past, pointing everyone to new, more hopeful horizons.

The Indian scholar Clifford E. Trafzner has complained that although "prophets played an integral part of the American Indian past" and, like Tijerina, belonged to a tradition that dovetailed remarkably well with that of Old and New Testament traditions, "since the preponderance of the documentary evidence about Indian prophets has been written by whites who held holy men and women in contempt, it was easy for historians to neglect the significance of Indian prophets in the historical development of Indian–white relations."[4]

Trafzner's aim, I think, is partly off. From Francis Parkman's malevolent portrayal of Pontiac's Delaware Prophet on, the problem between white authors and charismatic Native leaders has been one of distortion at least as much as neglect. Where his comment holds water is in criticizing their demonizing dismissals of sinister Iago-like figures who pull

attempted to unite tribes of the Old Northwest, and fueled the Indian war of 1763, "Native Americans and the American Revolution: Historic Stories and Shifting Frontier Conflict," in *Indians in American History*, edited by Frederick E. Hoxie (Arlington Heights, Ill.: Harlan Davidson, 1988). From the Indian perspective, their battlefield struggles were often prophecy-driven sacred revolts, to adopt the title and thesis of Joel W. Martin's *Sacred Revolt: The Muskogee's Struggle for a New World* (Boston: Beacon Press, 1991), and which early-nineteenth-century Creek Indian author George Stiggins makes a central theme in his *Creek Indian History: Narrative of the Geneology, Traditions and Downfall of the Ispocoga or Creek Indian Tribe of Indians* (Birmingham, Ala.: Birmingham Public Library Press, 1989), as does Gregory Evans Dowd in *A Spirited Resistance: The North American Indian Struggle for Unity, 1745–1815* (Baltimore: Johns Hopkins University Press, 1991). Comparative material on prophetic movements is found in Harold W. Turner, *Bibliography of New Religious Movements in Primal Societies*, Vol. II: *North America* (Boston: G. K. Hall, 1978), and in Shelley Anne Osterreich, compiler, *The American Indian Ghost Dance, 1870 and 1890: An Annotated Bibliography* (New York: Greenwood Press, 1991), and, for a more recent example, Willard Johnson's "Contemporary Native American Prophecy in Historical Perspective," *Journal of the American Academy of Religion* 64(3) (1996), pp. 575–612.
4 Clifford E. Trafzer, "Introduction," *American Indian Prophets* (Sacramento, Calif.: Sierra Oaks Publishing Company, 1986), p. x.

the strings or unduly influence the noble but inevitably doomed Indian paragons like Pontiac, Tecumseh, Geronimo, or Sitting Bull. In popular history, novels, and films, we often see these conjurors and oracles portrayed as menacing, frequently physically deformed, and psychologically twisted personalities who are bent on payback against a world that has rejected them. My resistance to that malicious stereotype may be another debt I owe to Tijerina. For whatever else might be said of the man, what never failed to strike me was the fearless, optimistic, guileless vigor of his personality, his constant graciousness and accessibility to me, and the undeniable justice of so much of his historical and social critique even when it was articulated through a prophetic discourse that I was otherwise resisting with all my might.

Proclamations about the future by these chosen few are a subset of mythic narrative and another way that tradition, or innovation, restores their authority over events yet to come. "If myth anchors the present in the past," Percy Cohen has written, "then prophecy anchors it in the future."[5] By their claim that the future is theirs to know and outsiders' to find out, American Indian sages and their prophecies offer their constituencies at least one secret weapon for staying a step ahead of the history that their interaction with Europeans has kicked into high gear. Folklorist Jarold Ramsey has coined the term "retroactive prophecy" to highlight "one of a numerous set of native texts, some mythological and others historical or personal, in which an event or deed in pre-Contact times is dramatized as being prophetic of some consequence of the coming of whites."[6]

Selecting stories from the Pacific Northwest, Southwest, and Great Basin that demonstrate "contact-era mythopoetic invention," Ramsey underscored their emphasis on the dire consequences of European

---

[5] Percy S. Cohen, "Theories of Myth," *Man* 4 (1969), p. 351.
[6] Jarold Ramsey, "Retroactive Prophecy in Western Indian Narrative," in *Reading the Fire: Essays in the Traditional Literatures of the Far West*, revi. ed. (Seattle: University of Washington Press, 1999), p. 195. Collecting folklore among the Hupa of northwestern California, John H. Bushnell called Native interpretations of Trinity River floods "post-hoc explanations" that actually commented on white desecration of sacred dance grounds ("Hupa Reaction to the Trinity River Floods: Post-Hoc Recourse to Aboriginal Belief," *Anthropological Quarterly* 42 (4) [October 1969], pp. 316–324).

contact: epidemics, liquor, money, armies, laws, missionaries, schools, and more. As Douglas H. Johnson has written of twentieth-century prophecy among the Nuer tribespeople of the Sudan:

> Prophecy is repeatedly validated by events; not only current events, but current understandings of what are seen as past events. As the past is contained in the present, so the present is contained in the future, and the prophet makes his own and succeeding generations aware of that continuum. In this way prophecy can be seen as a form of historical discourse, both about history and within history.[7]

Yet prophecy is only one of the ways that American Indian traditions tinker with past and future time. There are *prefiguring* rituals in which enterprises about to commence are safeguarded by symbolic manipulations. Whether they constitute a ceremony, tribal change of location, or some new venture, this "history to come" often becomes summarized in the metaphor of a "road" that first needs to be prayed over, with Pueblo peoples dribbling an anticipatory line of purifying cornmeal on the ground to "open" this future and render it auspicious (in the plains, the same forecasting procedure might use the ascending smoke from sage or cedar incense). The cornmeal road presages protected and positive outcomes. Not quite trod in advance, the route has nonetheless been purged, and even "acculturated," beforehand.[8] (Another reminder of the cultural and psychological gulf between white and Indian worlds: this Pueblo Indian preference for undramatic, safe and secure, *opened* roads that contrasts with that iconic theme of Anglo-America, endlessly recycled in novels and movies, of the jeopardy and transformative promise of

---

[7] Douglas H. Johnson, *Nuer Prophets: A History of Prophecy from the Upper Nile in the Nineteenth and Twentieth Centuries* (Oxford: Oxford University Press, 1994), p. 352. Julie Cruikshank makes this point in connection with Yukon Native responses to changing times: "Prophecy narratives are one more instance of the continuing use of tradition as a resource to frame explanations about the contemporary world. They offer a competing form of historical consciousness that deserves to be taken seriously." *The Social Life of Stories: Narrative and Knowledge in the Yukon Territory* (Lincoln: University of Nebraska Press, 1998), p. 137.

[8] Some of these prefiguring techniques are discussed in my "Orientations from Their Side: Dimensions of Native American Cartographic Discourse," in *Cartographic Encounters: Perspectives on Native American Mapmaking and Map Use*, edited by G. Malcolm Lewis (Chicago: University of Chicago Press, 1997), pp. 241–269.

an unknown *open road*, whether it be Mark Twain's Mississippi River or Jack Kerouac's Route 66.)

Under the shield of such prefiguring practices, human endeavors may proceed with a measure of confidence. The powers that be will watch over their own, in much the same way that, for the semimigratory Ojibwa studied by A. Irving Hallowell, oral traditions tell of treks between temporary campsites rendered safe and secure by mythic women who magically proceed everyone else to erect tent frames and prepare cooking fires at each location. Moving from one place to another, the travelers are comforted by their sameness; in a sense, the nomadic families never really leave home.

Another way of turning time around is by claiming *precognition* of the unfamiliar. When the U.S. government hunted down the raiding, freewheeling Navajo clans in 1863, hoping to round up the entire tribe in a southeastern New Mexico internment camp, some groups slipped through the dragnet. Led by Chief Hashkeniinii, one party of refugees hustled into the northern reaches of their territory. There they ventured for the first time behind their sacred Head of Earth Woman mountain and discovered a remarkable hideaway. Wandering up a narrow canyon, they found springs, unusual rock pillars, and finally a natural bridge. But in their eyes, they *recognized* that the Holy People had *already discovered* the area for them. The pillars represented familiar deities, each spring had its spirit inhabitant, the rocky overhang that echoed your words back was clearly such a sacred person, and that amazing rock arch was actually two stone rainbow beings caught in the act of love that produced the watery children that filled the San Juan and Colorado rivers. It was as if this animated geography was prepared and waiting for this eventuality – providing Navajos with sanctuary from history's storm.[9]

Examples like these suggest that American Indian manipulations of the past, present, and future are not necessarily sparked by Euro-American inducement or inspiration. Well before strangers showed up on their beaches, Native seers surely had occasion to bring envisioned futures into predestined accord with established traditions. But rarely

---

[9] This story and the liturgies it produced are found in Karl W. Luckert's *Navajo Mountain and Rainbow Bridge Religion* (Flagstaff: Museum of Northern Arizona, 1977).

was the prophetic turn of mind given such marvelous grist as that provided after 1492.

Throughout the Americas we find a fount of Native traditions that assume prior knowledge of the first sightings of Europeans. Sometime after New England Natives actually witnessed floating islands with billowing clouds fixed to upright trees whose banks discharged thunder and lightning, their soothsayers' dreams of walking islands with puffy white panels and sticks that spat fire were confirmed – or recomposed. In central British Columbia, the interior Salish remember by name the female shaman who awoke from a four-day "death" to describe the "people coming across the sea" who would bring electric stoves, airplanes, trains, and automobiles. In the same out-of-body experience, as if preparing for these eventualities, we also learn that "She was taught what prayers to use" for coping with the new arrivals.[10]

Sometimes these predictions reach into precontact times to account for the origins of all races. In an unapologetically racist Seminole version from the Deep South, the Great Spirit creates three men, of white, black, and red color, and hands each a box. Whites get pens, ink, and compasses; Indians get tomahawks, knives, and war clubs; blacks get hoes, buckets, and oxen whips so that they will toil for both groups.[11] New England Indian explanations focus on the black faces and tight, curly hair of these newcomers, who seem to them stuck in a menial status.

Material culture figures prominently in these prophecies. The white man's wares held endless fascination because of what they implied about the inner powers he possessed; predicting their possessions ahead of time was one way for Indians to assimilate them. Hence New England Indians passed on their foretellings of water that burned your throat and made you feel like you were flying, of pots that didn't smash into shards when dropped. European horses were even drawn into these recastings; Plains Indian stories describe their appearance as a gift from the supernaturals to a vision questor. A more secular strategy was adopted by the Crow for

---

[10] "Sexpinlhemx's Wife Foretells the Coming of the White Man," in *Our Tellings: Interior Salish Stories of the Nlha7kápmx People* (Vancouver: University of British Columbia Press, 1995), p. 123.

[11] Excerpted in George E. Lantford, compiler and editor, *Native American Legends: Southeastern Legends: Tales from the Natchez, Caddo, Biloxi, Chickasaw, and Other Nations* (Little Rock, Art: August House, 1989), pp. 140–141.

asserting cultural autonomy over the previously unknown. In the case of horses, the name for "elk" (*iichiile*) was quickly slapped on them. Then they renamed the wild animal they knew well and hunted, using a suffix for "real" or "prototypical" (*kaashe*); elk were now called "real elk" (*iichiilkaashe*). Through this mechanism of what one might call of "retroactive nomenclature," the suffix meaning "real" or "authentic" could impose the dignity of age and priority upon their own world, with everything innovative considered almost a subspecies or a second-best facsimile.[12]

Outsiders analyze the cultural role of prophecies less to ascertain their veracity than to understand their utility. For many New England Indians during the colonial period of intense Christian proselytizing, these "re-formulations of indigenous knowledge," as William S. Simmons characterizes a process behind their production that would not be unfamiliar to Indians from other regions as well, were ways in which Indian converts could reconcile their Native birth with their spiritual rebirth through "introducing Christian themes to their pre-European past."[13] Predictions of coming whites were commonly coupled with forecasts of the ramifications of their presence.

---

[12] In the east, William S. Simmons describes a related power reversal, as the Narragansetts explained the superiority of English technology – the metal plow, for instance – as due to their possessing spiritual authority, or *manitou*, a categorization, in fact, that made many by-products of European society, from metal wares to epidemics, congruent with their preexisting cosmology, in *Cautantowwit's House: An Indian Burial Ground on the Island of Conanicut in Narragansett Bay* (Providence: Brown University Press, 1970), p. 51. A similar incorporative attitude is reported from the Plateau, where "The idea that the white man did not invent the material culture of the Industrial Revolution but got them from the spirits who knew them long before exists among other Plateau tribes" (Harry Holbert Turney-High, "Two Kutenai Stories," *Journal of American Folklore* 54 [213–214] [July–December 1941], p. 194.), and Sergei Kon's "Shamanism and Christianity: Modern-Day Tlingit Elders Look to the Past" (*Ethnohistory* 38 [4] [1991], pp. 363–387) finds the same in the Northwest Coast. From the plains, the term "Lakotification" is applied by scholar William K. Powers to Sioux tendencies to innovate in much the same self-interested fashion, either by making new religious or social elements their own (which he calls "exonovation") or by readjusting their own symbolic categories in the light of new exigencies ("endonovation"). See "Innovating the Sacred: Creating Tradition in Lakota Religion," *European Review of Native American Studies* 9(2) (1995), pp. 21–24.

[13] William S. Simmons, "Of Large Things Remembered: Southern New England Legends of Colonial Encounters," in *The Art and Mystery of Historical Archaeology* (Boca Raton, Fla.: CRC Press, 1992), pp. 323, 319.

It could take a while for early signs to sink in. To make sense of
the white man's noisy, intrusive railroad trains and the leftover food
he'd seen them throw away rather than share with the poor during the
Depression, the Cherokee grandfather of Anderson Dirthrower harken-
ed back to his forefathers' encounter with early Europeans. At first,
they'd considered the newcomers to be magical offspring from the surf's
white foam, but they felt otherwise once the Indians gave them as much
land to sit on as a deerskin was large. Whites cunningly sliced the deerskin into thin strips so as to surround the land, ate the Indians' food, and
then evicted them from their homes. To understand their ways, advised
the old man, "you got to understand where the White Man comes from,
and his history." When Indians did conduct their own ethnohistorical investigations into Euro-American culture, they discovered that here were
poor, hungry commoners whose ancestors had killed the son of God and
who themselves had fled from an overbearing king. Cut loose from both,
his grandfather said, they brought to Indian country a overriding principle that explained their behavior: "The new rule was that you could
keep as much as you could get a hold of any way you could get a hold
of it."[14]

Earthly cataclysms might presage cultural ones. In the Pacific Northwest, for instance, volcanic activity in the Cascade Mountains in the
late eighteenth century alerted a Spokane prophet to a "different kind
of men ... who will bring with them a book and will teach you everything, and after that the world will fall to pieces."[15] More recently, the
Zuni "grandfathers" from New Mexico expressed forebodings of coming decay, when "Drinkers of dark liquids will come upon the land,
speaking nonsense and filth.... Population will increase until the land
can hold no more.... The tribes of men will mix.... Then our possessions will turn into beasts and devour us whole."[16] This sense of a world
taking revenge upon its intemperate usurpers is also found in a memory

[14] Anderson Dirthrower, "The White Man's Rule," in *Who Is the Chairman of this Meeting?: A Collection of Essays*, edited by Ralph Osborne (Toronto: Neewin Publishing
Company, 1972), p. 30.
[15] Quoted in Ramsey, "Retroactive Prophecy in Western Indian Narrative," p. 153.
[16] "The Zuni People," translated by Alvina Quam, in *The Zunis: Self Potrayals by the
Zuni People* (Albuquerque: University of New Mexico Press, 1972), p. 3.

of a Wailaki woman, Lucy Young, from central California:

My grandpa, before white people came, had a dream. He was so old he was all doubled up. Knees to chin, and eyes like indigo. Grown son carry him in great basket on his back, every place. My grandpa say: "White Rabbit" – he mean white people –"gonta devour our grass, our seed, our living. We won't have nothing more, this world."[17]

An equally bleak prediction climaxes a Jicarilla Apache tale of the great flood: "At the end of the world these people who travel with their eyes are going to come back and go to all directions. . . . For the telephone and telegraph are not going to be here any more. They are all going to burn. Next time the earth will be destroyed by fire."[18] Again, according to Ramsey, "The myths of such native groups, it is clear, had always served to uphold the people's world view *as a continuum*, by accommodating real and imagined changes in their world" and hence are "formally consistent with their mythological view of what we call history."[19]

Along with its swift reflex for recasting cosmic origins in the light of historical contingencies, prophecy also peers into the distance, even to the very end of time. Such apocalyptic foretellings are a trademark of the authority over history assumed by many American Indian revitalization prophets. One of the most famous was Smohalla, a Wanapum (Sahaptin) of the Columbia Plateau, who warned in the mid-1880s that "when God is ready, he will drive away all the people except the people who have obeyed his laws. . . . All the dead men will come to life again;

---

[17] Lucy Young, in Edith V. A. Murphey, "Out of the Past: A True Indian Story," *California Historical Society Quarterly* 20(4) (December 1941), p. 350.
[18] Morris Opler, *Myths and Tales of the Jicarilla Apache Indians*, Memoirs of the American Folk-lore Society, 31 (New York: G. E. Stechert Co., 1938), p. 113.
[19] Ramsey, *Reading the Fire*, p. 163. Prophetic discourse remains a beacon for some contemporary Indians. When outgoing Navajo tribal president Milton Bluehouse heard that supernatural "Holy Women" had appeared to two women, warning that caging cougars and wolves in the tribe's Window Rock zoo would bring trouble by upsetting the balance of nature, he started a controversy by ordering the animals set free. Explained the tribe's own native anthropologist, "Rather than focus on the sightings to determine if who saw it was nuts or not – that's what a Westerner would do – we look at it as a message: 'Are we going the way we should?'" "A Zoo in Peril Stirs a Debate About Navajo Tradition," *New York Times*, March 28, 1999, sec. 1, p. 37.

their spirits will come to their bodies again. We must wait here, in the homes of our fathers, and be ready to meet them in the bosom of our mother."[20]

This sort of prophetic "posthistory," as one might call it, is often part of a collective ideology, as among the Dunne-za, a Canadian sub-arctic people studied by anthropologist Robin Ridington. Their original *Naachin* or "Dreamer" was a messianic figure who blazed the "trail to heaven" and lived to tell about it. But those experiences were routinized into liturgy for a congregation that followed his blend of Christian ideas and old-style prophecies of terrible cataclysms, redemptive ethnic re-unions, and accounts to be settled.[21]

Behind nearly all these reformulations, one could argue, still lay the old historical agenda of mythic thought to assure its constituents, as we have already witnessed with the Tlingit people, that, in the words of Claude Lévi-Strauss, "the future will remain faithful to the present and the past."[22] That message was delivered to the late-nineteenth-century fieldworker Frank Hamilton Cushing after his unsuccessful attempt to purchase for the Smithsonian Institution ceremonial objects from the Hopis of Arizona's Oraibi Pueblo: "They gave me in substance their myth of creation which for the sake of clearness I have given rather as a myth than as an infuriated argument, interspersed with the most insulting messages to Washington."[23] Here we might also revisit the "hostile" Hopi leader Yukeoma's argument in 1911 to Commissioner of Indian Affairs Robert G. Valentine (discussed in Chapter 1) against conscription of Hopi children in government schools.

Hopi prophecies were his instruction manual. Yukeoma told Valentine of the emergence from the underworld of the hero twins, of inscribed stones given by the Red Headed Spirit to the Hopis as proof of their right to their land. Those traditions were the reason "why we don't

[20] Major J. W. MacMurray, "The Dreamers of the Columbia River Valley in Washington Territory," *Transactions of the Albany Institute* 11 (1887), p. 248.

[21] Robin Ridington, *Trail to Heaven: Knowledge and Narrative in a Northern Native Community* (Iowa City: University of Iowa Press, 1988).

[22] Claude Levi-Strauss, "When Myth Becomes History," in *Myth and Meaning* (New York: Schocken Books, 1979), p. 43.

[23] Quoted in Esther S. Goldfrank, "The Impact of Situation and Personality on Four Hopi Emergence Myths, *Southwestern Journal of Anthropology* 4 (1948), p. 244.

want the civilized way."[24] For this traditionalist, myth was the first, last, and only diplomatic argument a true Hopi could advance. If it went unheeded, then his people's prophecies would go on to warn Euro-Americans of the ultimate price they would have to pay.[25]

As to the incorporation of a prophetic movement's chartering narrative, whereby history becomes preserved as an outline for ceremonial practice, Native America offers a wide variation. In longhouses of the Iroquois League, it is de rigeur to narrate the transformative vision of Handsome Lake as if it were gospel. During the heyday of the Dream Drum religion of the Chippewa, its originating story was generally preached at some time or other during each ceremony, according to Tom Vennum, but the narrative emphasized the vision's message, not the messenger – the suffering fugitive known as Tailfeather Woman.[26] While during the postritual informal discussion immediately following an all-night peyote meeting there may be talk of Peyote Woman, who first brought the "medicine" north for Indians, its real focus is less on an orthodox history than on the phenomenological experience. And none of the "three styles" of prophetic personality that June Helm studied among the Dogrib in the late 1960s yielded any new, guiding master narratives or any rituals based upon them. Although the Dogrib gathered for quasi-Christian services and one man preached antiwhite sentiments, perhaps because none espoused any millenarian message, their activation of prophecy was never an issue.[27]

---

[24] Katherine C. Turner, *Red Men Calling on the Great White Father* (Norman: University of Oklahoma Press, 1951), p. 203.

[25] No prophetic discourse has been as open to outsiders and as controversial as that of the Hopi of Arizona. For nearly a century their prophecies and global warnings concerning the "balance of life" have been disseminated by outgoing Hopi spiritualists through diehard non-Indian supporters, environmentalists, and New Agers, a unique alliance comprehensively but acidly documented in Armin W. Geertz's *The Invention of Prophecy: Continuity and Meaning in Hopi Indian Religion* (Berkeley: University of California Press, 1994). Elsewhere, Geertz has identified the following traits of Hopi Prophecy: "it is clan based, it is rooted in the awareness of a continuum between past and present, it is collective, it is fatalistic, and it reflects changing political, social, and ideological contexts" ("A Container of Ashes: Hopi Prophecy in History," *European Review of Native American Studies*, 3[1] [1989], p. 2).

[26] Thomas Vennum, Jr., *The Ojibwa Dance Drum: Its History and Construction*, Smithsonian Folklife Studies, N. 2 (Washington, D. C.: Smithsonian Institution Press, 1982).

[27] June Helm, *Prophecy and Power Among the Dogrib Indians* (Lincoln: University of Nebraska Press, 1994).

A FOREST OF TIME

Some scholars have gone so far as to reconceive cultural encounters between Indians and Euro-American as, *au fond*, arguments lodged entirely within a prophetic discourse. In this view, it is first and foremost the clash of religious ideologies, together with their cosmologies and forecasts, that explains the miscommunications and strategic second-guessing of Indians and whites in conflict situations.[28] Perceiving how tensions between Indians and whites grew out of different philosophical premises, John Fenimore Cooper presciently dramatized their opposition in his early novel *The Pioneers*. According to historian Richard Slotkin's interpretation of the issues at stake between the citizens of Cooper's town of Templeton and its Indian neighbors:

> The different modes of perception derive from different mythological views of history. To the Christian Temple, the settlement of Templeton and the conversion or destruction of the Indians are part of a providential plan, figured in the creation of many by Jehovah and in the commandments to replenish the earth and to gather the souls of men into Christ's church. To the Indian, the settlement of Templeton is a breach in nature, a violation of natural law that must culminate in tragedy. The Delaware creation myth is the tale of a quest and an initiation, not a fall from grace.[29]

•

Casting a final glance over these chapters, let me highlight a few ideas and themes that have threaded through them.

---

[28] Literary scholar Tzvetan Todorov's sophisticated rereading of Meso-American encounters with Iberian Europe explores them as interpenetrations between colliding scriptural discourses in *The Conquest of America* (New York: Harper & Row, 1984), as does Stephen A. Colston's '"No Longer Will There Be a Mexico': Omens, Prophecies, and the Conquest of the Aztec Empire," in *American Indian Prophets: Religious Leaders and Revitalization Movements*, edited by Clifford E. Trafzer (Sacramento: Sierra Oaks Publishing Company, 1986), while Djelal Kadin focuses on the invaders' mythological justifications in *Columbus and the Ends of the Earth: Europe's Prophetic Rhetoric as Conquering Ideology* (Berkeley: University of California Press, 1992). Christopher L. Miller attempts something similar, if too neatly parallelistic, in *Prophetic Worlds: Indians and Whites on the Columbia Plateau* (New Brunswick, N. J.: Rutgers University Press, 1985).
[29] Richard Slotkin, *Regeneration Through Violence: The Mythology of the American Frontier, 1600–1860* (Middletown, Conn.: Wesleyan University Press, 1973), p. 488.

First, like the original Cambridge essay that launched it, this lengthier prolegomenon to American Indian ways of history has joined with the late historian H. Stuart Hughes's "vision of history," which stresses "the central importance of symbols in establishing common values of a given culture. . . . The symbol conveys the implicit principles by which the society lives, the shared understanding of assumptions which require no formal proof."[30]

The different Indian senses of the past that stand as separate trees with their respective branches in this American Indian forest are not assemblages of existential happenings that lack organic connection. Usually structured in ways that may reflect different combinations of socio-economic, political, religious, and hence historical determinants, they all stress selected cultural meanings, common aspirations, and preferable social processes through the media of well-worn multivocal "condensed" symbols that have swelled in content and stood the test of time. Such symbols and the ritualistic actions they empower serve to "naturalize" history, to retrospectively reify the contingent so that, for instance, ethnic communities come to accept their origins, commemorations, and destinies as foreordained by higher powers.[31]

Second, in the articulation of any Native society's historical consciousness, we must also remember that these master symbols and root metaphors have almost certainly undergone transformations, the "plasticity" of which Hughes also speaks in his book and whose inventive presence has been evinced throughout this work. Within these Native philosophies of history, moreover, high value is usually placed upon the maintenance of Indian conceptual autonomy over time, in as outwardly consistent and inwardly reassuring a fashion as possible. Sometimes this requires adjusting the facts and calls for retroactive enhancement in order for history to make sense in Indian terms, to integrate older

---

[30] H. Stuart Hughes, *History as Art and as Science: Twin Vistas of the Past* (Chicago: University of Chicago Press, 1975), p. 80. Further discussion is found in Robert Darnton's "The Symbolic Element in History," *The Journal of Modern History* 58(1) (March 1986), pp. 218–234.

[31] My chapters on myth and ritual would have been equally suitable places to cite this argument, as elaborated in Janet L. Dolgin and JoAnn Magdoff's "The Invisible Event," in *Symbolic Anthropology: A Reader in the Study of Symbols and Meanings* (New York: Columbia University Press, 1977).

claims into new sociopolitical climates, and to pass on essential meanings distilled from collective experience.

Suspecting that labels such as "tradition" or "sacred" are employed as "a flag of convenience to legitimate a position held on other grounds,"[32] or to exempt subject matter from empirical scrutiny, should not make us turn our backs on either the persistence of certain social phenomena or the inherently dynamic nature of culture itself. Uncovering the synthesized nature of indigenous claims does not mean that they are composed out of thin air. Study of their components and adhesive compounds identifies cultural processes that can also be upstreamed to identify their presence and consistency over earlier eras. True, a few "traditions" may be unmasked as individually perpetrated frauds, public relations strategies, or examples of collective self-delusion. But the fact remains that "history is not given and tradition is not static," as James Collins puts it, and modulations or recombinations of traditions do not make tribal agency and social identity "unreal or fictive, as terms such as 'constructed' or 'invented' can imply, but [they do] make it profoundly *historical*."[33] The trick lies in simultaneously tracking down hard facts *and* their cultural and historical contexts and nuances, without which they don't mean much.

Third, former times may be considered foreign countries by non-Indian historians,[34] but to Native peoples they usually constitute familiar, contiguous, and ever-present terrain, whose deceased occupants may even put in their two cents' worth. Despite my aversion to simplistic dichotomies, a pervasive distinction between Indian and non-Indian forms of history is the one between their "presentist" and "pastist" orientations, respectively. Sometimes the Native stories of earlier times swing between neighborhood gossip and lofty vision in order to personalize the past, to bring it in tune with inherited world view, or to warn about

---

[32] Jan Vansina, "On History and Tradition," in *Paths in the Rainforests: Towards a History of Political Tradition in Equatorial Africa* (Madison: University of Wisconsin Press, 1990), p. 258.

[33] James Collins, *Understanding Tolowa Histories: Western Hegemonies and Native American Responses* (New York: Routledge, 1998), pp. 50–51.

[34] It is salutary to confront the contrasts between Native historical attitudes and those taken for granted in David Lowenthal's *The Past Is a Foreign Country* (Cambridge: Cambridge University Press, 1985).

moral consequences so as to have maximum impact on the "history of the future." For Indian history is about nothing if not cultural survival, employing what the writer Gerald Vizenor likes to call the uniquely Indian skills of "trickster survivance."

While unusual permissions to "make history" may seem extended in American Indian practices for conceptualizing and representing the past, that does not necessarily mean that the academic sense of historical accuracy, as we have seen, is altogether jettisoned in the process. Indians have coexisted in many conceptual domains; their historical traditions have rarely seen any incompatibilities between the world of facts and that of dreams.[35] Generally, what remains of utmost importance to Indian historians has been psychological persistence, social congruence, group self-esteem, spiritual independence, cultural distinctiveness, and perpetuation of core values – in short, the continuing Native American acculturation of time and space. For outsiders who complain that this is not playing fair, Indians might well ask to be shown the historicity – often bearing catch phrases such as Iron, Bronze, Silver, or Gold Ages, "force majeure," "Third Reich," "divine right of kings," "manifest destiny," "Frontier Thesis," the "Monroe Doctrine," or a fledgling president's first "Hundred Days" – which is not underwritten by similar vested interests and cultural claims. One could even argue that the transparent didacticism of Indian narratives and histories simply makes them more up front about it.

Fourth, the study of Indian–white relations from a Native perspective reveals it less as separate and inviolate entities striking sparks off each other than as an essentially relational field of interacting and cross-borrowing cultural identities – often within contexts, to be sure, of unequal power relations, racial prejudice, gross injustice, and cross-cultural misreadings. Even so, today's tillers in historical fields must consider their work equally relational. Best-case scenario: they must invite Indians as full partners into their investigations.

---

[35] "The origin of cultural practices," write Richard Handler and Joselyn Linnekin, "is largely irrelevant to the experience of tradition; authenticity is always defined in the present. It is not pastness or giveness that defines something as traditional. Rather, the latter is an arbitrary symbolic designation; an assigned meaning rather than an objective quality," in "Tradition, Genuine and Spurious," *Journal of American Folklore* 97(385) (1984), p. 286.

When they do so, as ethnohistorian Ernest S. Burch, Jr., discovered, they can tap into fresh historical wells. Upon interviewing Inupiaq people in northwestern Alaska, for example, Burch uncovered a technology for wholesale intertribal warfare and the existence of early-nineteenth-century battles that refuted everything he'd learned from Arctic scholars. "The really upsetting thing about this," he writes, "is that if I had been willing from the beginning to pay attention to what elders were telling me, I would have known all of this ten or twenty years sooner. As it was, I missed an entire generation of people who probably knew more than my own informants did."[36] Updating this sense of urgency, Vine Deloria, Jr., asks historians "to look into the controversies of this century and record from those people still living their recollections of incidents of a half century ago. Rather than attempting to rebuild the memories of the Pueblos regarding Coronado and the revolt of 1688, people should right now be doing extensive writing and interviews of the elder Pueblo people concerning how they organized and eventually won their lands in 1924."[37]

And even if academic historians remain disinclined to conduct field-work, for their works on Indian–white relations to be anything but culturally cosmetic they must apprentice themselves to the sorts of so-cial, symbolic, economic, political, and folkloristic data that are the meat and potatoes of anthropology. "Only an anthropologist familiar with Indian culture and with social process," argue Mildred M. Wedel and Raymond J. DeMallie, "can discern the clouded facts, correctly analyze the misleading commentary, or extract significant cultural in-formation that appears incidentally in documents written for quite differ-ent purposes."[38] And, "If nothing else," adds Donald B. Smith, "from a good ethnological monograph, one can obtain a 'feel' for a native group,

[36] Ernest S. Burch, Jr., "From Skeptic to Believer: The Making of an Oral Historian," *Alaska History* 6(1) (Spring 1991), p. 11.
[37] Vine Deloria, Jr., "The Twentieth Century," *Red Men and Hat-Wearers: Viewpoints in Indian History*, Papers from the Colorado State University Conference on Indian History, August 1974, edited by Daniel Tyler (Boulder, Colo.: Pruett Publishing Co., 1976), p. 163.
[38] Mildred Mott Wedel and Raymond J. DeMallie, "The Ethnohistorical Approach in Plains Area Studies," in *Anthropology on the Great Plains*, edited by W. Raymond Wood and Margot Liberty (Lincoln: University of Nebraska Press, 1980), p. 110.

and an idea of what white society looks like, viewed from within a native community."[39]

Fifth, this book represents one generalist's dawning regard for the rich and scantily addressed history of American Indian intellectual life. It takes issue with the late Wilcomb E. Washburn's implication of Native silence, impotence, ignorance, or compliance when he neglects the Native side of the equation in focusing only on how "Indian history is, for good or ill, shaped by the white presence. Whether physically in terms of European immigrants, or intellectually, in terms of Western historical or anthropological theories."[40] It takes seriously the proposition that, in their own ways, Indian communities and individuals have been thoughtfully preoccupied with their movements through time. It endorses efforts to transcend old characterizations of Indians as victims or stereotypes and their traditions as monolithic and intractable.[41]

The many Indian pasts, I argue, are as much stories of philosophical, ideological, and symbolic creativity and synthesis, inevitably processed through definitions of self, community, and destiny, as they are beads of discrete incidents hung on narrative strings. No less than the "'contexts of assumption' which exist through time in complex interrelation with each other" that anthropologist George W. Stocking, Jr. holds up as a far more productive subject for non-Indian historians than determining their intellectual inheritance by citing an endless begatting of academic elders (what he terms the "forerunner syndrome"), a new breed of Indian historians must identify and investigate their own successive contexts of

[39] Donald B. Smith, *Le Sauvage: The Native People in Quebec, Historical Writing on the Heroic Period (1534–1663) of New France,* National Museum of Man, Mercury Series, History Division Paper N. 6 (Ottawa: National Museums of Canada, 1974), p. 91.

[40] Wilcomb E. Washburn, "Distinguishing History from Moral Philosophy and Public Advocacy," in *The American Indian and the Problem of History,* edited by Calvin Martin (New York: Oxford University Press, 1987), p. 92.

[41] This critique goes for favorable characterizations, too, such as the simplistically essentialistic descriptions of "the" Indian mind and world view in Calvin Martin's own contributions to his collection, *The American Indian and the Problem of History* (New York: Oxford University Press, 1986), which also focus on ontological contrasts between whites and Indians, to the neglect, critic Thomas Biolsi observes, of the impact of "five hundred years of depopulation, dislocation, ecological and cultural transformation, surplus extraction, class formation, political encapsulation, dispossession, and pauperization" (review article: "The American Indian and the Problem of Culture," *American Indian Quarterly* [Summer, 1989], pp. 265–266).

assumption, whose complexity may have intensified since first contact, literacy, and modernity, but that certainly possess their own developmental histories well before then.[42] As I observed earlier, however, in this effort scholars of American Indian ancestry can find themselves in a bind. For a precondition of this academic approach is that one should accept the past on its own terms, while the presentist bias of the traditions they study – and possibly of those they have personally inherited–is instead to formulate it as a collection of "natural" precedents for our times.

Sixth, and last, scholars, writers, and publishers should innovate new formats for representing on page or screen the multiple genres and mixed voices that are the warp and woof of Indian historicity and Indian–white relations. How to do conceptual, textual, illustrative, and typographic justice to the host of Indian ways of history that offer alternative, parallel, or altogether Other viewpoints can be a liberating challenge for future orchestrators of historical representations, especially where multiple interest groups and their memories, interpretations, and aesthetics are concerned. To this end, I concur with Claude Levi-Strauss's earlier comment that the homespun range of tribally produced histories may one day be seen as pioneers. These experiments exemplify the insistently incomplete and evolving nature of these materials, which conform with James Clifford's rhetorical questions concerning the processual nature of our subject:

> Is it possible that historical reality is not something independent of these differently centered perspectives, nor their sum total, and not the result of a critical sifting of different viewpoints by independent experts "at the end of the day"? Can we conceive of historical reality as an overlay of contextual stories whose ultimate meanings are open-ended because the contact relations that produced them are discrepant, unfinished?[43]

On a few occasions, I've used the verb "bequeathed" to characterize how traditionalist historians and others preoccupied with ensuring historical

---

[42] Stocking is quoted in Rosemary Levy Zumwalt's *American Folklore Scholarship: A Dialogue of Dissent* (Bloomington: Indiana University Press, 1988), pp. xii–xiii.

[43] James Clifford, "Fort Ross Meditation," in his *Routes: Travel and Translation in the Late Twentieth Century* (Cambridge: Harvard University Press, 1997), p. 319.

continuity often frame their responsibilities. Perhaps this analogy to material inheritance also has heuristic value in communicating the senses of property and duty that are often found in Indian notions of history. Conceiving of the past as a collective dowry, which subsequent generations must maintain in high repair and to which they must even contribute, as a sort of cultural capital from which they can draw ideological, spiritual, and psychological interest, may help us understand why Indian history must stay receptive to synthesis, accretion, and refurbishment.

This book proposes that devising ways to revisit the uniquely American Indian blends of spiritual, documentary and opportunistic contemplations of the past offers American intellectual history a new frontier. When they are explored, as illustrated by Robert Allen Warrior's pioneering comparison of the writings of John Joseph Matthews (Osage) and Vine Deloria, Jr.,[44] Ruth J. Heflin's comparative study of five generally contemporaneous Lakota writers,[45] or more informally, as with Deloria's memoir of lively brainstorming at the University of Arizona during Bob Thomas's tenure,[46] we find ourselves within subaltern American discourses. We feel freer to question whether we should even be speaking of indigenous senses of the past as alternative histories or alternatives *to* history. Instead of cramming them into familiar paradigms, might we not temper the hegemony of Western historiography by interpreting it *into them* every now and then?[47]

Without the opportunity for Indian peoples to tell their historical experiences in their many different ways, and without the burden upon non-Indian American historians to somehow weave Native ways of history into the research methodologies and narrative bedrock of their accounts, the fullness of the North American experience will remain unwitnessed and alternative visions for its future unrevealed. Just as

---

44 Robert Allen Warrior, *Tribal Secrets: Recovering American Indian Intellectual Traditions* (Minneapolis: University of Minnesota Press, 1995).

45 Ruth J. Heflin, *"I Remain Alive": The Sioux Literary Renaissance* (Syracuse, N.Y.: Syracuse University Press, 2000).

46 Vine Deloria, Jr., "Bob Thomas as Colleague," in *A Good Cherokee, a Good Anthropologist: Papers in Honor of Robert K. Thomas*, edited by Steve Pavlik (Los Angeles: American Indian Studies Center, 1998).

47 These sentences paraphrase Ashis Nandy in his "History's Forgotten Doubles," in "World Historians and Their Critics," Theme Issue of *History and Theory* 34 (1995), p. 60.

there is nothing new about my book's opening premise that historical practices are culture-specific, this broader challenge has also been expressed before. Historian Patricia Limerick followed up her insistence that her professional colleagues position cultural competition at the center of their narratives of the American West with her half-humorous proposal that America be dotted with "Managed Contention Sites" where multiple points of view and modes of interpretation might have at each other, thereby honoring the complexity of competing notions of "truth" and ways of getting at it.[48]

But if we listen carefully, we hear Indians themselves calling for a historical discourse that doesn't quarantine their pasts and their intellectual life from the broader American experience and its modes of recollection. When an elder stood up in 1954 to tell the nation's Commissioner of Indian Affairs that "We have a hard trail ahead of us in trying to Americanize you and your white brothers. But we are not afraid of hard trails," he could have been talking about American Indian ways of history.[49] When the Lakota author Luther Standing Bear wistfully imagined an alternative to his own indoctrination by the dominant society's educational system, he offered a prospectus we might well resurrect:

> So we went to school to copy, to imitate; not to exchange language and ideas, and not to develop the best traits that had come out of uncountable experiences of hundreds and thousands of years living upon this continent. Our annals, all-happenings of human import, were stored in our song and dance rituals, our history differing in that it was not stored in books, but in the living memory. So, while the white people had much to teach us, we had much to teach them, and what a school could have been established upon that idea![50]

[48] Patricia N. Limerick, *The Legacy of Conquest: The Unbroken Past of the American West* (New York: W. W. Norton and Company, 1987), p. 27, and "The Battlefield of History," *New York Times*, August 28, 1997, p. A19.

[49] Felix S. Cohen, "Americanizing the White Man," *The American Scholar* 21(2) (Spring 1952), p. 178.

[50] I found this quote at the beginning of a fine piece by one of my main mentors on Indian historicity, the late Alfonso Ortiz ("Introduction: Indian–White Relations: A View from the Other Side of the 'Frontier,'" in *Indians in American History*, edited by Frederick E. Hoxie [Arlington Heights, Ill.: Harlan Davidson, 1988], p. 1), so it seemed doubly appropriate to end this book with it. Luther Standing Bear, *Land of the Spotted Eagle* (Lincoln: University of Nebraska Press, [1933] 1978), p. 236.

Index

Abenaki, St. Francis, 76
Acoma Pueblo, 165, 192–4
American Indian Academics, 237–8
Amerindian Autohistory, 211
"ancestor stories," 68
Apess, William, 205–6
Arikara, 158
Assiniboine, 118
Athabaskan, 81
"attitudinal history," 108
Axtell, James, 27

Bahr, Donald, 40, 70–1
Bancroft, Hubert Howe, 9–10
Banyacya, Tomas, 220
Bascom, William, 66
Basso, Keith, 122, 145–6
Bear Butte, 134, 180
Beaulieu, David L., x
Beckwith, Martha Warren, xi
Bible ("the Book"), 192–6, 200–2
Blackfeet, xi
Bloomfield, Leonard, 112
Boas, Franz, 12
Bole Maru, 162
Booger Dance, 184–5
Bowers, Alfred W., 136, 141
Braudel, Fernand, 46, 98, 156–7
Brightman, Robert, 121–2

British structural-functionalism, 13
Brugge, David M., 96
Brumble, David H., 54
Burch, Ernest S., 235–6

"calendar sticks," 158
California Ghost Dance, 99–100,
    163
Cantwell, Robert, 173
Carrier, 199
Catlin, George, 7, 136
ceremonial canes, 158
Chaco Canyon, 155
Cherokee, 178, 184, 197, 203, 208
Cheyenne, 134, 180
Chipewyan, 80
Chippewa, 206
Chiricahua Apache, 93–4
Choctaw, 138
Chumash, 142, 147
Cibique Apache, 122
Clark, Ella E., 33
Clifford, James, 25, 238
clowning traditions, 185–6
Coast Salish, 113
Collins, James, 234
Colville, 124
"commemorative ceremonies," 177,
    180

"conjectural history," 11
"conjuncture," the, 156
Cooper, John Fenimore, 232
Copway, George, 7, 207
Coquille, 34
Cree, 36, 112, 121, 202
Creek, 133–4
Cronon, William, xii
"crossing the ice" migration epics, 73
Crow (also Absaroke), 58–59, 61,
    143, 144, 172–6, 180, 226–7
"culture hero," 180
"culture area," 65
Curtin, Jeremiah, 85–88, 98–101
Cushing, Frank Hamilton, 123, 197,
    230

d'Azevedo, Warren, 117
Dauenhauer, Nora Marks and
    Richard, 103
Day, Gordon M., 76
de Laguna, Frederica, 74–5, 90
De Voto, Bernard, 16
Delaware, 73, 201
Delgamuukw versus the Queen
    (legal case), 83
Deloria, Vine Jr., 24, 75, 131, 161,
    214, 236, 239
DeMallie, Raymond J., 12, 207–8,
    236
Dinetah, 141
Dirthrower, Anderson, 228
Dogrib, 231
Doris Duke Oral History Project, 29,
    210
Dream Drum religion, 231
Dundes, Alan, 119
Dunne-Za, 91, 230

"Earth Lodge Cult," 163
"Earthnaming" ceremony, 141
Eastern Pomo, 143
Eastern Shoshone, 135
Eaton, Rachel Caroline, 215
Echo-Hawk, Roger C., 74

Edmunds, R. David, 110
Edwards, Silas John, 202–3
Eggan, Fred, 95–6
Eliade, Mircea, 13–14, 88–9
Ellis, Florence H., 155
Elmendorf, William W., 93
"emic," 65
Emiko Ohnuki-Tierney, 34
Erdrich, Louise, 214
"ethno-ethnohistory," 21
ethnohistory, 18
"etic," 61
Evans-Pritchard, E. E., 15

Faw-Faw movement, 162
Fewkes, Dr. D. Walter, 117
"First Fruits" rituals, 177
Fixico, Donald L, 37
"floating gap," 71
Fogelson, Raymond D., 21, 35
folk history, 19
folk-tales (definition), 66
"folktale," 108–9
Fools Crow, 214
"forerunner syndrome," 237
Fort Laramie Treaty, 142
Foster, George, 56
Fukuyama, Francis, 26–8

Gay Head Wampanoag, 68–9
Geertz, Armin W., 48
Gill, Sam D., 37–8
Gossen Gary H., 112

Haile, Father Berard, 198
Hall, Edwin S., 120
Hallowell, A. Irving, 69–70, 225
Hamell, George R., 65
Hampton, Carol, 216–7
Handsome Lake, 5, 102–3
Havasupai, 147
Heckwelder, John, 6,9
Helm, June, 231
Hidatsa, xi, 136, 141, 148, 151, 180
"hidden transcripts," 109

"historical particularism," 12
"historical tale," 145
"historical consciousness," 20
"historical reenactment," 173
"historicity," 20
"history baskets," 160
Hittman, Michael, 202
Holden, Madronna, 113
Hopi, 37, 41, 48, 76, 77, 81–2,
    95–6, 117–8, 136, 140, 184,
    186, 191, 230–1
"Hopification," 140
Hudson, Charles, 19
Hudson Bay Cree Religious
    Movement, 201
Hughes, H. Stuart, 233
Hultkrantz, Ake, 135
Hunt, Edward Proctor, 192
Hupa, 210
Hymes, Dell, 79

Image of Limited Good, 56
"Indian time," 46
Indian autobiographies, 209
Indians academics, 216–7
Interior Salish, 135, 149
Inuit, 199
Inupiaq, 235–6
Inupiat, 120
Iron Teeth, 152–3
Iroquois, 4–5, 34, 101–3, 158
Iroquois League, 54, 102

Jacobs, Elizabeth, 45
Jefferson, Thomas, 148
Jennings, Francis, 7
Jicarilla Apache, 229
Johnson, Ella Elizabeth, 55
Johnston, Basil, 211

Kalapuya, 79
Katsina Cult, 142
Keyes, Greg, 96
Klah, Hosteen, 46
Koniaq, 70

Korom, Frank J., 198
Kroeber, Alfred L., 127–8
Kroeber, Karl, 92
Kutenai Calendar Records, 205
Kutenai, 53, 205
Kutenai-Salish, 60–1
Kwakiutl, 170

La Flesche, Francis, 10–11, 48
Lakota, xi
"Lakotification," 140
Legend, 69
"legend," 59, 65, 67
legendary narratives (definition), 66
Lemhi Shoshone, 114
Levi-Strauss, Claude, 14–15, 88–9,
    212, 230, 238
Limerick, Patricia N., 239–40
loci memoriae ("memory places"),
    130
longue duree, 98
Lowenstein, Tom
Lowie, Robert H., 59, 114, 118,
    174
Luckert, Karl W., 39, 42, 53, 225
Lurie, Nancy O., 38

Makah, 155
Malinowski, Bronsilaw, 13, 88
Malouf, Carling, 205
"Managed Contention Sites," 240
Mandan, 7, 94–5, 137–8, 157,
    161
Martin, Calvin, 170–1
masquerade, 183–6
Matachines Dance, 183–4
"material culture," 150
Mattina, Anthony, 124
McClellan, Catherine, 80–1
McNickle, D'Arcy, 212–3
Medicine Lodge Treaty, 37
memorate, 106–8
Menomini, xi
Mescalero Apache, 178
"migration charts," 158

Miller, Jay, 35
Mitchell, Frank, 32
mitewiwin ceremonials, 136
Mohave, 126–30
Mohegan, 118
Momaday, N. Scott, 215
Moore, John H., 133
Morrison, Kenneth M., 111
museums, 167–8
"myth as mirror" approach, 86–7
myth, 87–92
myths (definition), 66

Nanih Waiya, 138
Naskapi, 72
Natchez, 33, 96
Native American Church, 117, 200
Native American Graves Protection
    and Repatriation Act
    (NAGPRA), 165
Navajo, 98, 133, 141, 144, 198,
    203, 225
Navajo history, 29–31
Nelson, Byron Jr., 210–11
new religious movement, 181–3
"New Western Historians," 19
Nez Perce, 115
Norelputus, 86, 99–100
Northern Cheyenne, 39, 152
Northwest Coast, 139–40
Nunamiut Eskimo, 45

Oglala Sioux, 207
Ohnuki-Tierney, Emiko, 20–21, 34
Ojibwa, xi, 33, 137, 196, 211, 225
Okanagan, 195
Omaha, 48
Opler, Morris, E., 93–4
oral traditions, 65–7
"oral tradition," 59
oratory, 178
Ortiz, Alfonso, x, 98, 131–2, 185
Osage, 48, 178
Oto, 162
Ozette site, 155–6

Pacific Coast (Salish), 93
Paiute, 68
Parkman, Francis, 4–5, 9
Parks, Douglas R., 44, 92–3
Pawnee, 44, 74, 92–3, 157
Penobscot, 105–7
Pequot, 205
Perdue, Theda, 203
"persistent peoples," 131
Pima, 32, 70–1, 158
place names, 143–6
Plains Indian Ghost Dance, 162, 201
Plenty Coups, 61
Pocahontas, 77
Potawatomi, 112, 119
"power dreams," 127
Powhatan, 78
Pratt, Kenneth J., 42
prefiguring rituals, 224–5
Prescott, William Hickling, 2–3
"primordial ties," 132
Pryce, Paula, 149
"public rituals," 187
Pueblo Indian world view, 193–4
Pueblo Revolt of 1680, 81, 189–91

Radin, Paul, 55, 124
Rainbow Bridge Religion, 225
Ramsey, Jarold, 223
Red Earth, White Lies, 75
Red Jacket, 196–7
"reformulations of indigenous
    knowledge," 227
religious movements, 199–202
"remapping," 143–4
"retroactive prophecy," 223–4,
    228–9
Revard, Carter, 209
"revitalization movements," 100–1
Ridington, Robin, 91, 230
Rio Grande Pueblo, 183
Robinson, Harry, 195–6
Rodriquez, Sylvia, 184
Roessel, Ruth, x
Rooth, Anna Birgitta, 88–9

Rose, Wendy, xiii
Russell, Frank, 158

sacred landscapes, 146–7
Sahlins, Marshall, 22
Salinan, 116
Sando, Joe S., 211–2
Santa Fe Fiesta, 190
"scalped men," 92–3
"school of empathy"/"school of suspicion," 6–7
Schoolcraft, Henry Rowe, 8–9
Schwarz, Maureen Trudelle, 52
Scollon, Ronald and Suzanne B. K., 80
Scott, James C., 109
Seminole, 226
Sequoyah Syllabary, 203
Sequoyah, 203
Seton, Ernest Thompson, 60
Seven Arrows, 214
Shaker Religion, 201
Shalako Ceremony, 179
"shamans' duel," 116–120
Silko, Leslie Marmon, 213
Simmons, William S., 67, 227
Sioui, Georges E., 211
Skidi Pawnee, 36
Skinner, Alanson, xi
Slocum, John, 201
Slotkin, Richard, 232
Smith, Captain John, 77–8
Smith, Donald B., 236
Smohalla, 200, 229
Speck, Frank, 118
Spector, Janet D., 151
Standing Bear, Luther, xi–xii, 199, 240
Stands in Timber, John, 39
Star Quilt, 169, 171
Starr, Emmett, 208
Stocking, George, 237
Stony Indian, 198
Storyteller, 213
"string balls," 160

Strong, W.D., 72
"Sunrise Dance," 178
Sword, George, 207

Taos Pueblo, 132, 154, 174, 191
Tapahonso, Luci, 31, 40, 47
"temporal guide posts," 69–70, 72
Tewa, 98
The Pioneers, 232
The Way to Rainy Mountain, 215–6
Thomas, Robert K., 130
Three Affiliated Tribes, 94
Tierra Amarilla Raid, 218–20
Tijerina, Reies Lopez, 218
Tillamook, 45
Tlingit, 50, 81, 90, 103, 166
Tobacco Society, 172–6
Toelken, Barre, 34, 43, 52
Tohono O'odham, 37, 41, 168–9, 181
Tolowa, 143–4
Trauma of History, 187–8
"tribal history," 17
Tribal History, 209–10, 212
Trickster, 109–116, 123–5
Tsimshian, 123–4
Turner, Victor, 181–2, 187
Turner, Frederick Jackson, 16
Tuscarora, 55

University of Oklahoma Press, 17–18
"upstreaming," 155

Vansina, Jan, 22, 71
Van Winkle, Barrick, 84
Vennum, Thomas Jr., 137, 158, 231
Vikita ceremony, 181
Virgin of Guadalupe, 3–4

Wailaki, 229
Walam-Olum, 73–4
Walker, Deward E. Jr., 115
Walters, Anna Lee, 56
wampum belts, 159, 164
Wanapum, 200

Warren, William W., 206–7
Warrior, Robert Allen, 239
Washburn, Wilcomb E., 237
Washoe, 84
Wasson, George, 34
Wedel, Mildred Mott, 236
Welch, James, 214
Western Apache, 145–6, 202
Western Apache Writing System,
    202–303
Whale House, 166
White, Richard, 28
Whiteley, Peter M., 77, 140
Wiget, Andrew O., 81–2
Williamson, Margaret Holmes,
    77–8
Wind from an Enemy, Sky 213
Winnebago, 54, 55, 124

"winter counts," 160–1
Wintu, 85, 86, 98–101
"world systems," 171
Wovoka, 201

Yakima, 160
Yaqui, 204
Yaqui Deer Songs, 204
Yellowstone National Park, 59–63,
    103–4
Young, Lucy, 229
Young, M. Jane, 142–3
Yukeoma, 230–1
Yukon, 139
Yup'ik, 160

Zolbrod, Paul G., 53
Zuni, 18, 41, 142, 165, 179, 197, 228